EIGHTH EDITION

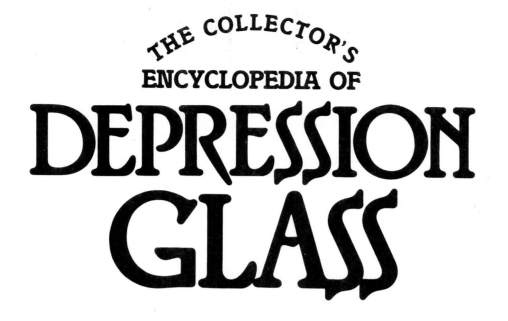

# THE COLLECTOR'S ENCYCLOPEDIA OF DEPRESSION GLASS

## By Gene Florence

COLLECTOR BOOKS
P.O. Box 3009
Paducah, KY 42001

The current values in this book should be used only as a guide. They are not intended to set prices, which vary from one section of the country to another. Auction prices as well as dealer prices vary greatly and are affected by condition as well as demand. Neither the Author nor the Publisher assumes responsibility for any losses that might be incurred as a result of consulting this guide.

Additional copies of this book may be ordered from:

Collector Books
P.O. Box 3009
Paducah, KY 42001

or

Gene Florence
P.O. Box 22186
Lexington, KY 40522

@ $19.95 Add $1.00 for postage and handling.

Copyright: Gene Florence, 1988

# ACKNOWLEDGMENTS

First of all, my thanks go to all the readers who have sent information and photographs of glassware for this book. The old saying that a "picture is worth a thousand words" is truer for glass than you think. I would much rather receive a poorly shot photo than a page of descriptions. Many have said that they had difficulty in getting the photo to come out; and therefore, they left it out when writing. Please enclose it, along with your SASE (self addressed stamped envelope) as I am well aware how difficult it is to get glass to show up. I will suggest that you take the glass outside in natural light, place it on a neutral surface and forget that you own a flash attachment! More good glassware photos have been ruined by the flash than for any other reason.

A special thanks to all the clubs and show promoters who have invited me to their shows. I have enjoyed them, attained knowledge from them, and I hope, contributed to them. Today, more and more shows are starting seminars to increase the knowledge of collectors attending. This trend is a valuable aid to collectors, if not overly done at the expense of dealer sales. In fact, increased attendance at the shows has been one of the results of seminars that peak collectors' interests!

A special thanks to my son, Chad, who volunteered his computer and time to teach me how to use its word processing system. My system decided that six years of information was all that my disc drives could handle. In any case, I now have six years of information on 8" disks, and no way to read them! After "Wordstar", I am now learning "Leading Edge". The rest of the family, especially Marc, has been hoping I would scrap my "archaic" computer. Since I was told by the computer repairman that my disc drives would make a great "boat anchor", they may get their wish sooner than I had planned.

Cathy, my wife, has become chief editor and critic. She still wonders if I invented run-on sentences. One of these days I am going to seclude myself for a month while writing. The phone has a persistent way of ringing right in the middle of a thought or sentence. In fact, I was just interrupted three times by the phone in the middle of that sentence!

"Grannie Bear", my Mom, spent weeks packing and listing glass for the marathon photography session we had for this book. That photography session would make a book in itself. I was there, and I still wonder how we photographed for three books in two locations during one week. My Dad, Charles, Sibyl, and Marie kept everything in line at home while we traveled. These books would never get finished were it not for their help!

Glass and information for this book were furnished by Earl and Beverly Hines, Dick and Pat Spencer, Bill and Lottie Porter, Mrs. Harold Workman and Gladys Florence.

Photographs for this book were made by Tom Clauser and Dana Curtis of Curtis and Mays Studio in Paducah, Kentucky. Glass arranging, unpacking, sorting, stacking, carting and repacking for the photography session was accomplished by Steve Quertermous, Kay Smith, Jane Fryberger, Dick and Pat Spencer, Beverly Hines, Wanda Farque, and Cathy Florence. Lottie and Bill Porter lent moral support and head shaking astonishment at what we were trying to accomplish!

If I have inadvertently left out someone who helped, please know that I am not unappreciative of your aid! I try to keep accurate records, but finding them sometimes presents a problem when it comes to deadline.

I also need to thank all the people at COLLECTOR BOOKS who have worked so long and hard to get this book together under deadline.

As we go to press for the Eighth edition, I wish to thank you, my readers, for continuing to make this the best selling glass book in America; and I wish you much success in your glass collecting!

# FOREWORD

Depression Glass as defined in this book is the colored glassware made primarily during the Depression years in the colors of amber, green, pink, red, blue, yellow, white and crystal. There are other colors and some glass made before, as well as after, this time frame; but primarily, the glass within this book was made from the 1920's through the 1930's. This book is mostly concerned with the inexpensively made glassware turned out by machine in quantity and sold through the five and dime stores or given away as promotional inducements to buy other products during that era known as The Depression.

There have been changes in the collecting of Depression Glass since my first book was sold in '72, some 350,000 copies ago! Prices have soared; seemingly plentiful patterns have been secreted into vast collections and wiped from the market place; heretofore inconsequental Depression patterns and previously ignored crystal colors have picked up buyers; indeed, ANYTHING that is Depression Glass, be it a particular pattern or not, suddenly has added value and collectibility. Collectors have become vastly more knowledgeable and sophisticated in their collecting. Many collectors are enhancing their collections of "A to W" (Adam to Windsor) with patterns of better glassware made during that same time frame. This broadening of interest on the part of collectors prompted me to research and write three more books on the field of Depression Glass, one on the KITCHENWARE items to be found during that era, one on the more ELEGANT glassware of the time, and one on RARE Depression Glass. In this edition, I am including some later patterns now being sought by collectors. These patterns were made in the 1950's and one, as late as the early 1960's. This is what the collector is requesting, so I am trying to provide what he wants. I am having to adjust my ways of thinking about this later glass just as many of you already have.

Information for this book has come via research, experience, fellow dealers, collectors and over 575,000 miles of travel pursuant to glassware. Too, some of the more interesting information has come from readers who were kind enough to share their photographs, old catalogue pages and special knowledge with me. These gestures I particularly treasure.

## PRICING

ALL PRICES IN THIS BOOK ARE RETAIL PRICES FOR MINT CONDITION GLASSWARE. THIS BOOK IS INTENDED TO BE ONLY A GUIDE TO PRICES AS THERE ARE SOME REGIONAL PRICE DIFFERENCES WHICH CANNOT REASONABLY BE DEALT WITH HEREIN.

You may expect dealers to pay from thirty to fifty percent less than the prices quoted. Glass that is in less than mint condition, i.e. chipped, cracked, scratched or poorly molded, will bring very small prices unless extremely rare; and then, it will bring only a small percentage of the price of glass that is in mint condition.

Prices have become pretty well nationally standardized due to national advertising carried on by dealers and due to the Depression Glass Shows which are held from coast to coast. However, **there are still some regional differences in prices due** partly **to glass being more readily available in some areas than in others.** Too, companies distributed certain pieces in some areas that they did not in others. Generally speaking, however, prices are about the same among dealers from coast to coast.

Prices tend to increase dramatically on rare items and, in general, they have increased as a whole due to more and more collectors entering the field and people becoming more aware of the worth of Depression Glass.

One of the more important aspects of this book is the attempt made to illustrate as well as realistically price those items which are in demand. The desire was to give you the most accurate guide to collectible patterns of Depression Glass available.

## MEASUREMENTS

To illustrate why there are discrepancies in measurements, I offer the following sample from just two years of Hocking's catalogue references:

| Year | | Ounces | | Ounces | | Ounces |
|------|---------|----------|--------------|-----------|----------------|--------|
| 1935 | Pitcher | 37,58,80 | Flat Tumbler | 5,9,13½ | Footed Tumbler | 10,13 |
| 1935 | Pitcher | 37,60,80 | Flat Tumbler | 5,9,10,15 | Footed Tumbler | 10,13 |
| 1936 | Pitcher | 37,65,90 | Flat Tumbler | 5,9,13½ | Footed Tumbler | 10,15 |
| 1935 | Pitcher | 37,60,90 | Flat Tumbler | 5,9,13½ | Footed Tumbler | 10,15 |

All measurements in this book are exact as to some manufacturer's listing or to acutal measurement. You may expect variance of up to ½ inch or 1-5 ounces. This may be due to mold variation or changes made by the manufacturer.

# Index

# ADAM   JEANNETTE GLASS COMPANY, 1932-1934

Colors:   Pink, green, crystal, yellow, some Delphite blue.  *(See Reproduction Section)*

The panic over the reproduced butter dish in pink Adam has long since subsided and the price of the older butter has started its rise once again. You can see an explanation of the new in the REPRODUCTION SECTION in the back of the book. As of the writing of this book, no green butters have been remade. Since they are so expensive, that is good for collectors.

The pink Adam/Sierra butter dish is shown on the left. Note the heavy Sierra lines in the photograph. Both patterns are on the top. The bottom is the normal Adam butter bottom. The top to both Adam and Sierra butter dishes are the same shape. Someone long ago probably made a mistake at the factory. The top has Sierra pattern on the inside and Adam pattern on the outside, giving two patterns on one piece. This could only happen by using the bottom half of the Sierra mould and the top half of the Adam mould on the same piece. I assume it was a mistake. Maybe it was an attempt to keep from making a new mould. In any case, it has given us a great collectible today! I might note that placing a Sierra butter top on an Adam bottom is not an Adam/Sierra butter. Again BOTH patterns have to be on the lid!

Adam lamps are being found less often than their counterparts in Floral. You can see what an Adam lamp would look like by turning to Floral pattern where one of those is pictured. These were made by frosting a sherbet and notching it for a switch. A metal cover with a bulb attached completed this lamp. There have been many frosted and notched sherbets found, but only a few bulbs. This bulb and cover are the harder parts fo find. Lamp prices continue to escalate because many people have complete sets except for the lamp and are willing to pay well to finish their set!

Cereal bowls and candy dishes are becoming hard to find in both colors, while iced teas in pink and sherbets in green are getting more difficult. Be sure to check the inner rims of cereal bowls for nicks. These bowls have to be mint to command the prices listed below. Those with inner rim roughness, as is usual, should be priced acordingly. I say *should* because YOU ultimately have to determine what to pay for less-than-mint glass—if you buy it at all. I realize Depression Glass is becoming more scarce in the marketplace and the ''wait for better'' attitude involves more risk than it once did.

The lids to the candy and the sugar bowl are interchangeable. Many collectors have had to buy a covered sugar to get a candy top. This adds another topless sugar to the supply. Of course, flies aren't the household nuisance they were in the '30's; so open sugar bowls don't pose the health hazard faced then!

Adam comes with two different pitchers. One has a round base; the one normally found has a square base. The round based pitcher has concentric rings in the base instead of the Adam motif. You will find this round based pitcher in crystal, also. In fact, many pieces of Adam are found in crystal. Crystal Adam is rare; however, no one collects it and the price is very low. Demand determines price more than rarity. This is a difficult concept for new collectors to learn, but take my word for it now. It will save you frustration later if you find a rare piece and can find no one else who wishes to own it. I know, I have been there!

| | Pink | Green | | Pink | Green |
|---|---|---|---|---|---|
| Ash Tray, 4¼″ | 22.50 | 16.50 | **Cup | 17.50 | 16.00 |
| Bowl, 4¾″ Dessert | 10.00 | 10.00 | Lamp | 225.00 | 225.00 |
| Bowl, 5¾″ Cereal | 30.00 | 30.00 | Pitcher, 8″, 32 oz. | 25.00 | 32.50 |
| Bowl, 7¾″ | 15.00 | 14.50 | Pitcher, 32 oz. Round Base | 40.00 | |
| Bowl, 9″, No Cover | 20.00 | 30.00 | Plate, 6″ Sherbet | 4.00 | 4.50 |
| Bowl, Cover, 9″ | 20.00 | 30.00 | ***Plate, 7¾″ Square Salad | 7.50 | 8.00 |
| Bowl, 9″ Covered | 40.00 | 60.00 | Plate, 9″ Square Dinner | 16.50 | 15.50 |
| Bowl, 10″ Oval | 16.00 | 18.00 | Plate, 9″ Grill | 12.50 | 12.00 |
| Butter Dish Bottom | 15.00 | 60.00 | Platter, 11¾″ | 12.00 | 14.00 |
| Butter Dish Top | 45.00 | 185.00 | Relish Dish, 8″ Divided | 10.00 | 11.50 |
| Butter Dish & Cover | 60.00 | 245.00 | Salt & Pepper, 4″ Footed | 41.50 | 77.50 |
| Butter Dish Combination | | | ****Saucer, 6″ Square | 3.50 | 4.00 |
| with Sierra Pattern | 500.00 | | Sherbet, 3″ | 17.50 | 27.50 |
| Cake Plate, 10″ Footed | 13.00 | 16.50 | Sugar | 10.00 | 12.50 |
| *Candlesticks, 4″ Pr. | 55.00 | 75.00 | Sugar/Candy Cover | 15.00 | 27.50 |
| Candy Jar & Cover, 2½″ | 57.50 | 75.00 | Tumbler, 4½″ | 17.00 | 15.00 |
| Coaster, 3¼″ | 14.50 | 12.50 | Tumbler, 5½″ Iced Tea | 42.50 | 30.00 |
| Creamer | 12.00 | 14.00 | Vase, 7½″ | 160.00 | 32.50 |

   *Delphite   $150.00
   **Yellow   $85.00
   ***Round Pink   $50.00       Yellow   $85.00
   ****Round Pink   $50.00       Yellow   $65.00

**Please refer to Foreword for pricing information**

6

# AMERICAN PIONEER  LIBERTY WORKS, 1931-1934

Colors:   Pink, green, amber, crystal.

American Pioneer is somewhat handicapped by its lack of availability in the marketplace. There are several collectors with unlimited funds who are getting stymied in finding this pattern. Green is the color most collected; amber is gaining steadily in popularity. The amber is even harder to find than the green. Those amber urns shown in the accompanying pictures are the only completed ones yet found. That should give you a hint as to how scarce they are!

Note the different shades of green. That candlestick lamp is one of a pair that was found in the Northeast. I purchased the pair, but it took over two years for the second one to be delivered. Some dealers are a little slow.

The footed piece behind the lamp is a mayonnaise. I originally listed that as a rose bowl and later changed my mind as to its use. Other publications finally caught up to that fact too. It's nice to know you are read, but irritating to be plagerized without credit for your years of hard work!

I have a picture of a large, green, ball-shaped vase in American Pioneer that was photographed at a show in Georgia several years ago. It stands 9″ high and is 30″ around. Unfortunately, the picture can't be reproduced for the book. It is larger than a bowling ball; if you see one of these, you will not forget it!

Luncheon items are the only commonly found items in all colors except amber. All pieces in amber are hard to find. There are two different sizes of covered casseroles. One measures 9¼″ and the other 8¾″. The lids are not interchangeable. I found that out the hard way. I bought a lid after searching for three years and it would not fit the bottom I had. Finally, I found another lid which did. The tops of these bowls flare a little differently, so I give you warning. It might be better to purchase the bowl complete than to try to put it together.

There may be other items in American Pioneer that I do not have listed; so if you find a new piece, be sure to let me know. I do appreciate the information you readers take the time to share with me.

| | Crystal, Pink | Green | | Crystal, Pink | Green |
|---|---|---|---|---|---|
| *Bowl, 5″ Handled | 10.00 | 12.00 | Lamp, 5½″ Round, Ball | | |
| Bowl, 8¾″ Covered | 70.00 | 85.00 | Shape (Amber $70.00) | 60.00 | |
| Bowl, 9″ Handled | 14.00 | 18.00 | Lamp, 8½″ Tall | 75.00 | 85.00 |
| Bowl, 9¼″ Covered | 80.00 | 100.00 | Mayonnaise, 4¼″ | 40.00 | 65.00 |
| Bowl, 10⅜″ Console | 35.00 | 50.00 | **Pitcher, 5″ Covered Urn | 110.00 | 135.00 |
| Candlesticks, 6½″ Pr. | 45.00 | 65.00 | ***Pitcher, 7″ Covered Urn | 130.00 | 165.00 |
| Candy Jar and Cover, 1 lb. | 65.00 | 85.00 | Plate, 6″ | 8.00 | 10.00 |
| Candy Jar and Cover, 1½ lb. | 70.00 | 95.00 | *Plate, 6″ Handled | 8.00 | 10.00 |
| Cheese and Cracker Set (Indented Platter and Comport) | 35.00 | 45.00 | *Plate, 8″ | 6.00 | 7.00 |
| | | | *Plate, 11½″ Handled | 10.00 | 14.00 |
| Coaster, 3½″ | 15.00 | 17.50 | *Saucer | 3.00 | 4.00 |
| Creamer, 2¾″ | 15.00 | 17.50 | Sherbet, 3½″ | 12.00 | 16.00 |
| *Creamer, 3½″ | 16.00 | 17.50 | Sherbet, 4¾″ | 18.00 | 22.50 |
| *Cup | 7.00 | 9.00 | Sugar, 2¾″ | 15.00 | 17.50 |
| Dresser Set (2 Cologne, Powder Jar, on Indented 7½″ Tray) | 150.00 | 175.00 | *Sugar, 3½″ | 16.00 | 17.50 |
| | | | Tumbler, 5 oz. Juice | 15.00 | 22.00 |
| Goblet, 4″, 3 oz. Wine | 30.00 | 35.00 | Tumbler, 4″, 8 oz. | 20.00 | 25.00 |
| Goblet, 6″, 8 oz. Water | 25.00 | 30.00 | Tumbler, 5″, 12 oz. | 25.00 | 35.00 |
| Ice Bucket, 6″ | 35.00 | 42.50 | Vase, 7″, 4 Styles | 55.00 | 75.00 |
| | | | Whiskey, 2¼, 2 oz. | 32.50 | |

  *Amber - Triple the price of pink
 **Amber  $225.00
***Amber  $275.00

**Please refer to Foreword for pricing information**

# AMERICAN SWEETHEART  MacBETH-EVANS GLASS COMPANY, 1930-1936

Colors:   Pink, Monax, red, blue; some Cremax and color rimmed Monax.

American Sweetheart continues to be a MAJOR COLLECTIBLE PATTERN in Depression Glass for several reasons. It comes in numerous colors; it has easily found items (as well as rare ones); it has never been reproduced; and it is in abundant supply in Monax (white) color. Cups, saucers, and most sizes of plates are still plentiful in Monax. Having basic pieces readily available along with the graceful shaping of the pattern itself makes this a beginning collector's dream! Thus, American Sweetheart's popularity is ever sustained.

Accessory pieces in Monax, however, are getting harder and harder to find. Soup bowls and two handled cream soups are disappearing faster than many collectors can locate them. Salt and pepper shakers and sugar lids have always been elusive, as their prices indicate. Supply on these latter items is sufficient for actual demand, at present, simply because newer collectors have been hesitant to pay those prices. To complete sets, these items will eventually have to be included.

For this eighth edition, I can report that several more of the MINIATURE versions of the CONSOLE BOWL (6½" wide x 1¾" tall) have turned up! The latest was found in Indiana for less the $20.00 and subsequently brought $550.00 in auction! (That reader certainly paid for the knowledge gained from his book purchase!) Isn't it AMAZING how many people STILL do not know that Depression Glass is valuable?

Time has a funny way of pointing out misconceptions about items that are hard to get. This has been particularly true of PINK TUMBLERS. For years, the 4¾" tumbler has seemed to be the harder-to-find size. Suddenly, it's the 4¼" size that's more limited in number. Both PITCHERS are now equally hard to obtain; yet there is always more demand for the smaller of the two.

The beige-like color found in some bowls and lampshades is referred to as CREMAX. This causes novice collectors some confusion since there is a PATTERN of glassware with that same name. Those lamp shades sometimes have shaded panels of color (blue, brown, green and orange) to highlight the pattern area.

No one has found another "VASE" like the one pictured. It's thought to have been some early factory worker's "lunch pail project" or simply a tumbler that failed to get properly cut. Whatever, it's UNIQUE and residing in California at present.

I have seen both red and blue TID-BIT SERVERS (priced on the following page). Many tid-bits have been "constructed" in recent years using old (or new) hardware and drilling into regular plates. Therefore, I only list those which I believe would be too costly to "make" today. Use your own good judgment when buying others.

| | Pink | Monax | | Pink | Monax |
|---|---|---|---|---|---|
| Bowl, 3¾" Flat Berry | 25.00 | | Plate, 15½" Server | | 160.00 |
| Bowl, 4½" Cream Soup | 30.00 | 40.00 | Platter, 13" Oval | 20.00 | 37.50 |
| Bowl, 6" Cereal | 9.50 | 8.50 | Pitcher, 7½", 60 oz. | 395.00 | |
| Bowl, 9" Round Berry | 21.00 | 37.50 | Pitcher, 8", 80 oz. | 360.00 | |
| Bowl, 9½" Flat Soup | 28.00 | 39.50 | Salt and Pepper, Footed | 265.00 | 195.00 |
| Bowl, 11" Oval Vegetable | 30.00 | 40.00 | Saucer | 2.50 | 1.50 |
| Bowl, 18" Console | | 265.00 | Sherbet, 3¾" Footed | 12.00 | |
| Creamer, Footed | 8.00 | 7.50 | Sherbet, 4¼" Footed | | |
| Cup | 9.50 | 7.00 | (Design Inside or Outside) | 9.50 | 13.00 |
| Lampshade | | 400.00 | Sherbet in Metal Holder | | |
| Plate, 6" or 6½" Bread & Butter | 2.00 | 2.50 | (Crystal Only) $3.00 | | |
| Plate, 8" Salad | 7.00 | 6.00 | Sugar, Open, Footed | 7.50 | 5.00 |
| Plate, 9" Luncheon | | 8.00 | Sugar Cover (Monax Only)* | | 150.00 |
| Plate, 9¾" Dinner | 15.00 | 12.00 | Tidbit, 3 Tier, 8", 12" & 15½" | | 165.00 |
| Plate, 10¼" Dinner | | 14.00 | Tumbler, 3½", 5 oz. | 40.00 | |
| Plate, 11" Chop Plate | | 9.00 | Tumbler, 4¼", 9 oz. | 45.00 | |
| Plate, 12" Salver | 9.00 | 9.00 | Tumbler, 4¾", 10 oz. | 50.00 | |

*Two style knobs.

**Please refer to Foreword for pricing information**

# AMERICAN SWEETHEART (Cont.)

Collector demand for BLUE and RED American Sweetheart has increased somewhat in the last few months, but more for the blue than the red. Collectors generally settle for a piece or two of each color rather than trying to accumulate a complete setting. (Yes! That WAS possible once as I have readers writing to tell me they remember eating from red American Sweetheart at their mother's or grandmother's homes at Christmas or other special family occasions. One reader remembered a red/white/and blue table setting each July 4th!)

Some blue and red sherbets and plates have appeared having the distinctive American Sweetheart SHAPE but not having the pattern. We can't call these anything but American Sweetheart BLANKS; and while they are novel, without the pattern, they can command only a fraction of the cost of the patterned pieces. The same can be said for the PLAIN PINK PITCHER in the SHAPE of American Sweetheart. If it does not have the pattern on it, it can't be considered to be anything other than "shaped" like American Sweetheart. However, several collectors have told me they are content to use these with their sets rather than the more costly patterned pitchers.

As you can see from the photograph, the starkly white MONAX American Sweetheart can also be found RIMMED WITH VARIOUS COLORS such as gold, pink, green, or "Smoke" which is a blue-gray color that reaches BLACK at the extreme edge. Of all the trims, the "Smoke" is the most highly prized coloring. Again new collectors, all "Smoke" will have a BLACK EDGE. There IS a bluish haze that appears at the rim of some Monax pieces. This does not mean these are "Smoke", merely that there has been some color "burnout" at the thinner rims of these Monax pieces.

The pink trimmed luncheon set pictured here was found in Washington Court House, Ohio, several years ago. Very few of these sets have ever been found complete. Years ago, fifteen-piece "luncheon sets" were sold in the various trim colors mentioned above as well as red and blue colors. The sets consisted of four cups, saucers and salad plates plus a creamer, sugar and salver (plate). It's a shame that not more of these sets are being found intact today!

Gold trimmed Monax American Sweetheart has traditionally had few collectors. However, now that gold-plated "silverware" is gaining popularity, it's very possible that the gold rimmed might turn out to be desirable after all! However, if you wish to get rid of the gold trim, you can easily do so by spending a few minutes erasing it with a pencil eraser. Don't scour it off as you risk scratching the glass and thus damaging its value.

|  | Red | Blue | Cremax | Smoke & Other Trims |
|---|---|---|---|---|
| Bowl, 6″ Cereal |  |  | 8.00 | 27.50 |
| Bowl, 9″ Round Berry |  |  | 30.00 | 65.00 |
| Bowl, 18″ Console | 650.00 | 725.00 |  |  |
| Creamer, Footed | 75.00 | 85.00 |  | 60.00 |
| Cup | 60.00 | 80.00 |  | 55.00 |
| Lampshade |  |  | 400.00 |  |
| Lamp (Floor with Brass Base) |  |  | 600.00 |  |
| Plate, 6″ Bread and Butter |  |  |  | 15.00 |
| Plate, 8″ Salad | 40.00 | 65.00 |  | 25.00 |
| Plate, 9″ Luncheon |  |  |  | 30.00 |
| Plate, 9¾″ Dinner |  |  |  | 50.00 |
| Plate, 12″ Salver | 115.00 | 135.00 |  | 75.00 |
| Plate, 15½″ Server | 225.00 | 285.00 |  |  |
| Platter, 13″ Oval |  |  |  | 95.00 |
| Saucer | 20.00 | 22.50 |  | 13.50 |
| Sherbet, 4¼″ Footed (Design Inside or Outside) |  |  |  | 30.00 |
| Sugar, Open Footed | 65.00 | 75.00 | 57.50 |  |
| Tidbit, 3 Tier, 8″, 12″ & 15½″ | 425.00 | 525.00 |  |  |

**Please refer to Foreword for pricing information**

# ANNIVERSARY   JEANNETTE GLASS COMPANY, 1947-1949

Colors:   Pink, recently crystal and iridescent.

Anniversary, strictly speaking, was made later than the Depression era glassware. However, as with some other later patterns, it's being collected by Depression enthusiasts; so it is included here.

You often see the iridized Anniversary displayed at flea markets. This was newly made in the early 1970's when I first started buying Depression Glass. It was marketed at the local "dish barn" in boxed sets. Often this is marked "Carnival Glass" by sellers; and many times it is priced as such. If you like it, remember its age and pay accordingly. It should sell in the range of crystal or lower.

Some Anniversary pieces including the fruit bowl, candy dish, pin-up vase, butter dish, and wine glass are not easily found. Collecting patterns (such as Anniversary) which are not considered "major" patterns is in vogue with newer collectors. Let your local dealer or those that attend the glass shows know what you are trying to collect. Most dealers are happy to look for specific items they know they can sell immediately. This holds true for any pattern.

The bottom to the Anniversary butter is harder to locate than the top; and there is little demand for later issued crystal Anniversary except for the butter dish and the pin-up vase. The supply of vases has about dried up; so be on the lookout for these. Many of these were used and are water stained. There is nothing that will totally remove this stain—no matter what you are told.

| | Crystal | Pink | | Crystal | Pink |
|---|---|---|---|---|---|
| Bowl, 4⅞" Berry | 1.50 | 3.00 | Pickle Dish, 9" | 3.00 | 6.00 |
| Bowl, 7⅜" Soup | 4.00 | 8.50 | Plate, 6¼" Sherbet | 1.25 | 2.00 |
| Bowl, 9" Fruit | 7.00 | 12.00 | Plate, 9" Dinner | 3.50 | 5.00 |
| Butter Dish Bottom | 10.00 | 20.00 | Plate, 12½" Sandwich Server | 4.00 | 7.00 |
| Butter Dish Top | 12.50 | 22.00 | Relish Dish, 8" | 4.50 | 6.50 |
| Butter Dish and Cover | 22.50 | 45.00 | Saucer | 1.00 | 1.50 |
| Candy Jar and Cover | 17.50 | 30.00 | Sherbet, Footed | 2.50 | 5.00 |
| *Comport, Open, 3 Legged | 3.50 | 7.50 | Sugar | 2.00 | 4.50 |
| Cake Plate, 12½" | 5.50 | 8.50 | Sugar Cover | 4.00 | 7.50 |
| Cake Plate and Cover | 10.00 | 12.50 | Vase, 6½" | 9.00 | 17.50 |
| Candlestick, 4⅞" Pr. | 12.50 | | Vase, Wall Pin-up | 10.00 | 15.00 |
| Creamer, Footed | 3.50 | 7.50 | Wine Glass, 2½ oz. | 5.00 | 10.00 |
| Cup | 2.50 | 4.50 | | | |

*Old form; presently called compote or candy.

# AUNT POLLY   U.S. GLASS COMPANY, Late 1920's

Colors:   Blue, green, iridescent.

The oval vegetable bowl, sugar cover and shakers are difficult to find in blue Aunt Polly. Most of the pieces listed have surfaced in either green or iridescent, but not all have appeared in both. Iridescent Aunt Polly holds its own in price due to scarcity. The iridescent butter, in fact, is quite rare! However, there is little demand for either green or iridescent at present except sugar and creamer or butter dish collectors.

The biggest drawback to collecting Aunt Polly is the absence of cups and saucers. For some reason, patterns that lack these items seem to discourage collectors. Another problem with Aunt Polly is shown by my photograph. The color varies. There are three distinct shades of green and two in blue. It is difficult enough to find Aunt Polly without worrying about color discrepancies!

The blue butter top and bottom are equally hard to find. However, in green and iridescent, only the top is difficult since the bottom is the same one found in other U.S. Glass patterns such as Strawberry and Floral and Diamond. That means that there are more bottoms available.

The two-handled candy lid fits the sugar also.

| | Green, Iridescent | Blue | | Green, Iridescent | Blue |
|---|---|---|---|---|---|
| Bowl, 4⅜" Berry | 6.00 | 10.00 | Creamer | 20.00 | 32.50 |
| Bowl, 4¾", 2" High | 8.50 | 12.50 | Pitcher, 8", 48 oz. | | 135.00 |
| Bowl, 5½" One Handle | 12.50 | 15.00 | Plate, 6" Sherbet | 4.00 | 6.00 |
| Bowl, 7¼" Oval, Handled Pickle | 9.00 | 17.50 | Plate, 8" Luncheon | | 12.00 |
| Bowl, 7⅞" Large Berry | 15.00 | 22.00 | Salt and Pepper | | 160.00 |
| Bowl, 8⅜" Oval | 25.00 | 45.00 | Sherbet | 7.50 | 8.50 |
| Butter Dish and Cover | 195.00 | 150.00 | Sugar | 20.00 | 25.00 |
| Butter Dish Bottom | 45.00 | 75.00 | Sugar Cover | 40.00 | 75.00 |
| Butter Dish Top | 150.00 | 75.00 | Tumbler, 3⅝", 8 oz. | | 18.00 |
| Candy, Cover, 2-Handled | 35.00 | 50.00 | Vase, 6½" Footed | 20.00 | 30.00 |

**Please refer to Foreword for pricing information**

14

## "AURORA" HAZEL ATLAS GLASS COMPANY, Late 1930's

Colors:    Cobalt blue, pink.

Aurora is one of those small sets that a few people are attracted to because of the color. If you like cobalt blue and cannot afford some of the more collected patterns, Aurora might just fill your color requirements; but do not be too surprised if it is harder to find than you might imagine.

My wife likes this. She collected what's shown here to use at "small meal" times when you just need a salad, sandwich and drink! She's derived a lot of pleasure from searching, buying, owning and using this set. I will have to tell you that she blends the cobalt Petalware mustard bottom with this to serve fruit or custard desserts when she uses the "Aurora". I admit the pattern has grown on me.

You will find that the small, deeper bowls are surprisingly sparse.

|  | Cobalt/ Pink |  | Cobalt/ Pink |
|---|---|---|---|
| Bowl, 4½" Deep | 11.00 | Plate, 6½" | 4.00 |
| Bowl, 5⅜" Cereal | 5.00 | Saucer | 2.50 |
| Creamer, 4½" | 9.00 | Tumbler, 4¾", 10 oz. | 12.50 |
| Cup | 5.00 | | |

## AVOCADO, No. 601 INDIANA GLASS COMPANY, 1923-1933

Colors:    Pink, green, crystal, white. *(See Reproduction Section)*

In my travels, I have had many collectors tell me that they never see this pattern at all. There is more of it in central Indiana than any place I know; but some of the most avid collectors are in Florida and Texas! It was made in Dunkirk, Indiana, in the late 1920's and early 1930's; and it was on its way to being one of the most collected patterns in Depression Glass until Indiana remade it in 1974.

Today, this pattern is still avidly sought by a few collectors instead of the many that were before Indiana made that mistake. Be sure to see the Reproduction Section for detailed information. The pink pitcher and tumbler were made first and later several other colors were added. The reproduced pink has a more orange-pink color than the original; but fourteen years later, pink avocado has never recovered from that 1974 blow. Since then, the company has marketed green sherbets, creamer, sugar and sherbet plates. Possibly, it's only a matter of time until they market the rest of the pieces again. Thus, the price rise for this glassware has slowly plodded along. Traditionally, this is what happens when a pattern is reproduced--at least until the "differences" between old and new become common knowledge. Unfortunately, when the original company remakes their own product, any differences are negligible! I'm not saying the glass is worthless as an investment, rather that it will take another forty or fifty years before it can be considered to be antique. Had the company had the foresight to remake the pattern in heretofore unknown colors, then they could have enhanced the collectibility of BOTH the older glass and the new. As it is, they have damaged the investment possibilities of their older product—thereby souring everyone's taste for their glass. Indiana's Depression Glass patterns are something of a pariah among the vast field of collectors today.

Green pitcher and tumbler sets have dried up into collections. They represent some of the few pieces in Avocado to be making advancements in price. Milk white pieces of Avocado were probably a product of Indiana's milk white production of the 1950's; and a few pieces have turned up with an apple design rather than the Avocado. These were collectible as a novelty until Indiana recently remade these in AMBER for Tiara.

|  | Pink | Green |  | Pink | Green |
|---|---|---|---|---|---|
| Bowl, 5¼" 2-Handled | 20.00 | 23.00 | *Pitcher, 64 oz. | 400.00 | 650.00 |
| Bowl, 6" Footed Relish | 15.00 | 20.00 | ***Plate, 6¾" Sherbet | 9.50 | 11.50 |
| Bowl, 7" 1 Handle Preserve | 13.00 | 16.00 | **Plate, 8¼" Luncheon | 13.00 | 15.00 |
| Bowl, 7½" Salad | 25.00 | 39.50 | Plate, 10¼" 2-Handled Cake | 25.00 | 35.00 |
| Bowl, 8" 2-Handled Oval | 15.00 | 20.00 | Saucer | 18.00 | 20.00 |
| Bowl, 9½", 3¼" Deep | 65.00 | 85.00 | ***Sherbet | 40.00 | 45.00 |
| ***Creamer, Footed | 25.00 | 27.50 | ***Sugar, Footed | 25.00 | 27.50 |
| Cup, Footed | 25.00 | 26.00 | *Tumbler | 80.00 | 125.00 |

   *Caution on pink. The orangeish-pink is new!
   **Apple Design   $10.00. Amber has been newly made.
   ***Just remade in green.

**Please refer to Foreword for pricing information**

# BEADED BLOCK   IMPERIAL GLASS COMPANY, 1927-1930's

Colors:   Pink, green, crystal, ice blue, vaseline, iridescent, amber, red, opalescent and milk white.

You can finally see that white Beaded Block pitcher that I have mentioned before but have never been able to show you! This one was found in Michigan for fifty cents (nails and screws included) at a garage sale!

The red lily bowl remains elusive. All but one of these that I know about have come from the Dayton, Ohio, area.

There are several items, the 6″ vases in pink and blue and the white lily bowl, that I want you to notice here. If you look closely, you will notice that these items all have straight edges with no scallops around the edges. Only the lily bowl seems to be Beaded Block and that is marked IG on the bottom which means it was made after 1951. The vases are nice "go-with" pieces but are not truly Beaded Block. Imperial called these tall footed pieces "footed jellies" rather than compotes. These used to be found on grocery shelves containing a product and topped with a metal lid. You'll notice they have "zipper-like" ridged sides rather than the beading.

Imperial also called the two-handled bowl a "jelly" rather than a soup.

Beaded Block comes in a multitude of colors and has the dubious distinction of being mistaken for "Carnival", "Vaseline" or "Pattern" glassware—all terms guaranteed to make the item more costly when bought from unknowing or misinformed dealers. Take care when buying. YOU ultimately decide what a piece is worth to you. If you feel a piece is priced exhorbitantly, pass it by unless you can convince the dealer to moderate the price!

| | Crystal*,Pink, Green, Amber | Other Colors | | Crystal*, Pink, Green, Amber | Other Colors |
|---|---|---|---|---|---|
| Bowl, 4½″ 2-Handled Jelly | 6.00 | 12.50 | Bowl, 7½″ Round, Plain Edge | 7.50 | 14.00 |
| **Bowl, 4½ Round Lily | 8.50 | 15.00 | Bowl, 8¼″ Celery | 9.50 | 15.00 |
| Bowl, 5½″ Square | 6.00 | 8.50 | Creamer | 12.50 | 20.00 |
| ***Bowl, 5½ 1 Handle | 6.50 | 8.50 | Pitcher, 5¼″, Pint Jug | 85.00 | |
| Bowl, 6″ Deep Round | 8.50 | 15.00 | Plate, 7¾ Square | 5.00 | 8.00 |
| Bowl, 6¼″ Round | 6.50 | 14.00 | Plate, 8¾″ Round | 10.00 | 15.00 |
| Bowl, 6½″ Round | 6.50 | 14.00 | Stemmed Jelly, 4½″ | 8.00 | 15.00 |
| Bowl, 6½″ 2-Handled Pickle | 10.00 | 15.00 | Stemmed Jelly, 4½″, Flared | | |
| Bowl, 6¾″ Round, Unflared | 8.50 | 12.50 | Top | 9.00 | 16.00 |
| Bowl, 7¼″ Round, Flared | 8.00 | 14.50 | Sugar | 12.50 | 20.00 |
| Bowl, 7½″ Round, Fluted | | | Vase, 6″ Bouquet | 10.00 | 18.00 |
| Edges | 17.50 | 20.00 | | | |

*All pieces 25% to 40% lower.
**Red: $75.00.
***White: $150.00.

---

# "BOWKNOT"   MANUFACTURER UNKNOWN, Probably late 1920's

Color:   Green

I asked if anyone had a cereal bowl last time and surprisingly there were quite a few readers who did! Thanks; I now have one for future books. In looking for pieces of glassware in patterns that are not avidly collected, I have the same problem as many of you. Dealers at Depression Glass shows cannot afford to take up table space for Bowknot cereals when the same space can display Cherry bowls that many people are searching for when maybe only one person is looking for Bowknot. That is why you need to ask for the glass you want. It may be back at the shop just waiting for a buyer! The same is true in advertising. It costs more to advertise a Bowknot cereal than Cherry because space is costly and few collectors are looking for Bowknot while many are looking for Cherry.

My wife is totally charmed with this pattern—liking the shapes and what she terms the pattern's "Depression era look". Maybe she equates its dearth of pieces to the lack of everything else during the Depression!

| | Green | | Green |
|---|---|---|---|
| Bowl, 4½″ Berry | 9.00 | Sherbet, Low Footed | 9.00 |
| Bowl, 5½″ Cereal | 12.00 | Tumbler, 5″, 10 oz. | 11.00 |
| Cup | 5.00 | Tumbler, 5″, 10 oz. Footed | 11.00 |
| Plate, 7″ Salad | 7.50 | | |

**Please refer to Foreword for pricing information**

# BLOCK OPTIC, "BLOCK"   HOCKING GLASS COMPANY, 1929-1933

Colors:   Green, pink, yellow, crystal and some blue.

Block Optic continues to be one of the most popular patterns of Depression Glass! It never seems to attract the frenetic activity of some other patterns. Rather, it just quietly continues to attract new collectors and to steadily sell while other patterns go through "ups and downs". Were you to graph the activity generated by Block Optic, you'd just see a gently rising line.

New collectors are turning to patterns which are affordable without mortaging the homestead. This is good for Depression Glass and will make dealers rethink their concepts about buying only major patterns. It is now difficult not to consider Block Optic as one of those major patterns. I have always tried to carry various patterns to shows where I set up a booth. A whole four-piece set in a minor pattern can be bought for the price of one hard-to-find piece in most highly collected patterns. The prices for Block have now placed it in the moderate price range of the highly collected patterns.

Note the five styles of creamer and sugars shown. There are three styles (footed, cone shape with fancy handles; footed, rounded shape with plain handles; and flat bottomed) in the green picture. The pink picture shows two other styles (footed, cone shaped with plain handles; and footed, round shape with fancy handles). The mate to the yellow creamer is missing; but that should show the various styles to look for in your travels.

There are four styles of cups which are also shown. Three are pictured in green: a flared top which takes a 6⅛" saucer with no indent; a small round cup which takes a 5¾" saucer with cup indent; and a large, plain handle, round cup taking a 6⅛" saucer with no indent. In the pink, the large round cup with a fancy handle, taking a 6⅛" saucer with indent is shown.

Pink Block Optic is now being sought almost as often as the green; and because of that, several items are being found in shorter supply than previously thought, such as the pink ice tub and the 80 oz. pitcher. To that scarcity, add the newly discovered 3½" short wine (which is just like the rarely seen one in green Cameo)! Further, collectors of pink Block Optic are having difficulty in finding stemware of all types. There are far fewer cocktails and wines in pink than there ever were in green.

Recently, there was a green frosted set discovered which means that sugar/creamer and cup collectors have a new type to find. This frosted effect was done by dipping the glass in camphoric acid; this is called "satinizing" in collecting circles.

Yellow Block, though pretty, creates a problem in that there are so few different pieces to collect. It presents a challenge; and you can find enough to set a table. There are some accessory pieces such as candy and shakers. Speaking of shakers, has anyone seen any of the bulbous style floating around recently?

The blue butter dish remains one-of-a-kind to date.

| | Green | Yellow | Pink | | Green | Yellow | Pink |
|---|---|---|---|---|---|---|---|
| Bowl, 4¼" Berry | 5.00 | | 4.50 | Plate, 8" Luncheon | 3.00 | 3.75 | 2.50 |
| Bowl, 5¼" Cereal | 8.50 | | 6.00 | Plate, 9" Dinner | 13.00 | 25.00 | 17.00 |
| Bowl, 7" Salad | 14.00 | 20.00 | 12.00 | Plate, 9" Grill | 6.50 | 12.50 | 9.50 |
| Bowl, 8½" Large Berry | 15.00 | | 12.00 | Plate, 10¼" Sandwich | 12.50 | | |
| *Butter Dish and Cover, 3" x 5" | 37.50 | | | Salt and Pepper, Footed | 22.50 | 55.00 | 45.00 |
| Butter Dish Bottom | 22.50 | | | Salt and Pepper, Squatty | 40.00 | | |
| Butter Dish Top | 15.00 | | | Sandwich Server, Center Handle | 40.00 | | 35.00 |
| Candlesticks, 1¾" Pr. | 50.00 | | 40.00 | Saucer, 5¾", With Cup Ring | 7.00 | | 5.00 |
| Candy Jar & Cover, 2¼" Tall | 30.00 | 40.00 | 30.00 | Saucer, 6⅛", With Cup Ring | 7.00 | | 4.50 |
| Candy Jar & Cover, 6¼" Tall | 37.50 | | 50.00 | Sherbet, Non-Stemmed (Cone) | 3.00 | | |
| Comport, 4" Wide Mayonnaise | 20.00 | | 40.00 | Sherbet, 3¼", 5½ oz. | 4.50 | 7.50 | 6.00 |
| Creamer, 3 Styles: Cone | | | | Sherbet, 4¾", 6 oz. | 11.00 | 12.00 | 9.00 |
| Shaped, Round, Rayed-Foot | | | | Sugar, 3 Styles: As | | | |
| and Flat (5 Kinds) | 10.00 | 9.50 | 8.50 | Creamer | 9.00 | 9.50 | 8.00 |
| Cup, Four Styles | 5.00 | 6.00 | 4.00 | Tumbler, 3" & 3½", 5 oz. Flat | 12.00 | | 11.00 |
| Goblet, 3½" Short Wine | | | 50.00 | Tumbler, 4", 5 oz. Footed | 15.00 | | 12.00 |
| Goblet, 4" Cocktail | 18.00 | | 20.00 | Tumbler, 9 oz. Flat | 10.00 | | 10.00 |
| Goblet, 4½" Wine | 18.00 | | 20.00 | Tumbler, 9 oz. Footed | 13.50 | 13.00 | 11.00 |
| Goblet, 5¾", 9 oz. | 16.00 | | 12.50 | Tumbler, 10 oz. Flat | 13.00 | | 11.00 |
| Goblet, 7¼", 9 oz. Thin | | 19.00 | | Tumbler, 6", 10 oz. Footed | 15.00 | 17.00 | 14.00 |
| Ice Bucket | 27.50 | | 22.50 | Tumbler, 14 oz. Flat | 20.00 | | |
| Ice Tub or Butter Tub, Open | 25.00 | | 65.00 | Tumble-up Night Set: 3" | | | |
| Mug, Flat Creamer, No Spout | 25.00 | | | Tumbler Bottle and Tumbler, | | | |
| Pitcher, 7⅝", 68 oz., Bulbous | 55.00 | | 40.00 | 6" High | | 45.00 | |
| Pitcher, 8½", 54 oz. | 25.00 | | 27.50 | Vase, 5¾" Blown | 150.00 | | |
| Pitcher, 8", 80 oz. | 37.50 | | 45.00 | Whiskey, 1⅝", 1 oz. | | | 20.00 |
| Plate, 6" Sherbet | 1.50 | 2.00 | 1.00 | Whiskey, 2¼", 2 oz. | 16.00 | | 16.00 |

*Blue  $350.00 - Crystal $85.00

**Please refer to Foreword for pricing information**

# "BUBBLE", "BULLSEYE", "PROVINCIAL"

## ANCHOR HOCKING GLASS COMPANY, 1934-1965

Colors:  Pink, light blue, dark green, red, crystal and any Hocking color.

Bubble continues to be a delight for new collectors. It is one of the few patterns that can be collected in blue for an affordable price, although the creamer's price usually shocks a budding collector. The flanged bowl which measures 9″ is missing from most collections and is rarely seen. New collectors should not be surprised to see Bubble in any color made by Hocking. The 8⅜″ berry bowl was made in many colors. It is found in pink most often; however, remember that any other piece in pink is a "find". Notice the price of a cup and saucer for example. I have had reports of pink dinner plates, but I have never seen one. Send me a picture if you have one!

More of the topaz (yellow) Bubble seems to be surfacing; thus far, no one has been able to date its production years. It seems possible that it is late 1950's—judging from the glass it has been found with; but that is speculation.

Green Bubble appeared in the 1950's and early '60's during the Forest Green production. Green Bubble is presently selling well. I've asked several buyers their reasons for buying it and received answers ranging from "I'm using it for my Christmas table," to "The price is bound to go up on this, too!" For some reason, no one has tried to pry me away from the iridized green sugar in the picture—not even a collector of sugar and creamers! I still have not heard of other iridized green, but looking at the sugar, I would be surprised to find a set of anything that ugly!

Crystal Bubble sells for about half the price of the green; but the pitcher in crystal is harder to find than the Royal Ruby one. Royal Ruby was issued in the 1960's under the name "Provincial". Red "Bubble" is enjoying a recent surge of interest on the part of collectors. Red Bubble would have even more devotees if there were more pieces available. The lack of creamer, sugar and serving pieces (except for berry bowls) has been a deterrent, I'm sure. Many collectors mix the crystal and red for special occasions; so if you have not tried that, you might consider it.

For those of you who would like to use Depression Glass for every day dishes, I highly recommend crystal Bubble since it costs little more than today's dishes and it is durable and only a little harder to replace. Besides, you'll enjoy both the search for pieces and the use of pattern. Westmoreland made some glasses called "Thousand Eye" that will "go with" the Bubble nicely.

| | Dark Green | Light Blue | Ruby Red | | | Dark Green | Light Blue | Ruby Red |
|---|---|---|---|---|---|---|---|---|
| Bowl, 4″ Berry | 4.00 | 9.00 | | | Plate, 6¾″ Bread and | | | |
| Bowl, 4½″ Fruit | 5.50 | 7.00 | 5.00 | | Butter | 1.50 | 2.00 | |
| Bowl, 5¼″ Cereal | 5.50 | 7.50 | | | Plate, 9⅜″ Grill | | 10.00 | |
| Bowl, 7¾″ Flat Soup | | 8.50 | | | Plate, 9⅜″ Dinner | 4.50 | 5.00 | 5.50 |
| Bowl, 8⅜″ Large Berry | | | | | Platter, 12″ Oval | | 10.00 | |
| (Pink—$3.00) | 7.50 | 9.00 | | *** | Saucer | 1.00 | 1.00 | 1.50 |
| Bowl, 9″ Flanged | | 75.00 | | | Sugar | 6.50 | 12.50 | |
| Candlesticks (Crystal - | | | | | Tidbit (2 Tier) | | | 16.50 |
| $10.00 Pr.) | 17.50 | | | | Tumbler, 6 oz. Juice | | | 6.00 |
| Creamer | 7.00 | 20.00 | | | Tumbler, 9 oz. Water | | | 5.50 |
| *Cup | 3.00 | 2.50 | 4.00 | | Tumbler, 12 oz. Iced Tea | | | 8.50 |
| Lamp, 2 Styles, Crystal Only - $30.00 | | | | | Tumbler, 16 oz. | | | |
| **Pitcher, 64 oz. Ice Lip | | | 35.00 | | Lemonade | | | 14.00 |

*Pink—$60.00
**Crystal—$40.00
***Pink—$17.50

# CAMEO, "BALLERINA" or "DANCING GIRL"   HOCKING GLASS COMPANY,

## 1930-1934

Colors:   Green, yellow, pink and crystal w/platinum rim.   *(See Reproduction Section)*

It has been an exciting year for Cameo collectors! Several 3½" short wines have been found in green; a couple of sandwich servers have found their way into the market place; and several heretofore unphotographed pieces are being seen in my new book on *Very Rare Glassware of the Depression Years*. Shown for the first time were the yellow milk pitcher, two new style lamps and a crystal relish. The lamps were made using a tall sherbet and water tumbler similar to the lamp base made from the water goblet on the next page.

Saucers still are in demand at the highly touted price of $85.00. Remember, there has to be a defined cup ring in which the cup resides. The sherbet plate with no indent is what was normally sold and used as saucers. To date the ringed saucers have only been found in green.

Cameo is still one of the most collected patterns of Depression Glass and may have reached the point where it is THE most collected pattern. It is difficult to judge that; but as I travel the country, there has been little to convince me otherwise. There are more unique and unusual pieces in this pattern than in many others which makes owning a COMPLETE set virtually impossible as well as costly. Basic sets can still be easily put together and enjoyed without completely exhausting your pocketbook.

Collectors seldom notice grill plates, but take a look at the TWO-HANDLED one located on page 27. This handled one is difficult to find!

The Cameo shakers were reproduced; but the pattern proved to be so weak that they were easily distinguished from the old. So far, this mould has not been improved; and if you will look in the Reproduction Section, you will see that the pattern is so weak—it does not photograph well.

A special thanks to Frank McClain for his photography of Lynn and Jerry Mantione's pink Cameo and green sandwich server. The pink pitcher is the first to come to light, but it suffers from a weak pattern. Blank pitchers in yellow and pink have been found for years; but until now, the Cameo design has been missing! Pink Cameo is rare; but with time and money, a set can be assembled.

The odd lid pictured fits only the "rope" top juice pitcher, but should it? Some have supposedly turned up with the water pitcher, but I have yet to see one that fits correctly.

The small size children's sets are NEW! (See Reproduction Section at back).

|  | Green | Yellow | Pink | Crys/ Plat |
|---|---|---|---|---|
| Bowl, 4¼" Sauce |  |  |  | 4.25 |
| Bowl, 4¾" Cream Soup | 45.00 |  |  |  |
| Bowl, 5½" Cereal | 22.00 | 22.50 |  | 6.00 |
| Bowl, 7¼" Salad | 35.00 |  |  |  |
| Bowl, 8¼" Large Berry | 23.00 |  | 110.00 |  |
| Bowl, 9" Rimmed Soup | 27.50 |  |  |  |
| Bowl, 10" Oval Vegetable | 14.00 | 27.50 |  |  |
| Bowl, 11", 3-Legged Console | 40.00 | 55.00 | 25.00 |  |
| Butter Dish and Cover | 140.00 | 850.00 |  |  |
| Butter Dish Bottom | 85.00 | 325.00 |  |  |
| Butter Dish Top | 55.00 | 525.00 |  |  |
| Cake Plate, 10", 3 Legs | 15.00 |  |  |  |
| Cake Plate, 10½" Flat | 75.00 |  |  |  |
| Candlesticks, 4" Pr. | 72.50 |  |  |  |
| Candy Jar, 4" Low and Cover | 42.50 | 57.50 | 375.00 |  |
| Candy Jar, 6½" Tall and Cover | 95.00 |  |  |  |
| Cocktail Shaker (Metal Lid) Appears in Crystal Only |  |  |  | 350.00 |
| Comport, 5" Wide Mayonnaise | 20.00 |  | 150.00 |  |

**Please refer to Foreword for pricing information**

| | Green | Yellow | Pink | Crys/ Plat |
|---|---|---|---|---|
| Cookie Jar and Cover | 37.50 | | | |
| Creamer, 3¼" | 16.50 | 12.50 | | |
| Creamer, 4¼" | 17.50 | | 60.00 | |
| Cup, 2 Styles | 11.00 | 6.50 | 55.00 | 5.00 |
| Decanter, 10" With Stopper | 95.00 | | | 150.00 |
| Decanter, 10" With Stopper, Frosted (Stopper Represents ⅓ Value of Decanter) | 25.00 | | | |
| Domino Tray, 7" With 3" Indentation | 77.50 | | | |
| Domino Tray, 7" With No Indentation | | | 150.00 | 90.00 |
| Goblet, 3½" Wine | 300.00 | | | |
| Goblet, 4" Wine | 47.50 | | 175.00 | |
| Goblet, 6" Water | 37.50 | | 125.00 | |
| Ice Bowl or Open Butter, 3" Tall x 5½" Wide | 115.00 | | 400.00 | 200.00 |
| Jam Jar, 2" and Cover | 120.00 | | | 125.00 |
| Pitcher, 5¾", 20 oz. Syrup or Milk | 145.00 | 400.00 | | |
| Pitcher, 6", 36 oz. Juice | 42.50 | | | |
| Pitcher, 8½", 56 oz. Water | 37.50 | | 1000.00 | 350.00 |
| Plate, 6" Sherbet | 2.00 | 2.00 | 60.00 | 1.75 |
| Plate, 7" Salad | | | | 3.00 |
| Plate, 8" Luncheon | 7.50 | 7.50 | 23.00 | 3.50 |
| Plate, 8½" Square | 27.50 | 100.00 | | |
| Plate, 9½" Dinner | 12.00 | 6.50 | 50.00 | |
| Plate, 10" Sandwich | 10.00 | | 30.00 | |
| Plate, 10¼" Rimmed Dinner | 75.00 | | 100.00 | |
| Plate, 10½" Grill | 7.50 | 6.50 | 35.00 | |
| Plate, 10½" Grill With Closed Handles | 47.50 | 6.00 | | |
| Plate, 10½" With Closed Handles | 7.00 | 6.00 | | |
| Platter, 12", Closed Handles | 14.00 | 27.50 | | |
| Relish, 7½" Footed, 3 Part | 20.00 | 85.00 | | 95.00 |
| *Salt and Pepper, Footed Pr. | 50.00 | | 550.00 | |
| Sandwich Server, Center Handle | 2,250.00 | | | |
| Saucer With Cup Ring | 87.50 | | | |
| Saucer, 6" (Sherbet Plate) | 2.00 | 2.00 | 60.00 | |
| Sherbet, 3⅛" molded | 9.50 | 25.00 | 30.00 | |
| Sherbet, 3⅛" blown | 11.00 | | | 55.00 |
| Sherbet, 4⅞" | 24.00 | 30.00 | 65.00 | |
| Sugar, 3¼" | 11.50 | 10.00 | | |
| Sugar, 4¼" | 17.50 | | 60.00 | |
| Tumbler, 3¾", 5 oz. Juice | 21.50 | | 65.00 | |
| Tumbler, 4", 9 oz. Water | 18.00 | | 60.00 | 8.00 |
| Tumbler, 4¾", 10 oz. Flat | 20.00 | | 75.00 | |
| Tumbler, 5", 11 oz. Flat | 20.00 | 37.50 | 72.50 | |
| Tumbler, 5¼", 15 oz. | 45.00 | | 100.00 | |
| Tumbler, 3 oz. Footed Juice | 42.50 | | 90.00 | |
| Tumbler, 5", 9 oz. Footed | 19.00 | 12.00 | 80.00 | |
| Tumbler, 5¾", 11 oz. Footed | 42.50 | | | |
| Tumbler, 6⅜", 15 oz. Footed | 300.00 | | | |
| Vase, 5¾" | 125.00 | | | |
| Vase, 8" | 17.50 | | | |
| Water Bottle (Dark Green) Whitehouse Vinegar | 15.00 | | | |

*Beware Reproductions

# CHERRY BLOSSOM  JEANNETTE GLASS COMPANY, 1930-1939

Colors: Pink, green, Delphite (opaque blue), crystal, Jadite (opaque green), red. *(See Reproduction Section)*

I received one very irate letter over my comments about Cherry Blossom in the last edition; I guess most people know by now that I have always been honest with my readers. If the price declines, I report that just as I do when the price goes up! This time, I can truthfully say that the price of most Cherry Blossom is on the increase again. This is in spite of all the reproductions being thrown into the market from Taiwan. I believe the buying public has finally understood that by ignoring these copies, the manufacturers don't find the reproduction business as lucrative as they thought. Ask anyone in the retail trade how long it takes to move unwanted merchandise once you see it is not selling! **Price cuts** on reproductions is what I have been seeing at the flea markets!

What I have been noticing lately is that people who started collections years ago are coming back to BASIC Depression Glass patterns after a few years of non-collecting; and there are many new collectors who are just getting started! This makes for a steady market and rising prices which is music to the ears of many dealers. For a time, it was more profitable to have money "gaining interest" in stocks or CD's. Now, people are returning to the antique market.

Be sure to read the Reproduction Section for all of the pieces made to date. I will endeavor to pass along to you some tell-tale signs that shriek "REPRODUCTION" in the back of the book.

The letters AOP in the price listing refer to pieces having an "all over pattern"; PAT means "pattern at the top" only.

You will find a few pieces of crystal Cherry Blossom; but it is not considered to be collectible.

Cherry Blossom is still a very popular pattern with collectors; and sales of blue Delphite are being reported.

| | Pink | Green | Delphite | | Pink | Green | Delphite |
|---|---|---|---|---|---|---|---|
| Bowl, 4¾" Berry | 9.00 | 12.00 | 9.00 | Plate, 9" Grill | 16.50 | 18.00 | |
| Bowl, 5¾" Cereal | 22.00 | 25.00 | | Plate, 10" Grill | | 50.00 | |
| Bowl, 7¾" Flat Soup | 36.00 | 38.50 | | Platter, 9" Oval | 650.00 | | |
| * Bowl, 8½" Round Berry | 13.00 | 16.00 | 35.00 | Platter, 11" Oval | 18.00 | 22.00 | 30.00 |
| Bowl, 9" Oval Vegetable | 18.00 | 20.00 | 40.00 | Platter, 13" and 13" Divided | 28.00 | 30.00 | |
| ** Bowl, 9" 2-Handled | 12.00 | 17.00 | 12.50 | Salt and Pepper (Scalloped | | | |
| ** Bowl, 10½", 3 Leg Fruit | 37.50 | 40.00 | | Bottom) | 1,000.00 | 700.00 | |
| Butter Dish and Cover | 52.50 | 67.50 | | Saucer | 2.50 | 3.00 | 3.00 |
| Butter Dish Bottom | 15.00 | 20.00 | | Sherbet | 10.00 | 12.50 | 11.00 |
| Butter Dish Top | 37.50 | 47.50 | | Sugar | 10.00 | 11.00 | 15.00 |
| Cake Plate (3 Legs) 10¼" | 13.00 | 15.00 | | Sugar Cover | 10.00 | 11.00 | |
| Coaster | 10.00 | 8.50 | | Tray, 10½" Sandwich | 10.00 | 12.00 | 13.00 |
| Creamer | 11.00 | 12.50 | 15.00 | Tumbler, 3¾", 4 oz. Footed | | | |
| Cup | 13.50 | 16.00 | 12.50 | AOP, Round or Scalloped | 11.00 | 14.00 | 15.00 |
| Mug, 7 oz. | 160.00 | 140.00 | | Tumbler, 4½", 9 oz. Round | | | |
| *** Pitcher, 6¾" AOP, 36 oz. | | | | Foot AOP | 21.00 | 25.00 | 14.00 |
| Scalloped or Round Bottom | 30.00 | 37.50 | | Tumbler, 4½", 8 oz. Scalloped | | | |
| Pitcher, 8" PAT, 42 oz. Flat | 32.00 | 40.00 | | Foot AOP | 21.00 | 25.00 | |
| Pitcher, 8" PAT, 36 oz. Footed | 37.50 | 44.00 | 65.00 | Tumbler, 3½", 4 oz. Flat PAT | 13.00 | 20.00 | |
| Plate, 6" Sherbet | 5.00 | 5.00 | 8.50 | Tumbler, 4¼", 9 oz. Flat PAT | 13.00 | 17.00 | |
| Plate, 7" Salad | 13.00 | 15.00 | | Tumbler, 5", 12 oz. Flat PAT | 37.50 | 50.00 | |
| **** Plate, 9" Dinner | 11.50 | 14.00 | 11.00 | | | | |

 *Yellow—$350.00
 **Jadite—$275.00
 ***Jadite—$300.00
 ****Translucent Green—$175.00   Jadite—$40.00

## CHERRY BLOSSOM - CHILD'S JUNIOR DINNER SET

| | Pink | Delphite |
|---|---|---|
| Creamer | 27.50 | 30.00 |
| Sugar | 27.50 | 30.00 |
| Plate, 6" | 7.00 | 8.25 (design on bottom) |
| Cup | 22.00 | 26.00 |
| Saucer | 3.50 | 4.50 |
| 14 Piece Set | 195.00 | 205.00 |

Original box sells for $15.00 extra with pink sets.

**Please refer to Foreword for pricing information**

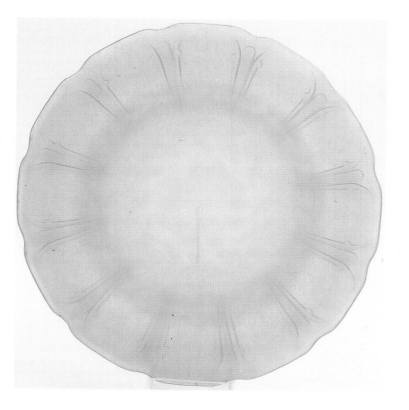

# CHINEX CLASSIC   MacBETH-EVANS DIVISION OF CORNING GLASS WORKS, Late 1930's - Early 1940's

Colors:   Ivory, ivory w/decal decoration

Chinex has an embossed, scroll-like design in the dishes which will distinguish them from the Cremax pattern with which it is often confused. The scrolling is found only on the lid of the butter dish. The base of the butter has only the pie crust-type edging which leads people to believe they've discovered a Cremax butter bottom. The decaled butter has the same decal on the top and bottom if it is floral decorated; but the castle decorated butter has the design only on the inside bottom.

Collectors have asked me to show more of this elusive pattern; so here it is. The pink and blue decorated roses are quite striking whereas the plain with floral decal centers seems lacking in comparison. I assume that sets can be gathered in these colors. I only buy one of each piece for photographing so you can see them.

Castle decal is the most desirable, but the hardest to find. Many collectors like the brown tone shown in the top picture; I am more impressed with the blue bordered pieces. I had never noticed this before, but there are two shades of blue! Both colors were present when I purchased these pieces or I may never have noticed this. The lighter blue is found on flat pieces; the other items are a darker blue. Look at the plates for color comparison. The top to the castle decal butter is missing, but it hides the design anyway. For photography that is acceptable; but I need the top if any one has one for sale.

The opaque beige pieces with the colored designs leads to many table setting possibilities if you can find enough to set the table. That will not be an easy task. This pattern is not as plentiful as we once thought. I did get a letter from a collector in a midwestern state recently stating that this pattern was available in that area except it was all undecorated and no one wanted the plain!

| | Browntone or Plain Ivory | Decal Decorated | Castle Decal |
|---|---|---|---|
| Bowl, 5¾" Cereal | 4.00 | 6.00 | 10.00 |
| Bowl, 7" Vegetable | 12.50 | 17.50 | 25.00 |
| Bowl, 7¾" Soup | 10.00 | 15.00 | 22.50 |
| Bowl, 9" Vegetable | 9.50 | 15.00 | 22.50 |
| Bowl, 11" | 15.00 | 25.00 | 32.50 |
| Butter Dish | 47.50 | 60.00 | 75.00 |
| Butter Dish Bottom | 10.00 | 20.00 | 25.00 |
| Butter Dish Top | 32.50 | 40.00 | 50.00 |
| Creamer | 4.50 | 7.50 | 10.00 |
| Cup | 3.50 | 5.00 | 8.00 |
| Plate, 6¼" Sherbet | 1.50 | 2.00 | 4.00 |
| Plate, 9¾" Dinner | 3.00 | 6.00 | 12.00 |
| Plate, 11½" Sandwich or Cake | 6.50 | 10.00 | 15.00 |
| Saucer | 1.50 | 2.50 | 3.00 |
| Sherbet, Low Footed | 5.00 | 9.00 | 12.50 |
| Sugar, Open | 4.00 | 7.50 | 10.00 |

# "CHRISTMAS CANDY", NO. 624  INDIANA GLASS COMPANY, 1950's

Colors:  Teal and crystal.  *(See Reproduction Section)*

I remember reading somewhere that this pattern was made in the 1930's, but all my resources say much later. I saw a boxed set years ago at the Michigan Depression Glass Society show in Ypsilanti, but I can't remember the story behind it. At the time, I felt it was too new to get excited about; I remember it was only marked No. 624 and listed as "Seafoam" color.

Since I have been showing this pattern in the "pocket" guide, I have had many requests to include it in the big book. I have been trying to find more information.

The demand for crystal is almost nil according to several dealers, but they cannot keep the teal in stock! I do not find Christmas Candy in my area at all. What I have found has been in the Indianapolis area. I do know it sells well in other areas, especially Texas.

|  | Crystal | Teal |
|---|---|---|
| Bowl, 7⅜" Soup | 5.00 | 17.50 |
| Creamer | 7.50 | 12.50 |
| Plate, 6", Bread and Butter | 2.50 | 7.50 |
| Plate, 8¼" Luncheon | 5.50 | 12.50 |
| Plate, 9⅝" Dinner | 7.50 | 17.50 |
| Plate, 11¼", Sandwich | 10.00 | 27.50 |
| Saucer | 1.50 | 3.00 |
| Sugar | 7.50 | 12.50 |

# CIRCLE  HOCKING GLASS COMPANY, 1930's

Colors:  Green, pink, crystal.

It appears that green is the only color in which you can hope to collect a set of Circle. Several collectors have told me that it is impossible to find this in pink. As you can see, I have only found a couple of pieces myself; but I only bought the sugar because I did not have one in green and not because it was pink! Granted, it will probably take a while to gather even a collection of green; but it can be done (sans dinner plates) and it's still very reasonably priced for a Depression ware pattern.

I have been told by collectors that the dinner plates are impossible to find at any price. One of the problems with the pattern is that dealers do not carry Circle to shows since there are fewer collectors. It always pays to ask each dealer if they have your pattern. Maybe they have some back in their shop. Many responsible dealers carry a book of people's wants and actively search for glass to fill these needs.

The rounded cup takes a saucer WITH a cup ring, whereas the flat bottomed cup takes one WITHOUT. The bi-colored stemmed ware has been found from coast to coast. I suspect there are more pieces to be found in this pattern than are listed here. Please let me know of any others you find!

| | Green/Pink | | Green/Pink |
|---|---|---|---|
| Bowl, 4½" | 3.25 | Plate, 8¼" Luncheon | 3.50 |
| Bowl, 5½" Flared | 5.00 | Plate, 9½" Dinner | 6.00 |
| Bowl, 8" | 7.50 | Saucer | 1.00 |
| Creamer | 5.00 | Sherbet, 3⅛" | 3.50 |
| Cup (2 Styles) | 3.00 | Sherbet, 4¾" | 5.00 |
| Decanter, Handled | 27.50 | Sugar | 5.00 |
| Goblet, 4½" Wine | 7.50 | Tumbler, 4 oz. Juice | 4.00 |
| Goblet, 8 oz. Water | 8.50 | Tumbler, 8 oz. Water | 5.00 |
| Pitcher, 80 oz. | 16.50 | | |
| Plate, 6" Sherbet | 2.00 | | |

**Please refer to Foreword for pricing information**

# CLOVERLEAF   HAZEL ATLAS GLASS COMPANY, 1930-1936

Colors:   Pink, green, yellow, crystal, black.

Black Cloverleaf is very difficult to photograph in order to get the design to show. I included a few pieces which had the designs highlighted in gold in hopes these would show better. We may have to go back to the old method of white powder in the design if this does not work.

Since I bought (and sold) a large collection of Cloverleaf a few years ago, I can make a few observations. This collection of seven years was built on the fact that if a piece were found or advertised at any price, it was purchased—no matter what it cost. There were seventeen 7″ green bowls and only seven 8″ bowls. There were twenty yellow cereals and only nine green. Previously, it had been thought that the yellow cereals and the green 7″ bowls were the rare ones. Not so! My travels have confirmed what the collection underscored. Several pieces that were suppposed to exist have subsequently been removed from my list. If they weren't in this collection, I seriously doubt they exist.

The green, flat, 9 oz. tumbler is even more difficult to locate than I had previously thought and is missing in many collections today. Collectors are settling for the more commonly found flared style; demand for these has increased the price.

Black Cloverleaf sherbet plates carry the design in the center. The saucer does not. See the design in the sherbet plate standing to right of the 8″ plate. Not everybody knows Depression Glass; so remember to check all black glass displays for Cloverleaf ash trays and sherbet plates. You might be lucky enough to find sherbet plates in a stack of saucers as I once did.

| | Pink | Green | Yellow | Black |
|---|---|---|---|---|
| Ash Tray, 4″, Match Holder in Center | | | | 60.00 |
| Ash Tray, 5¾″, Match Holder in Center | | | | 72.50 |
| Bowl, 4″ Dessert | 8.00 | 12.50 | 17.50 | |
| Bowl, 5″ Cereal | | 20.00 | 20.00 | |
| Bowl, 7″ Deep Salad | | 30.00 | 35.00 | |
| Bowl, 8″ | | 45.00 | | |
| Candy Dish and Cover | | 40.00 | 90.00 | |
| Creamer, 3⅝″ Footed | | 7.50 | 12.50 | 12.50 |
| Cup | 5.00 | 6.00 | 8.00 | 11.50 |

| | Pink | Green | Yellow | Black |
|---|---|---|---|---|
| Plate, 6″ Sherbet | | 3.50 | 5.00 | 22.50 |
| Plate, 8″ Luncheon | 5.00 | 5.00 | 10.00 | 10.50 |
| Plate, 10¼″ Grill | | 15.00 | 17.50 | |
| Salt and Pepper, Pr. | | 22.50 | 85.00 | 57.50 |
| Saucer | 2.00 | 2.50 | 3.00 | 3.00 |
| Sherbet, 3″ Footed | 4.50 | 4.00 | 8.50 | 15.00 |
| Sugar, 3⅝″ Footed | | 7.50 | 12.50 | 12.50 |
| Tumbler, 4″, 9 oz. Flat | | 30.00 | | |
| Tumbler, 3¾″, 10 oz. Flat Flared | 13.50 | 25.00 | | |
| Tumbler, 5¾″, 10 oz. Footed | | 16.00 | 20.00 | |

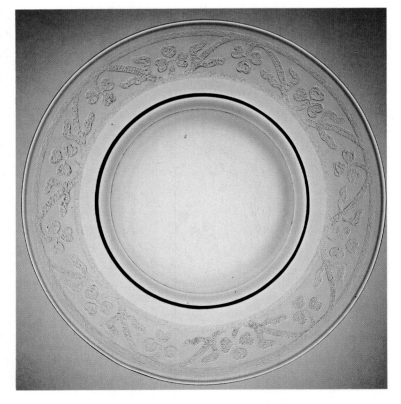

**Please refer to Foreword for pricing information**

# COLONIAL, "KNIFE AND FORK"   HOCKING GLASS COMPANY, 1934-1936

Colors:    Pink, green, crystal and opaque white.

Scarcities of Colonial pattern are driving collectors up the wall. I looked at two very large collections of Colonial green and one of pink and crystal in the last few months. Amazingly, the green sets were complete with dinner plates and cream soups; but they were missing cereal and soup bowls as well as the harder-to-find tumblers. Several tumblers ought to be bought at any cost—if you find them! They are, in green, the 4 oz. (5¼" tall) claret, in green and crystal, the 10 oz. tumbler (measuring 2¾" across the top) and the 12 oz. tumbler (measuring 3" across the top). The 15 oz. lemonade is merely difficult in green; but it is virtually impossible to find in pink or crystal. All sizes of crystal are hard to find.

Colonial attracts new collectors even with all those hard-to-find pieces. It sets a beautiful table and makes a dramatic display for the china cabinet. Green is still the most collectible color.

Spooners, (one pictured in green), are 5½" tall whereas a sugar bowl without its lid will measure only 4½" tall. Often they are confused. Also, the lid of the butter will fit the wooden cheese dish. However, the cheese dish lid is ½" shorter than the butter lid.

| | Pink | Green | Crystal |
|---|---|---|---|
| Bowl, 3¾" Berry | 23.50 | | |
| Bowl, 4½" Berry | 7.00 | 9.00 | 4.50 |
| Bowl, 5½" Cereal | 35.00 | 40.00 | 15.00 |
| Bowl, 4½" Cream Soup | 35.00 | 40.00 | |
| Bowl, 7" Low Soup | 35.00 | 40.00 | 15.00 |
| Bowl, 9" Large Berry | 13.00 | 20.00 | 10.00 |
| Bowl, 10" Oval Vegetable | 20.00 | 22.00 | 12.00 |
| Butter Dish and Cover | 450.00 | 45.00 | 30.00 |
| Butter Dish Bottom | 325.00 | 27.50 | 20.00 |
| Butter Dish Top | 125.00 | 17.50 | 10.00 |
| Cheese Dish | | 95.00 | |
| Creamer, 5", 8 oz. (Milk Pitcher) | 13.50 | 17.50 | 7.00 |
| Cup (White 7.00) | 9.00 | 9.00 | 6.00 |
| Goblet, 3¾", 1 oz. Cordial | | 25.00 | 12.50 |
| Goblet, 4", 3 oz. Cocktail | | 20.00 | 10.00 |
| Goblet, 4½", 2½ oz. Wine | | 20.00 | 10.00 |
| Goblet, 5¼", 4 oz. Claret | | 20.00 | 12.00 |
| Goblet, 5¾", 8½ oz. Water | 30.00 | 22.50 | 12.00 |
| Mug, 4½", 12 oz. | 300.00 | 650.00 | |
| Pitcher, 7", 54 oz. Ice Lip or None | 37.50 | 40.00 | 22.50 |
| *Pitcher, 7¾", 68 oz. Ice Lip or None | 45.00 | 50.00 | 25.00 |

| | Pink | Green | Crystal |
|---|---|---|---|
| Plate, 6" Sherbet | 3.50 | 4.00 | 2.50 |
| Plate, 8½" Luncheon | 6.00 | 7.00 | 3.25 |
| Plate, 10" Dinner | 27.50 | 47.50 | 17.50 |
| Plate, 10" Grill | 17.50 | 20.00 | 10.00 |
| Platter, 12" Oval | 20.00 | 16.00 | 10.00 |
| Salt and Pepper, Pr. | 100.00 | 110.00 | 45.00 |
| Saucer (White 3.00) (Same as Sherbet Plate) | 3.50 | 4.00 | 2.50 |
| Sherbet, 3" | 12.50 | | |
| Sherbet, 3⅜" | 6.00 | 11.00 | 4.50 |
| Spoon Holder or Celery | 85.00 | 90.00 | 55.00 |
| Sugar, 5" | 15.00 | 11.00 | 6.00 |
| Sugar Cover | 25.00 | 15.00 | 10.00 |
| Tumbler, 3", 5 oz. Juice | 10.00 | 20.00 | 8.00 |
| **Tumbler, 4", 9 oz. Water | 10.00 | 16.00 | 8.00 |
| Tumbler, 10 oz. | 25.00 | 33.00 | 15.00 |
| Tumbler, 12 oz. Iced Tea | 33.00 | 42.00 | 18.00 |
| Tumbler, 15 oz. Lemonade | 45.00 | 65.00 | 23.00 |
| Tumbler, 3¼", 3 oz. Footed | 10.00 | 14.00 | 7.00 |
| Tumbler, 4", 5 oz. Footed | 15.00 | 22.00 | 9.00 |
| ***Tumbler, 5¼", 10 oz. Footed | 25.00 | 35.00 | 15.00 |
| Whiskey, 2½", 1½ oz. | 7.00 | 9.00 | 5.00 |

*Beaded top in pink $900.00        **Royal Ruby $75.00        ***Royal Ruby $100.00

**Please refer to Foreword for pricing information**

# COLONIAL BLOCK   HAZEL ATLAS GLASS COMPANY, Early 1930's

Colors:    Green, crystal and pink; white in 1950's.

Until I included Colonial Block pattern in my book, I received many inquiries about a round "Block Optic" butter dish marked with HA in the bottom which is the marking for Hazel Atlas and not Anchor Hocking. This is confusing to new collectors, so I include that here.

The butter tub shown in the foreground seems to be harder to find than the regular butter dish, although both sell for the same price. There are more collectors for the green, but the pink is more scarce. Many collectors started accumulating this pattern by mistake. It was often, and still is, confused with Block Optic. Notice Colonial Block is heavier and has more pronounced lines than Hocking's Block.

There is still some confusion over the pitcher shown here. It is probable that Hazel Atlas did indeed manufacture these as Colonial Block pitchers since many are turning up marked HA. It was previously thought they were the product of U.S. Glass; a similar pitcher was manufactured by U.S. Glass. Newer collectors are more willing to accept pieces that "go-with" these patterns than collectors who started years ago. Several reasons come to mind—economics being the major one. Years ago, five or ten dollars was a lot to pay for this old glassware. Today, five hundred or more is not uncommon for rarely found items.

Pay particular attention to the Colonial Block goblet. Often you see these labeled "Block" and so priced. They are NOT "Block Optic" and should only command a $8.00 or $9.00 price at best.

| | Pink, Green | White | | Pink, Green | White |
|---|---|---|---|---|---|
| Bowl, 4″ | 5.00 | | Candy Jar w/Cover | 27.50 | |
| Bowl, 7″ | 12.50 | | Creamer | 8.50 | 5.50 |
| Butter Dish | 30.00 | | Goblet | 8.50 | |
| Butter Dish Bottom | 7.50 | | Pitcher | 25.00 | |
| Butter Dish Top | 22.50 | | Sugar | 9.00 | 4.50 |
| Butter Tub | 30.00 | | Sugar Lid | 6.00 | 3.00 |

# COLONIAL FLUTED, "ROPE"   FEDERAL GLASS COMPANY, 1928-1933

Colors:    Green and crystal

Colonial Fluted has both good and bad news. The good news is that many new collectors have taken my advice and started looking for this. The bad news is that there is little available that is not worn or badly scratched. Therefore, the price on several items has increased. The bowls seem to be in real short supply.

Colonial Fluted makes a great luncheon set to use for bridge parties. Parties are also a great way to introduce Depression Glass to friends. Who knows, maybe a friend has a garage full of this old "junque" just awaiting your knowledge to expound its virtues. Believe me, it does still happen that way. I have letters which prove it!

That's a vegetable bowl to the right of the background—lest you think at long last we had discovered a dinner plate to go with a "luncheon" plate. Most of the depth of the piece was lost by the camera. There are some dinner plates out there bearing the Federal mark. One has the panels but no roping; the other has the roping but no panels. Thus, neither quite fits this pattern although some people are blending them into their sets quite successfully.

Many pieces are marked with a "F" within a shield which was the Federal Glass symbol.

| | Green | | Green |
|---|---|---|---|
| Bowl, 4″ Berry | 4.00 | Plate, 6″ Sherbet | 1.50 |
| Bowl, 6″ Cereal | 6.00 | Plate, 8″ Luncheon | 3.25 |
| Bowl, 6½″, Deep (2½″) Salad | 13.00 | Saucer | 1.00 |
| Bowl, 7½″ Large Berry | 10.00 | Sherbet | 4.50 |
| Creamer | 4.50 | Sugar | 3.00 |
| Cup | 3.50 | Sugar Cover | 8.00 |

# COLUMBIA  FEDERAL GLASS COMPANY, 1938-1942

Colors:  Crystal, some pink.

A correction in the size of the 11″ chop plate needs to be noted. It has previously been listed as 11¾″, but it really measures 11″. All measurements were originally taken from company catalogues; but over the last sixteen years, I have discovered that we are more precise in our measuring today than they were then. This makes it difficult for collectors, and even more so for beginning collectors because an ounce in a tumbler or an inch on a plate may mean several dollars in price. We always were taught to round up on ½ or more, but that may not have been the case years ago. As a former math teacher, I know that it was taught, but LEARNED is a different matter entirely! A plate that actually measures 8½″ may have been listed as 8″ or 9″.

Pictured in the center is a tumbler with a plain, bulbous top seated on an inch high beaded bottom. These have turned up in boxed sets of Columbia; so, it will have to be assumed they were meant to be Columbia tumblers though there were not catalogued as such. Several of the snack plates have been found in the Denver area along with an unusual bowl similar in style. I purchased a snack plate for the next book, since it has been several years since I have shown one. The collector only had two of the bowls, and I was unable to talk him out of one of those. You might be on the lookout for them in that area.

Butter dishes can come with various flashed-on colors (blue, iridescent, red, purple, amethyst, green) and with decal decorated tops. I might add that the butter bottom is now being found more often than the top.

Those pink luncheon pieces are extremely hard to find; luckily there are few collectors of pink.

| | Crystal | Pink | | Crystal | Pink |
|---|---|---|---|---|---|
| Bowl, 5″ Cereal | 10.00 | | Butter Dish Top | 10.00 | |
| Bowl, 8″ Low Soup | 11.00 | | Cup | 4.50 | 10.00 |
| Bowl, 8½″ Salad | 11.00 | | Plate, 6″ Bread & Butter | 1.50 | 5.00 |
| Bowl, 10½″ Ruffled Edge | 14.00 | | Plate, 9½″ Luncheon | 4.00 | 15.00 |
| Butter Dish and Cover | 15.00 | | Plate, 11″ Chop | 6.00 | |
|   Ruby Flashed (17.50) | | | Saucer | 1.00 | 5.50 |
|   Other Flashed (16.00) | | | Snack Plate | 25.00 | |
| Butter Dish Bottom | 5.00 | | Tumbler | 9.00 | |

# CREMAX  MacBETH-EVANS DIVISION OF CORNING GLASS WORKS, Late 1930's-Early 1940's

Colors:  Cremax, cremax with fired-on color trim.

I have not had the luck in finding pieces of Cremax that I did in finding Chinex this time. If you like challenges, this is the pattern to choose! Actually, this is rare glass; but, it is so hard to find that few people make the attempt.

There are various floral decals to be found other than those pictured here which further compounds the issue of gathering a set together. The castle decal is the most highly prized (as in Chinex), but is even harder to find in this pattern.

Look at the demi-tasse cup and saucers shown. Only one cup was found on its own colored saucer. All the others were found on plain Cremax saucers. The blue cup was switched for a more photogenic look.

There is no butter dish in Cremax although the edge of the base of the Chinex butter is similar to the Cremax pattern.

This PATTERN is called Cremax. MacBeth-Evans also used the word cremax to describe the beige-like COLOR used in some of its patterns such as American Sweetheart, Dogwood, and Petalware. Be aware of this overlap of meaning.

| | Cremax | Decal Decorated | | Cremax | Decal Decorated |
|---|---|---|---|---|---|
| Bowl, 5¾″ Cereal | 2.50 | 6.00 | Plate, 9¾″ Dinner | 3.00 | 6.00 |
| Bowl, 9″ Vegetable | 5.50 | 9.50 | Plate, 11½″ Sandwich | 3.50 | 6.00 |
| Creamer | 3.00 | 5.50 | Saucer | 1.00 | 1.00 |
| Cup | 3.00 | 3.50 | Sugar, Open | 3.00 | 5.50 |
| Plate, 6¼″ Bread and Butter | 1.00 | 2.00 | | | |

**Please refer to Foreword for pricing information**

# CORONATION, "BANDED RIB", "SAXON"   HOCKING GLASS COMPANY, 1936-1940

Colors:   Pink, green, crystal and Royal Ruby.

After four years of showing rare green Coronation, no one has written me about any newly discovered pieces of green. Evidently, the green was experimental and little of it ever found its way out of the factory. I have not found any pieces other than the bowl and plates shown. Once again, I would like to thank Anchor Hocking for the photograph of the four green pieces which are part of the glassware in their morgue (so called, since discontinued and experimental products are often kept there by companies after their lifespan). These pieces of glassware often give vital clues to patterns or colors produced by a company when all catalogues fail to include this information.

Notice that the handles on the pink bowls in Coronation are closed whereas red bowls all have open handles. The green bowl has no handles! Why? Who knows? Maybe they were made at different times since Anchor Hocking promoted a whole line of Royal Ruby products in the late 1930's and early 1940's; perhaps it was felt the open handles made the red bowls more attractive or easier to hold. A very large supply of the red bowls was found in a warehouse in original factory boxes in 1975.

You who are just learning Depression Glass should pay careful attention to the tumbler shown here in Coronation because it's often confused with the more costly Lace Edge tumbler (pictured with Lace Edge). You will notice that the rays are well up the sides of the Coronation tumbler but only up about a third of the glass on the Lace Edge tumbler.

There is no ruby saucer to match the Royal Ruby Coronation cup that you will find simply because this cup was sold with a crystal saucer. Every time I make a statement like that I wonder about having to retract it later, because the one thing I have learned in seventeen years of writing is never say never! Old ads clearly show it on crystal saucers, however.

The Coronation pitcher still is difficult to find, but other pink pieces are abundant for today's market.

| | Pink | Royal Ruby | Green | | Pink | Royal Ruby | Green |
|---|---|---|---|---|---|---|---|
| Bowl, 4¼" Berry | 3.00 | 5.00 | | Pitcher, 7¾", 68 oz. | 150.00 | | |
| Bowl, 6½" Nappy | 3.50 | 7.50 | | Plate, 6" Sherbet | 1.25 | | |
| Bowl, 8" Large Berry, | | | | Plate, 8½" Luncheon | 3.00 | 6.00 | 20.00 |
| Handled | 7.00 | 11.50 | | Saucer (Same as 6" Plate) | 1.25 | | |
| Bowl, 8" No Handles | | | 50.00 | Sherbet | 3.50 | | 35.00 |
| Cup | 3.50 | 4.50 | | Tumbler, 5", 10 oz. Footed | 12.00 | | 50.00 |

# CUBE, "CUBIST"   JEANNETTE GLASS COMPANY, 1929-1933

Colors:   Pink, green, crystal, amber, white, ultramarine, canary yellow and blue.

Experimental pieces of Cube have shown up this time! There are powder jars in blue and canary yellow (vaseline) as well as one powder base in an ugly, opaque orange/white. Since it's rare, it is a shame that a top to this did not surface also. The canary yellow can be seen in my book on "Rare" glass.

This pattern is often mistaken for Fostoria's "American" pattern. The design is similar, but Fostoria's glass is better grade glassware. ("American" pattern listings can be found in my book on *Elegant Glassware of the Depression Era*.) The 2" creamer and sugar in crystal are abundant but seldom collected, and the tray that they reside on always drives novice "American" collectors "bananas". The quality of the glass is the sure-fire giveaway. Jeannette's Cube is dull whereas the Fostoria is crystal clear. There is an abundance of these small creamer and sugars in opaque white and amber also; so do not mistake these for being a rare color if you are just starting to collect.

Pitchers and tumblers in Cube are hard to find, especially the green ones. Since there are more collectors of pink than green, there is little price discrepancy between the tumblers. In most cases, demand pushes up price faster than scarcity.

Cube has everything going for it except a dinner plate. A few collectors are put off by patterns without one; but Cube has everything else including accessory pieces such as the candy dish, butter, shakers and even a powder jar!

| | Pink | Green | | Pink | Green |
|---|---|---|---|---|---|
| Bowl, 4½" Dessert | 4.00 | 5.00 | Plate, 8" Luncheon | 3.00 | 5.00 |
| Bowl, 4½" Deep | 4.50 | | Powder Jar and Cover | | |
| *Bowl, 6½" Salad | 7.00 | 11.00 | 3 Legs | 12.50 | 16.00 |
| Butter Dish and Cover | 40.00 | 45.00 | Salt and Pepper, Pr. | 25.00 | 27.50 |
| Butter Dish Bottom | 10.00 | 12.50 | Saucer | 1.25 | 1.50 |
| Butter Dish Top | 30.00 | 32.50 | Sherbet, Footed | 4.50 | 6.00 |
| Candy Jar and Cover, | | | **Sugar, 2" | 2.00 | |
| 6½" | 21.50 | 25.00 | Sugar, 3" | 5.00 | 6.00 |
| Coaster, 3¼" | 3.50 | 4.50 | Sugar/Candy Cover | 6.50 | 8.50 |
| **Creamer, 2" | 2.00 | | Tray for 3" Creamer | | |
| Creamer, 3" | 5.00 | 7.00 | and Sugar, 7½" | | |
| Cup | 4.50 | 7.00 | (Crystal Only) | 4.00 | |
| Pitcher, 8¾", 45 oz. | 140.00 | 150.00 | Tumbler, 4", 9 oz. | 35.00 | 40.00 |
| Plate, 6" Sherbet | 1.50 | 2.50 | | | |

*Ultramarine—$40.00
**Amber—$3.00

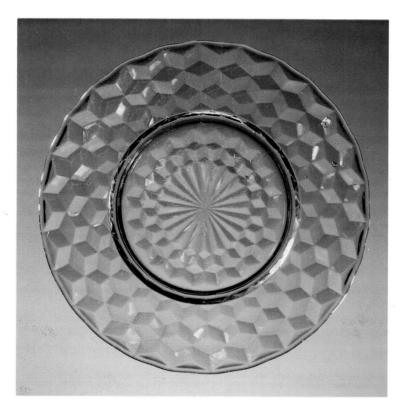

45

# "CUPID"   PADEN CITY GLASS COMPANY, 1930's

Colors:   Pink, green, light blue, black, canary yellow.

Cupid is a pattern I enjoy finding! Lately, the pieces I have seen for sale have been badly scratched or priced in the stratosphere. One great thing about buying Cupid is that you cannot make a mistake buying a duplicate. A dozen people will buy any "mistakes"!

No new pieces have been added to the listing; but, though damaged, I did find the green samovar last fall at a good price, $15.00!

Most Cupid that has surfaced so far is in the form of serving pieces. I assume we may never see plates, cups, and saucers in Cupid as we do in some of Paden City's other patterns. Hopefully, some one will prove me wrong!

Cupid collectors seem to be happy with only finding an occasional piece! I guess that is "laid back" collecting in the truest sense.

The center handled bowls were called candy bowls by Paden City. They probably would be a little messy with sweet potato casserole or mashed potatoes being passed at the table. The center handled trays were called sandwich trays; that might work!

|  | All Colors |  | All Colors |
|---|---|---|---|
| Bowl, 8½" Oval-Footed | 45.00 | Ice Tub, 4¾" | 60.00 |
| Bowl, 9¼" Footed Fruit | 50.00 | Lamp, Silver Overlay | 150.00 |
| Bowl, 9¼" Center-Handled | 45.00 | Mayonnaise, 6" Diameter, Fits on | |
| Bowl, 11" Console | 50.00 |    8" Plate | 60.00 |
| Cake Plate, 11¾" | 45.00 | Plate, 10½" | 30.00 |
| Cake Stand, 2" High, Footed | 40.00 | Samovar | 200.00 |
| Candlestick, 5" Wide, Pr. | 50.00 | Sugar, 4¼" Footed | 32.50 |
| Candy w/Lid, Footed, 4¾" High | 70.00 | Sugar, 5" Footed | 35.00 |
| Candy w/Lid, 3 Part | 65.00 | Tray, 10¾" Center-Handled | 40.00 |
| Comport, 6¼" | 30.00 | Tray, 10⅞" Oval-Footed | 50.00 |
| Creamer, 4½" Footed | 32.50 | Vase, 8¼" Elliptical | 100.00 |
| Creamer, 5" Footed | 35.00 | Vase, Fan-Shaped | 75.00 |
| Ice Bucket, 6" | 65.00 | | |

**Please refer to Foreword for pricing information**

46

# "DAISY", NUMBER 620   INDIANA GLASS COMPANY

Colors:   Crystal, 1933; amber, 1940; dark green and milk glass, 1960's, 1970's.

Daisy grill plates with an indent for the cream soup have recently been discovered! I was beginning to wonder if the grill plates existed at all. Why the ring for a cream soup and not a cup is a mystery to me; but a boxed set of four grills and cream soups has been found at a show in Belleville, Illinois.

The green bowl in the picture is dated 1981 in the bottom and was received with a floral arrangement when I was in the hospital in 1983. I was amused later when I saw that date embossed in the bottom; so, Indiana still makes these bowls even if they are sold to florists! We're grateful for the date, of course; and I have told you in past editions that Indiana marketed Daisy in avocado green under the name of "Heritage" (not to be confused with Federal's "Heritage" pattern) as late as the '70's. Since Federal's Heritage in green is rare, this has caused a problem with new collectors or dealers when found in original boxes labeled Heritage. Many boxed sets have been found in this 1970's issue. Some collectors are beginning to collect this Daisy "Heritage" green which is fine; just know that it is newer glass and pay accordingly.

Few collectors even consider the antique 1930's crystal "Daisy"; most prefer the amber made during the war years. In this color, the 12 oz. tumblers and the cereal bowls are believed to be the most difficult pieces to find; yet I know a lady who feels the relish is even harder to find than those. For glass to be antique, it must be at least fifty years old. By that distinction, a lot of *Depression Glass* can now be considered antique. I can still remember going to "antique" shows where our glass was supposed to be banned because it was not old enough to be displayed! Actually, some of my best bargains were found at those shows.

| | Green, Crystal | Amber | | Green, Crystal | Amber |
|---|---|---|---|---|---|
| Bowl, 4½" Berry | 4.00 | 7.00 | Plate, 9⅜" Dinner | 3.50 | 6.00 |
| Bowl, 4½" Cream Soup | 3.00 | 7.50 | Plate, 10⅜" Grill w/Indent | 4.00 | 20.00 |
| Bowl, 6" Cereal | 10.00 | 20.00 | Plate, 11½" Cake or | | |
| Bowl, 7⅜" Deep Berry | 6.00 | 10.00 | Sandwich | 5.00 | 9.00 |
| Bowl, 9⅜" Deep Berry | 9.00 | 22.50 | Platter, 10¾" | 5.00 | 10.00 |
| Bowl, 10" Oval Vegetable | 6.00 | 12.50 | Relish Dish, 8⅜", 3 Part | 10.00 | 20.00 |
| Creamer, Footed | 4.50 | 6.50 | Saucer | 1.00 | 1.50 |
| Cup | 2.50 | 4.50 | Sherbet, Footed | 2.50 | 7.00 |
| Plate, 6" Sherbet | 1.00 | 2.00 | Sugar, Footed | 3.00 | 6.50 |
| Plate, 7⅜" Salad | 2.00 | 5.50 | Tumbler, 9 oz. Footed | 7.00 | 14.00 |
| Plate, 8⅜" Luncheon | 2.00 | 5.00 | Tumbler, 12 oz. Footed | 15.00 | 27.50 |

# DIANA   FEDERAL GLASS COMPANY, 1937-1941

Colors:   Pink, amber and crystal.

Diana's potential has been overlooked in the past. As you can see from the picture, there are numerous pieces to be found and a quick glance at the price listing will show you that it's still inexpensive—which can't be said of many Depression Glass patterns.

Occasionally, frosted items turn up. In fact, one entire set showed up in pink. Frosted glass, which was made by dipping the glass in camphoric acid, has always been less attractive to today's collectors. It is usually ignored by most in all patterns; but it must have been popular in the Depression years since there's so much of it still found.

The pink demitasse sets are becoming more and more difficult to find; and the sets on the metal racks are seldom seen on the market.

There are other pieces that are not readily available. The tumblers in amber and shakers in all colors are difficult with sherbets being not far behind. The sherbets are cone shaped when you find them. There is a slight controversy as to whether they belong to this pattern or not; but that only stimulates and whets the appetite for collectors! A little controversy is not a bad thing in this collecting world.

| | Crystal | Pink | Amber | | Crystal | Pink | Amber |
|---|---|---|---|---|---|---|---|
| *Ash Tray, 3½"      *Green—$3.00 | 2.00 | 3.00 | | Plate, 6" Bread & Butter | 1.00 | 1.50 | 1.50 |
| Bowl, 5" Cereal | 2.50 | 3.50 | | Plate, 9½" | 4.00 | 6.00 | 6.50 |
| Bowl, 5½" Cream Soup | 2.50 | 5.00 | 6.00 | Plate, 11¾" Sandwich | 4.50 | 6.00 | 6.50 |
| Bowl, 9" Salad | 5.00 | 6.50 | 5.50 | Plate, 12" Oval | 5.00 | 7.00 | 8.00 |
| Bowl, 11" Console Fruit | 5.00 | 6.50 | 8.00 | Salt and Pepper, Pr. | 17.50 | 40.00 | 75.00 |
| Bowl, 12" Scalloped Edge | 4.50 | 7.50 | 8.50 | Saucer | 1.00 | 1.50 | 1.50 |
| Candy Jar and Cover, Round | 12.00 | 20.00 | 25.00 | Sherbet | 2.50 | 5.50 | 6.00 |
| Coaster, 3½" | 2.00 | 3.50 | | Sugar, Open Oval | 2.50 | 3.50 | 3.50 |
| Creamer, Oval | 2.00 | 4.50 | 4.50 | Tumbler, 4⅛", 9 oz. | 5.00 | 12.00 | 15.00 |
| Cup | 2.50 | 4.00 | 4.00 | Junior Set: 6 cups and | | | |
| Cup, 2 oz. Demitasse and 4½" Saucer Set | 6.50 | 18.00 | | Saucers with Round Rack | 50.00 | 120.00 | |

**Please refer to Foreword for pricing information**

# DIAMOND QUILTED, "FLAT DIAMOND"

**IMPERIAL GLASS COMPANY, Late 1920's-Early 1930's**

Colors: Pink, blue, green, crystal, black; some red and amber.

Diamond quilted in black has caught the fancy of several collectors lately. There are many collectors of black glass, but few dinnerware sets can be collected. Actually, this set is more of an expanded luncheon set due to a lack of dinner plates.

Old catalogues only list Diamond Quilted punch bowls in pink. The existence of the actual glass always over-rules whatever was said by the catalogue. So, enjoy this last view of a green one since it now has a new home in the Carolinas. The major difficulty in collecting the green is color variation. Some of the green is dark and other pieces are yellowish in shade. The greens "clash" with each other which makes it difficult to order by mail. Be aware of that if you collect the green!

Blue Diamond Quilted is very attractive and never fails to "sell itself". There are few blue collectors however due to its limited supply. Amber items are surfacing, but not enough as yet to be collectible as a set. This is also true of the red. The price of these colors in Diamond Quilted is held in check by their limited numbers and the few collectors searching for them. The sky is the limit on blue should more collectors begin to search it out.

Most blue and black Diamond Quilted pieces have the quilting on the inside of the dish. However, you have to turn the black plate over on its face to see the quilting.

Candle holders were made in two styles. One is shown in green and the other is shown in the old catalogue ad below. Several arguments have surfaced over the candlesticks below. They are not Windsor Diamond however.

Lest you confuse the pattern, Hazel Atlas also made a quilted pitcher and three sizes of tumblers in cobalt blue, pink and green. The quilting effect on these stops and becomes a straight line before it reaches the top of the dish. Too, these are a heavier glass.

| | Pink, Green | Blue, Black | | Pink, Green | Blue, Black |
|---|---|---|---|---|---|
| Bowl, 4¾" Cream Soup | 6.50 | 15.00 | Mayonnaise Set: Ladle, | | |
| Bowl, 5" Cereal | 4.50 | 8.00 | Plate, Comport | 27.50 | |
| Bowl, 5½" One Handle | 5.50 | 8.50 | Pitcher, 64 oz. | 35.00 | |
| Bowl, 7" Crimped Edge | 5.50 | 10.00 | Plate, 6" Sherbet | 2.50 | 3.50 |
| Bowl, Rolled Edge Console | 13.50 | 30.00 | Plate, 7" Salad | 4.00 | 6.50 |
| Cake Salver, Tall 10" | | | Plate, 8" Luncheon | 4.00 | 10.00 |
| Diameter | 35.00 | | Punch Bowl and Stand | 300.00 | |
| Candlesticks (2 Styles), Pr. | 9.50 | 22.50 | Plate, 14" Sandwich | 8.50 | |
| Candy Jar and Cover, | | | Sandwich Server, | | |
| Footed | 40.00 | | Center Handle | 17.50 | 35.00 |
| Compote and Cover, 11½" | 50.00 | | Saucer | 2.00 | 3.50 |
| Creamer | 6.00 | 9.50 | Sherbet | 4.00 | 8.50 |
| Cup | 4.00 | 6.00 | Sugar | 6.00 | 9.50 |
| Goblet, 1 oz. Cordial | 8.00 | | Tumbler, 9 oz. Water | 6.50 | |
| Goblet, 2 oz. Wine | 8.00 | | Tumbler, 12 oz. Iced Tea | 7.50 | |
| Goblet, 3 oz. Wine | 8.00 | | Tumbler, 6 oz. Footed | 6.00 | |
| Goblet, 6", 9 oz. | | | Tumbler, 9 oz. Footed | 9.50 | |
| Champagne | 7.50 | | Tumbler, 12 oz. Footed | 12.50 | |
| Ice Bucket | 37.50 | 55.00 | Vase, Fan, Dolphin Handles | 25.00 | 40.00 |
| | | | Whiskey, 1½ oz. | 6.50 | |

**Covered Bowl**—6¾ in. diam., deep round shape with 3 artistic feet, dome cover, fine quality brilliant finish **pot glass**, allover block diamond design, transparent Rose Marie and emerald green. **I C5603**—Asstd. ½ doz. in carton, 20 lbs.
**Doz $6.95**

**I C989**—3 piece set, 2 transparent colors (rose and green), good quality, 10½ in. rolled rim bowl, TWO 3½ in. wide base candlesticks. Asstd. 6 sets in case, 30 lbs. ............ SET (3 pcs) **65c**

**Please refer to Foreword for pricing information**

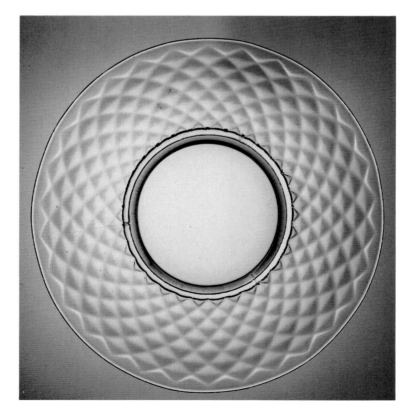

# DOGWOOD, "APPLE BLOSSOM", "WILD ROSE"   MacBETH-EVANS GLASS COMPANY, 1929-1932

Colors:   Pink, green, some crystal, Monax, Cremax and yellow.

Dogwood in RED was the latest surprise in this popular pattern! Since red has been found in American Sweetheart and "S" Pattern, it stands to reason that red Dogwood was also made at that time by MacBeth-Evans. The only piece to surface so far is a 8½" berry bowl. It, too, is shown in the "Rare" book. There is sure to be more found, so let me know!

I thought I had a bigger story on Dogwood, but it only rates second to the red. Have you ever considered going to the Phillipines to look for Depression Glass? When you get off the floor from rolling around laughing, I will explain. The Dogwood pitchers in the American Sweetheart style are supposed to be rare, and they are in the United States. Maybe most of them were shipped to the Phillipines and that is why they are rare here. I met a dealer at a southern Depression Glass show who had been stationed there in 1985. He brought back three or four of these pitchers bought there for very reasonable prices along with other Depression Glass. In fact, I have shipped five books there in the last few months. Word is getting out! Air mail postage costs are more than the cost of the book itself and that is how all the books have been ordered! Collecting closets full of shoes may soon be passed over in favor of Depression Glass in the Phillipines!

Dogwood always attracts admiration, particularly the pitcher and tumblers which have the silk screened Dogwood design on them. Both pink and green are pictured here. Remember, the pitchers MUST have the Dogwood design, not just SHAPE, to be considered to be Dogwood. Those plain pitchers were simply made by the same company.

Pink grill plates come in both styles—all over design or design at the rim only. Green comes only with the rim design. Luncheon plates are plentiful and have been as long as I have been searching for Depression Glass.

The 10¼" fruit bowl, which is so rarely seen any more, is unhappily the one turning up frosted and drilled through to be used as a lamp shade! I suspect that is one of the reasons it is so rare. In any case, the lamp shade is difficult to sell and the bowl is greatly in demand.

New collectors should know that PINK cups, saucers, creamers and sugars come in both a thick and thin variety—the thin having a slightly rolled edge. Both styles of pink cups are pictured along with the thick creamer and sugar. The green comes in only the thin style.

The platter shown is a rarely seen piece. A batch of nine was found a few years ago in the town of Charleroi, Pennsylvania. The owner used them as steak platters.

Only a yellow luncheon plate and a cereal bowl have surfaced in that color.

There is also a smaller, 11" cake plate in Dogwood like the one pictured in "S" pattern. It has to be considered a rare piece. The heavy 13" cake plate has also been found in Cremax color, but the pattern is underneath and does not show through.

There is little demand for the Monax items; they remain more interesting than desirable. We turned the bowl over in the picture so you could see the design. The Monax salver is turning out to be more plentiful than first believed and makes an excellent decorated cake base. It "shows off" your cake.

The 4¾" stemmed wine goblet was not made by MacBeth-Evans; but it's so close to Dogwood pattern that I wanted collectors to be aware of it. A reader sent me a photo showing footed cone-shaped tea and water tumblers having this same design. So be aware of those.

| | Pink | Green | Monax Cremax | | Pink | Green | Monax Cremax |
|---|---|---|---|---|---|---|---|
| *Bowl, 5½" Cereal | 15.00 | 18.50 | 12.00 | Plate, 10½" Grill AOP or | | | |
| Bowl, 8½" Berry | 37.50 | 75.00 | 30.00 | Border Design Only | 13.00 | 13.50 | |
| Bowl, 10¼" Fruit | 200.00 | 100.00 | 55.00 | Plate, 12" Salver | 20.00 | | 15.00 |
| Cake Plate, 11" Heavy Solid Ft. | 175.00 | | | Platter, 12" Oval (Rare) | 245.00 | | |
| Cake Plate, 13" Heavy Solid Ft. | 65.00 | 55.00 | 100.00 | Saucer | 4.00 | 5.00 | 15.00 |
| Creamer, 2½" Thin | 12.50 | 37.50 | | Sherbet, Low Footed | 20.00 | 60.00 | |
| Creamer, 3¼" Thick | 13.50 | | | Sugar, 2½" Thin | 11.00 | 37.50 | |
| Cup, Thin or Thick | 10.00 | 18.00 | 30.00 | Sugar, 3¼" Thick | 10.50 | | |
| Pitcher, 8", 80 oz. Decorated | 120.00 | 400.00 | | Tumbler, 3½", 5 oz. Decorated | 200.00 | | |
| Pitcher, 8", 8 oz. (American | | | | Tumbler, 4", 10 oz. Decorated | 25.00 | 60.00 | |
| Sweetheart Style) | 400.00 | | | Tumbler, 4¾", 11 oz. | | | |
| Plate, 6" Bread and Butter | 4.50 | 5.50 | 20.00 | Decorated | 30.00 | 65.00 | |
| *Plate, 8" Luncheon | 4.75 | 5.00 | | Tumbler, 5", 12 oz. Decorated | 35.00 | 75.00 | |
| Plate, 9¼" Dinner | 17.50 | | | Tumbler, Molded Band | 11.00 | | |

*Yellow—$50.00

**Please refer to Foreword for pricing information**

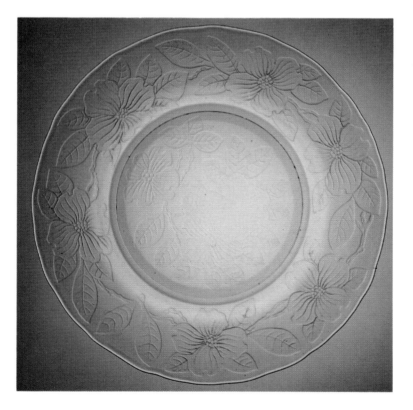

# DORIC   JEANNETTE GLASS COMPANY, 1935-1938

Colors:   Pink, green, some Delphite and yellow.

Doric tumblers continue their rise in price. I am amazed at how few of these are found; and there are collectors who would "kill" for mint green tumblers! Pink collectors abound, but they can find most of their tumblers without the difficulties encountered by the collectors of green.

The cereal bowl is shown in green behind the shakers. The cream soup is two-handled as are all cream soups. I point this out since I have seen cereals priced as cream soups twice in this last year.

Although rare, there is little demand for the Delphite. Exceptions are the sherbet and three-part candy which are commonly found. That pitcher in Delphite is still the only one known.

Take a good look at the other pitchers shown here! That yellow footed pitcher is unique at this writing. There ought to be others awaiting discovery. Also, the footed green Doric pitcher is something of a wizard at hiding. Now, in the pink footed pitchers you will notice there are two styles due to a variation at the lip.

One of the major problems in collecting Doric is that many pieces have mold roughness when found. The cereal bowls and footed tumblers are the worst offenders. For those who have difficulty with terminology, look at the pink picture. The tumbler on the left is the 4½", 9 oz. while the one on the right is the footed tumbler. This heavy ringed base is not as pronounced as most footed tumblers, but is used in this case to distinguish it from the flat one.

The square Doric dish shown in pink can be found on a metal tray having "two stories" so to speak. It was called a relish tray and comes in two sizes. One was pictured in previous editions.

Sugar dish and candy lids in this pattern do not interchange since the candy lid is taller and has a more traditional cone shape.

The pink Doric shaker lids are original; the green lids are newly made. I point this out merely to let people know that new lids are now being made available for Depression Glass shakers. Original lids are preferable unless they're corroded or caved in.

There is a three part, iridized candy dish that was made as recently as the '70's and was selling in my area at the local dish barn for about 79 cents. If there is a dish barn in your area, it would pay you to go through it from time to time and acquaint yourself with what is available and see where some flea market dealers obtain their wares.

| | Pink | Green | Delphite | | Pink | Green | Delphite |
|---|---|---|---|---|---|---|---|
| Bowl, 4½" Berry | 5.00 | 5.50 | 27.50 | Plate, 6" Sherbet | 2.50 | 3.00 | |
| Bowl, 5" Cream Soup | | 160.00 | | Plate, 7" Salad | 12.50 | 12.50 | |
| Bowl, 5½" Cereal | 20.00 | 25.00 | | Plate, 9" Dinner (Serrated 50.00) | 7.50 | 9.50 | |
| Bowl, 8¼" Large Berry | 9.50 | 12.50 | 77.50 | Plate, 9" Grill | 7.50 | 10.00 | |
| Bowl, 9" 2-Handled | 9.50 | 10.00 | | Platter, 12" Oval | 12.00 | 13.50 | |
| Bowl, 9" Oval Vegetable | 12.00 | 16.00 | | Relish Tray, 4" x 4" | 5.00 | 7.50 | |
| Butter Dish and Cover | 55.00 | 67.50 | | ** Relish Tray, 4" x 8" | 6.50 | 9.50 | |
| Butter Dish Bottom | 17.50 | 25.00 | | Salt and Pepper, Pr. | 25.00 | 27.50 | |
| Butter Dish Top | 37.50 | 42.50 | | Saucer | 2.00 | 2.50 | |
| Cake Plate, 10", 3 Legs | 12.50 | 12.50 | | Sherbet, Footed | 7.50 | 9.00 | 5.00 |
| Candy Dish and Cover, 8" | 25.00 | 27.50 | | Sugar | 9.00 | 10.00 | |
| * Candy Dish, 3-Part | 4.50 | 5.50 | 4.50 | Sugar Cover | 9.00 | 15.00 | |
| Coaster, 3" | 10.00 | 12.00 | | Tray, 10" Handled | 7.50 | 9.50 | |
| Creamer, 4" | 7.50 | 8.50 | | Tray, 8" x 8" Serving | 7.50 | 9.00 | |
| Cup | 5.50 | 6.50 | | Tumbler, 4½", 9 oz. | 30.00 | 50.00 | |
| Pitcher, 6", 36 oz. Flat | 25.00 | 30.00 | 750.00 | Tumbler, 4", 10 oz. Footed. | 25.00 | 50.00 | |
| Pitcher, 7½", 48 oz. Footed | 300.00 | 600.00 | | Tumbler, 5", 12 oz., Footed. | 40.00 | 60.00 | |
| (Also in Yellow at $900.00) | | | | | | | |

*Candy in metal holder—$40.00. Iridescent made recently

**Please refer to Foreword for pricing information**

# DORIC AND PANSY   JEANNETTE GLASS COMPANY, 1937-1938

Colors:   Ultramarine; some crystal and pink.

I repeat what I said in the Seventh edition with even more emphasis than before. For those of you with travel plans to England or Canada, keep a weather eye out for Doric and Pansy salts, peppers and butter dishes. It might help pay for your trip should you find some. I have reports of at least four sets coming out of England! Maybe that's why there are few to be found here; they were shipped out of the country. Too, these may have traveled with service personnel. My mail from England regarding Depression Glass in general is picking up. So, look for it if you're there!

Having gone to Canada last year, I might say that there "used to be" a lot of Doric and Pansy in England. Canadian collectors are having English friends buy it and ship it back to them! I talked to one dealer who had received six butter dishes in the last year! The harder-to-find pieces may be only harder to find in the United States! As with "Phillippine" Dogwood pitchers, we may simply have mass shipped some pieces outside the United States!

Many Doric and Pansy shakers are weakly patterned; they need to have SOME pattern design to be called Doric and Pansy, however. I've seen a few that had the shape and color only. They really can't be called Doric and Pansy shakers in that case.

Ultramarine Doric and Pansy is not easily found, but once found, it doesn't always "match". Due to the unstable ways of heating the glass back then, there were various shades of ultramarine from one batch to the next. The greener tinted colored glass is usually shunned by collectors for the bluer color.

With the increased interest in collecting children's toys and miniature dishes, owners of the "Pretty Polly Party Dishes" in Doric and Pansy should be feeling very smug. If you haven't completed your set, I suggest you do so quickly before the prices climb any further.

Only berry sets and the children's set have been found in pink.

| | Green, Teal | Pink Crystal | | Green, Teal | Pink, Crystal |
|---|---|---|---|---|---|
| Bowl, 4½" Berry | 10.00 | 6.50 | Plate, 6" Sherbet | 7.00 | 6.00 |
| Bowl, 8" Large Berry | 60.00 | 17.50 | Plate, 7" Salad | 25.00 | |
| Bowl, 9" Handled | 25.00 | 10.00 | Plate, 9" Dinner | 18.00 | 5.00 |
| Butter Dish and Cover | 450.00 | | Salt and Pepper, Pr. | 300.00 | |
| Butter Dish Bottom | 100.00 | | Saucer | 3.00 | 2.25 |
| Butter Dish Top | 350.00 | | Sugar, Open | 110.00 | 55.00 |
| Cup | 15.00 | 7.50 | Tray, 10" Handled | 15.00 | |
| Creamer | 115.00 | 55.00 | Tumbler, 4½", 9 oz. | 35.00 | |

## DORIC AND PANSY
### "PRETTY POLLY PARTY DISHES"

| | Teal | Pink | | Teal | Pink |
|---|---|---|---|---|---|
| Cup | 25.00 | 20.00 | Creamer | 30.00 | 22.50 |
| Saucer | 4.00 | 3.00 | Sugar | 30.00 | 22.50 |
| Plate | 7.00 | 5.00 | 14-Piece Set | 190.00 | 150.00 |

**Please refer to Foreword for pricing information**

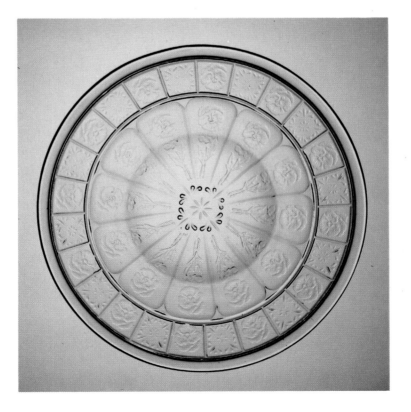

# ENGLISH HOBNAIL   WESTMORELAND GLASS COMPANY, 1920's - 1970's

Colors:   Crystal, pink, amber, turquoise, cobalt, green, blue and red.

Westmoreland is no more! All of the glass and the moulds have been sold through auction. Only time will tell if English Hobnail will be made by some other company. I have not been able to find out where the moulds for this pattern went; so be sure to subscribe to a monthly publication to keep abreast of current news in the glass world. I suspect we will see a rise in all prices of Westmoreland glass.

This is a beautiful pattern which has had tremendous longevity, meaning there is much old to be found and much new! For instance, red English Hobnail was causing quite a stir in collecting circles until Westmoreland made 17 pieces, including the pitcher, for LeVay Distributing Company in the late '70's.

Pink is about the only COLOR in which you can hope to collect an entire set and there are at least two different shades of that. There are three distinct greens, two ambers (the lighter version being made in the 1960's), two turquoise, and a number of fired-on colors, plus round and squared shapes. No, I'm not trying to put you off collecting this, just letting you know what you'd be in for once you decide to collect it. Actually, I like this pattern. My wife used the crystal goblets for several years at our table.

You can enjoy owning an occasional piece of English Hobnail without coveting an entire set. Many people buy the candy dishes or cologne bottles, a lamp or serving tray, a pitcher or shakers just to add color to a room or set of china.

To help new collectors distinguish English Hobnail from Miss America, I offer the following observations. English Hobnail pieces have center rays of varying distance; the hob tips are more rounded giving it a smoother "feel"; and the goblets have rims that flair slightly plus moving directly from the hobs to the plain glass rim. Miss America rays flair equidistant from the center; the hobs are sharp to touch and the goblets don't flair at the rim and have three sets of rings above the hobs before entering a plain glass rim.

| | Cobalt, Amber, Turquoise*, Pink, Green | | | Cobalt, Amber, Turquoise*, Pink, Green |
|---|---|---|---|---|
| **Ash Tray, Several Shapes | 18.50 | | Goblet, 5 oz. Claret | 18.00 |
| Bowls, 4½", 5" Square | | ** | Goblet, 6¼", 8 oz. | 20.00 |
| and Round | 9.50 | | Grapefruit, 6½" Flange Rim | 14.00 |
| Bowl, Cream Soup | 13.50 | | Lamp, 6¼" Electric | 50.00 |
| Bowls, 6" Several Styles | 10.00 | ** | Lamp, 9¼" | 100.00 |
| Bowls, 8" Several Styles | 20.00 | | Lampshade, 17" Diameter | |
| **Bowls, 8" Footed and | | | (Crystal) | 125.00 |
| 2-Handled | 40.00 | | Marmalade and Cover | 32.50 |
| **Bowls, 11" and 12" | | | Pitcher, 23 oz. | 125.00 |
| Nappies | 35.00 | | Pitcher, 39 oz. | 145.00 |
| Bowls, 8", 9" Oval Relish | 15.00 | | Pitcher, 60 oz. | 175.00 |
| Bowl, 12" Oval Relish | 17.50 | | Pitcher, ½ gal. Straight | |
| Candlesticks, 3½" Pr. | 30.00 | | Sides | 200.00 |
| Candlesticks, 8½" Pr. | 50.00 | ** | Plate, 5½", 6½" Sherbet | 3.50 |
| Candy Dish, ½ lb. | | | Plate, 7¼" Pie | 4.00 |
| Cone-Shaped | 45.00 | ** | Plate, 8" Round or Square | 7.50 |
| Candy Dish and Cover, | | | Plate, 10" Dinner | 20.00 |
| Three Feet | 65.00 | | Salt and Pepper, Pr., | |
| Celery Dish, 9" | 16.50 | | Round or Square Bases | 67.50 |
| Celery Dish, 12" | 20.00 | | Salt Dip, 2" Footed and | |
| **Cigarette Box | 25.00 | | with Place Card Holder | 20.00 |
| **Cologne Bottle | 25.00 | | Saucer | 3.50 |
| Creamer, Footed or Flat | 20.00 | ** | Sherbet | 12.50 |
| Cup | 15.00 | | Sugar, Footed or Flat | 20.00 |
| Decanter, 20 oz. with | | | Tumbler, 3¾", 5 oz. or 9 oz. | 13.00 |
| Stopper | 75.00 | | Tumbler, 4", 10 oz. Iced Tea | 15.00 |
| Demitasse Cup and Saucer | 30.00 | | Tumbler, 5", 12 oz. Iced Tea | 20.00 |
| Egg Cup | 25.00 | | Tumbler, 7 oz. Footed | 13.50 |
| Goblet, 1 oz. Cordial | 22.50 | | Tumbler, 9 oz. Footed | 15.00 |
| Goblet, 2 oz. Wine | 15.00 | | Tumbler, 12½ oz. Footed | 20.00 |
| Goblet, 3 oz. Cocktail | 15.00 | | Vase | 100.00 |
| | | | Whiskey, 1½ oz. and 3 oz. | 20.00 |

*Add about 50% more for Turquoise
**Cobalt double price listed

**Please refer to Foreword for pricing information**

# FIRE-KING DINNERWARE "ALICE", "JANE RAY", "SQUARE"

## ANCHOR HOCKING GLASS CORPORATION, 1940's-1960's

Colors: Jade-ite, blue, white w/trims.

I am combining these three patterns into one grouping for now. Strictly speaking, these were made later than Depression glass, but many collectors are turning to these because they are readily available and inexpensive. As is the case in other patterns, demand creates a rise in price, but there is still an abundance of this glassware commonly called "Oatmeal" glass in many areas. It was packed in Mother's Oats and before instant and cold cereals were available, everyone (seemingly) ate oatmeal.

The dinner plates in "Alice" are in shorter supply than any other piece. I suspect this is because they were a little large to fit in boxes of oats and had to be purchased.

"Alice" is pictured below, "Jane Ray" top right and "Square" bottom right.

**"Alice" price***

| | Jade-ite |
|---|---|
| * Cup | 1.25 |
| ** Plate, 8½" | 4.00 |
| *** Saucer | .50 |

*Add $1.50 for White w/Trim   **Add 25¢ for White w/Trim   ***Add 50¢ for White w/Trim

**"Square" prices**

| | All Colors |
|---|---|
| Bowl, 4¾", Dessert | 3.00 |
| Bowl, 7⅜", Salad | 5.00 |
| Cup | 2.00 |
| Plate, 8⅜", Luncheon | 2.75 |
| Plate, 9¼", Dinner | 3.50 |
| Saucer | .50 |

**"Jane Ray" prices**

| | Jade-ite |
|---|---|
| Bowl, 4⅞", Dessert | 1.50 |
| Bowl, 5⅞", Oatmeal | 2.00 |
| Bowl, 7⅝", Soup | 3.00 |
| Bowl, 8¼", Vegetable | 4.00 |
| Cup | 1.25 |
| Creamer | 2.00 |
| Plate, 7¾", Salad | 1.50 |
| Plate, 9⅛", Dinner | 2.50 |
| Platter, 12" | 5.00 |
| Saucer | .50 |
| Sugar | 1.50 |
| Sugar Cover | 2.50 |

# FIRE-KING DINNERWARE "PHILBE" HOCKING GLASS COMPANY,
## 1937-1938

Colors:    Blue, green, pink and crystal.

The five pitchers shown here represent all but one that are known. There is another pink juice. The two large blue illustrate color variation since there are two distinct shades of blue. The darker blue shown with the platinum trim is similar to "Mayfair" blue whereas the untrimmed pitcher is closer in color to Federal Glass Company's "Madonna" blue. You can probably see this distinction more closely if you will look at the juice pitchers shown in the blue Mayfair picture (page 121) in which the same shades of blue are exhibited.

This is the one pattern that collectors write me to ask if I have any for sale—more than any other pattern in the book! I wish I had! It has been one of my favorites since I saw a set on display at Anchor Hocking on my first research trip in 1972. I have often wondered if the color caught my eye more than the pattern, but never seeing a set of it together again, I am not sure!

Does anyone out there have a green candy top? I found a bottom (and a water tumbler) that you can see in the photo. That's all the Philbe I have found except for the blue pitcher which came from Ohio.

The picture of the blue cookie jar is courtesy of Anchor Hocking. I had one in green that I sold for $10.00 years ago. These two are the only ones that I have ever seen or heard about in my travels.

If you could say any pieces of this pattern were commonly found, then you'd have to lump the green grill plates, the pink oval bowl and the blue 6½" footed tea into that group. Amazingly, the footed tea is more common than the footed water. (This is also true in the pink Mayfair which is the same shape as this "Philbe".) I say the same shape because unfortunately the Philbe water and tea tumblers are conspicously missing in the photo! They were unpacked after this photograph was taken and all the glass repacked. No one would believe me if I told the story behind the photography sessions; but some day I may try a short story on that! Make that a short novel! We had six collectors, and their glass in boxes, the photographer, two editors from Collector Books, along with the publisher who popped in and out, Cathy and me trying to sort and arrange this glass. That was problem enough, but there was also glass belonging to twenty other people besides all that! Thankfully, all glass has been returned intact and we all think we did a 98% good job of getting everything photographed properly. We did overlook the Philbe tumblers, however.

Many of the dinnerware pieces have shapes similar to Cameo, another Hocking pattern. Notice the cup and saucer that is shown for the first time! I found it at Washington Court House, Ohio, (about ten years ago) which is where many of the other blue pieces shown here were found. It was sold to a dealer in Georgia who sold it to a cup and saucer collector in Michigan before we photographed the Fourth book. She brought it to Paducah to photograph for this book. Glass travels in a very short circle, if you can keep up with it.

|  | Crystal | Pink Green | Blue |
|---|---|---|---|
| Bowl, 5½" Cereal | 15.00 | 30.00 | 40.00 |
| Bowl, 7¼" Salad | 20.00 | 40.00 | 60.00 |
| Bowl, 10" Oval Vegetable | 20.00 | 40.00 | 90.00 |
| Candy Jar, 4" Low, with Cover | 75.00 | 200.00 | 300.00 |
| Cookie Jar with Cover | 100.00 | 300.00 | 500.00 |
| Creamer, 3¼" Footed | 30.00 | 65.00 | 75.00 |
| Cup | 20.00 | 52.50 | 100.00 |
| Goblet, 7¼", 9 oz. Thin | 37.50 | 117.50 | 150.00 |
| Pitcher, 6", 36 oz. Juice | 200.00 | 500.00 | 850.00 |
| Pitcher, 8½", 56 oz. | 300.00 | 600.00 | 1,100.00 |
| Plate, 6" Sherbet | 15.00 | 30.00 | 50.00 |
| Plate, 8" Luncheon | 18.00 | 25.00 | 35.00 |
| Plate, 10" Heavy Sandwich | 20.00 | 35.00 | 50.00 |
| Plate, 10½" Salver | 20.00 | 35.00 | 50.00 |
| Plate, 10½" Grill | 20.00 | 30.00 | 45.00 |
| Plate, 11⅝" Salver | 20.00 | 30.00 | 45.00 |
| Platter, 12" Closed Handles | 22.00 | 50.00 | 100.00 |
| Saucer, 6" (Same as Sherbet Plate) | 15.00 | 30.00 | 50.00 |
| Sugar, 3¼" Footed | 30.00 | 65.00 | 75.00 |
| Tumbler, 4", 9 oz. Flat Water | 25.00 | 100.00 | 125.00 |
| Tumbler, 3½" Footed Juice | 30.00 | 90.00 | 125.00 |
| Tumbler, 5¼", 10 oz. Footed | 20.00 | 65.00 | 50.00 |
| Tumbler, 6½", 15 oz. Footed Iced Tea | 25.00 | 45.00 | 40.00 |

**Please refer to Foreword for pricing information**

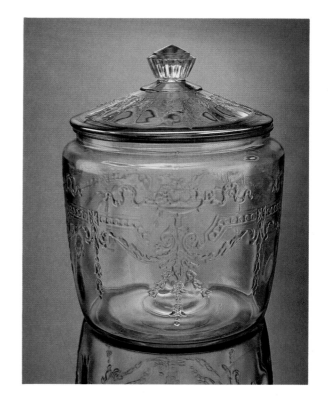

# FIRE-KING OVEN GLASS    ANCHOR HOCKING GLASS CORPORATION, 1941-1950's

Colors:    Pale blue, crystal; some ivory and Jade-ite.

We again owe thanks to Anchor Hocking for the picture of the blue skillet and nipple cover. Now that we know these items were made, possibly our search will prove more fruitful! Only a few nipple covers have turned up and no blue skillets have been reported as yet although the Jade-ite skillet is turning out to be available with searching.

Novice collectors should know there are four different custard cups; and the mugs come in a thick and thicker versions.

The uncovered casseroles were called "bakers" while those sold with lids were called "casseroles".

The handles on the large roaster sit opposite rather than atop each other so as to create a larger gripping surface. (The "tabs" are to keep the handles from sliding on each other.) These work best if you think of a clock with the tabs at the quarter hour.

The one-cup measure without a spout is called a "dry" measure and is rare.

Juice saver pie plates have a rim to keep the juices from spilling out of the pie when cooking. There is a lack of these today which means either the public did not buy the idea or they worked so well that usage finally caught up with them.

The child's bake set ("Sunny Suzy Glass Baking Set") pictured in the 4th edition is selling for $50.00-$60.00 in its original box.

I have re-listed the 4⅜" individual pie plate and the 5⅜" deep dish pie plate (as listed by Anchor Hocking) under "bowls" since I had so many calls and inquiries regarding these. These are shown on the left beside the mug and the one-spout measuring cup. The smaller of these "bowls" is hard to find.

| | Blue | | Blue |
|---|---|---|---|
| Baker, 1 pt., Round or Square | 3.50 | Custard Cup, 5 oz. | 3.00 |
| Baker, 1 qt. | 4.50 | Custard Cup, 6 oz., 2 Styles | 3.50 |
| Baker, 1½ qt. | 8.50 | Loaf Pan, 9⅛" Deep | 20.00 |
| Baker, 2 qt. | 10.00 | Measuring Bowl, 16 oz. | 18.00 |
| Bowl, 4⅜", Individual Pie Plate | 9.00 | Nurser, 4 oz. | 12.00 |
| Bowl, 5⅜", Cereal or Deep Dish Pie | | Nurser, 8 oz. | 15.00 |
| Plate | 10.00 | Pie Plate, 8⅜" | 7.00 |
| Cake Pan (Deep), 8¾" (Roaster) | 14.00 | Pie Plate, 9" | 8.00 |
| Casserole, 1 pt., Knob Handle Cover | 10.00 | Pie Plate, 9⅝" | 9.00 |
| Casserole, 1 qt., Knob Handle Cover | 10.00 | Pie Plate, 10⅜" Juice Saver | 50.00 |
| Casserole, 1½ qt., Knob Handle Cover | 12.00 | Perculator Top, 2⅛" | 3.50 |
| Casserole, 2 qt., Knob Handle Cover | 15.00 | Refrigerator Jar & Cover, 4½" x 5" | 7.50 |
| Casserole, 1 qt., Pie Plate Cover | 12.50 | Refrigerator Jar & Cover, 5⅛" x 9⅛" | 15.00 |
| Casserole, 1½ qt., Pie Plate Cover | 15.00 | Roaster, 8¾" | 30.00 |
| Casserole, 2 qt., Pie Plate Cover | 18.00 | Roaster, 10⅜" | 47.50 |
| Casserole, 10 oz., Tab Handle Cover | 12.00 | Table Server, Tab Handles (Hot Plate) | 10.00 |
| Coffee Mug, 7 oz., 2 Styles | 17.50 | Utility Bowl, 6⅞" | 8.00 |
| Cup, 8 oz., Dry Measure, No Spout | 50.00 | Utility Bowl, 8⅜" | 10.00 |
| Cup, 8 oz. Measuring, 1 Spout | 10.00 | Utility Bowl, 10⅛" | 15.00 |
| Cup, 8 oz., Measuring, 3 Spout | 16.00 | Utility Pan, 8⅛" x 12½" | 12.00 |

**Please refer to Foreword for pricing information**

# FIRE-KING OVEN WARE, "TURQUOISE BLUE"   ANCHOR HOCKING
## GLASS CORPORATION, 1950's

Color: Turquoise blue.

Turquoise Blue is the name found on original labels. The backs of the pieces are embossed "Oven Ware" and the labels say "Heat-Proof". These are our everyday dishes. In fact my oldest son just destroyed a cereal bowl last night. The dishes are fairly durable, but not when dropped from a six foot height! This was a regular cereal bowl. The bowl that he generally uses for cereal is the 8" vegetable bowl! Regular 5" cereal bowls are not nearly large enough for a seventeen year old who starts out with a whole quart of milk before he looks for the cereal box.

You can use this pattern in the microwave. The relish and the egg plates are usually trimmed in gold so they are not good candidates for the microwave unless you get a thrill from watching sparks fly.

The "Splash Proof" tear-shaped mixing bowls were issued under the name "Swedish Modern" in 1957. They do work and are great for mixing and pouring pancake mix!

You will find that all bowls are hard to find with the soup and cereals being the hardest. The 9" dinner plate is the easiest size of the plates to accumulate, but the 10" will take a while to find. As a lover of food, I prefer the 10" plate as my dinner plate.

| | Blue | | Blue |
|---|---|---|---|
| Bowl, 4½", Berry | 2.75 | Creamer | 3.50 |
| Bowl, 5", Cereal | 4.00 | Cup | 2.00 |
| Bowl, 6⅝", Soup/Salad | 6.50 | Egg Plate | 10.00 |
| Bowl, 8", Vegetable | 9.00 | Mug, 8 oz. | 5.00 |
| Bowl, Tear, Mixing, 1 pt. | 4.00 | Plate, 6⅛" | 2.50 |
| Bowl, Tear, Mixing, 1 qt. | 5.00 | Plate, 7" | 3.50 |
| Bowl, Tear, Mixing, 2 qt. | 6.00 | Plate, 9" | 4.00 |
| Bowl, Tear, Mixing, 3 qt. | 7.00 | Plate, 9", w/Cup Indent | 3.50 |
| Bowl, Round, Mixing, 1 qt. | 4.00 | Plate, 10" | 7.50 |
| Bowl, Round, Mixing, 2 qt. | 5.00 | Relish, 3 Part | 6.00 |
| Bowl, Round, Mixing, 3 qt. | 6.00 | Saucer | .50 |
| Bowl, Round, Mixing, 4 qt. | 7.00 | Sugar | 3.50 |

# FIRE-KING OVEN WARE, "SWIRL"   ANCHOR HOCKING GLASS
## CORPORATION, 1955-1960's

Colors: Blue, pink, white w/gold trim, ivory w/trims and Jade-ite.

"Swirl" and Turquoise Blue pieces are all embossed Oven Ware. Each of the colors had a name as found on original labels. The blue is "Azur-ite"; pink is "Pink"; white is "22K-Gold"; the red-trimmed is "Sun Rise". I had not found a labeled piece of the red-trimmed, but a reader found a set with labels and wrote about her find. I appreciate any additional information you have on any pattern in the book!

As with the rest of the Fire-King listings, this is later-made glass. Just realize that it is really not Depression Glass. I hope to take care of putting all of this later-made glass in perspective in another book in the near future.

There may be a little higher price on the blue in some areas, but most of the colors are selling in the same price range for now. I suspect some of the trimmed lines may be found to be more limited in production.

| | Jade-ite | Other Colors |
|---|---|---|
| Bowl, Berry, 4⅞" | 2.00 | 3.00 |
| Creamer | 2.00 | 3.50 |
| Cup | 1.75 | 2.50 |
| Plate, 6⅞", Salad | 1.25 | 1.75 |
| Plate, Dinner, 9⅛" | 2.50 | 3.75 |
| Platter, 12" | 7.50 | 10.00 |
| Saucer | .50 | .75 |
| Sugar | 1.50 | 2.00 |
| Sugar Cover | 1.50 | 2.00 |

**Please refer to Foreword for pricing information**

# FLORAGOLD, "LOUISA"    JEANNETTE GLASS COMPANY, 1950's

Colors:    Iridescent, some shell pink, ice blue and crystal.

There is a pattern in Carnival glass very similar to this which is known as "Louisa"—hence the crossed nomenclature. This creates some difficulty for collectors, but the listing here is for the glassware made in the 1950's. Rose bowls found with or without curved-in tops belong to the older Carnival glass era.

Recently, compotes in two styles have been uncovered. One has a ruffled top and the other has a straight edged top. Very few of these were made in a special run and most were given to employees of the factory. The smaller butter dish (5½" x 3" tall) with the squashed knob pictured in earlier editions is still unique at this time.

I have been asked time and again what the difference is between the 10 oz. and 11 oz. tumblers. One ounce is obvious. The 10 oz. has a narrow band around the top which the 11 ounce does not have. The 15 oz. tumbler is very hard to find except in crystal where they sell in the $6.00-$7.00 range. If some one can figure out how to iridize these, then this supply might even dry up. (Don't worry; the factory is already closed!)

There is a tid-bit in Floragold made from two ruffled bowls rather than the usual plate type. These are set around a white, wooden post. Each sell for approximately $20.00.

Cups were sold with that large bowl or the pitcher in Christmas promotions and were called "egg nog" sets. Therefore, cups are much more plentiful than saucer/sherbet plates. The sherbet plate and the saucer are the same and there is no indent for the cup.

That is a 8½" squared bowl in the picture next to the plate. Depth is lost at this camera angle. There is no 8½" ruffled bowl!

The salt and pepper can also be found with brown lids. Both white and brown are plastic and crack when over tightened. That is why the tops are worth as much as the shakers. All Floragold shakers originally had plastic tops!

The vase looks like a large tumbler whose top was inwardly scalloped. You will notice that the vase has had a big price jump since the last book, since few are being found. The vase is shown in the pattern shot for comparison purposes to the large tumbler.

| | Iridescent | | Iridescent |
|---|---|---|---|
| Bowl, 4½" Square | 4.50 | Creamer | 6.00 |
| Bowl, 5½" Round Cereal | 20.00 | Cup | 4.50 |
| Bowl, 5½" Ruffled Fruit | 4.50 | Pitcher, 64 oz. | 25.00 |
| Bowl, 8½" Square | 12.00 | Plate, 5¾" Sherbet | 6.00 |
| Bowl, 9½" Deep Salad | 25.00 | Plate, 8½" Dinner | 17.50 |
| Bowl, 9½" Ruffled | 6.50 | Plate or Tray, 13½" | 12.50 |
| Bowl, 12" Ruffled Large Fruit | 6.50 | Indent on 13½" Plate | 25.00 |
| Butter Dish and Cover, ¼ lb. | | Platter, 11¼" | 13.50 |
| Oblong | 17.50 | *Salt and Pepper, Plastic Tops | 35.00 |
| Butter Dish and Cover, Round | 35.00 | Saucer, 5¾" (No Ring) | 6.00 |
| Butter Dish Bottom | 12.00 | Sherbet, Low Footed | 8.00 |
| Butter Dish Top | 23.00 | Sugar | 5.00 |
| Candlesticks, Double Branch Pr. | 32.50 | Sugar Lid | 7.50 |
| Candy or Cheese Dish and Cover, | | Tumbler, 10 oz. Footed | 12.00 |
| 6¾" | 35.00 | Tumbler, 11 oz. Footed | 12.00 |
| Candy, 5¼" Long, 4 Feet | 4.50 | Tumbler, 15 oz. Footed | 45.00 |
| Candy Dish, 1 Handle | 6.50 | Vase or Celery | 150.00 |
| Coaster/Ash Tray, 4" | 4.50 | | |
| *Tops $8.50 each. | | | |

69

# FLORAL, "POINSETTIA"   JEANNETTE GLASS COMPANY, 1931-1935

Colors:   Pink, green, Delphite, Jadite, crystal, amber, red and yellow.

I spent a weekend at the Harbourfront Flea Market in Hamilton, Ontario, last year and met several collectors who had English friends searching for Depression Glass at flea markets and sales just as we do here. The stories I heard in Canada about Floral were similar to those I related in Doric and Pansy. The rarer pieces such as vases, rose bowls, flat pitchers and tumblers—are all being found in England and being shipped back to Canada or to the United States in containers. That is, unless these pieces are found by collectors there before they are sent back. More and more of my books are finding their way to collectors in England as the English are becoming aware of our glass. Not only green, but many unusual pieces in crystal are being found. English green Floral, however, seems to be a lighter color green (see difference in the photograph) and almost all pieces found there have ground or polished bottoms indicating earlier glass or special productions. If the glass could only talk, we could tie up a lot of loose ends about the how and why of Floral in England!

I can say for a fact that if you are looking for Floral lemonade pitchers, go to the Northwest. That seems to be true for the pink lamps also. Green lamps are not found any place I am aware of and I have covered a lot of this country.

There are few of the rarer pieces that are not being found in England or Canada. However, the comports, ice tubs and cream soups are being found *here* if found at all. Note the large size of the cream soup. I met a family member of the man who supposedly designed the cream soups. I should have asked why it was so large. It looks as if a bowl were used and handles added as an afterthought. He probably designed the Doric cream soups also. Both are rare today and both are very large which may mean that they were not acceptable to the public.

The dresser set pictured is the only one of those to be found complete. One powder dish measures 3″ and the other 4¼″. Several dresser trays have been found, however, so there must be other powder jars with the lids still with them. I see a few around with no lids.

Sugar and candy lids in this pattern are interchangeable.

The 11″ platter comes with scalloped indentations reminiscent of the Cherry Blossom platter. The normally found platter has smooth sides.

Unusual items in Floral (so far) include the following:
  a) an entire set of DELPHITE Floral
  b) a YELLOW, two-part relish dish
  c) an AMBER plate, cup and saucer
  d) green and crystal JUICE PITCHERS w/ground bottoms (shown)
  e) footed vases in green and crystal, flared at the rim (shown); some hold flower frogs with THE PATTERN ON THE FROGS (shown)
  f) a crystal lemonade pitcher
  g) lamps (shown in green and pink)
  h) a green GRILL plate
  i) an octagonal vase with a patterned, round foot (shown)
  j) a RUFFLED EDGED berry and master berry bowl
  k) pink and green Floral ICE tubs (shown)
  l) oval vegetable with cover
  m) a rose bowl (shown)
  n) a 9″ comport in pink and green (shown)
  o) 9 oz. flat tumblers in green (shown)
  p) 3 oz. footed tumblers in green (shown)
  q) 8″ round bowl in cremax and opaque red
  r) CARAMEL colored dinner plate
  s) cream soups (shown in pink)

# FLORAL, "POINSETTIA" (Cont.)

| | Pink | Green | Delphite | Jadite |
|---|---|---|---|---|
| Bowl, 4" Berry (Ruffled 50.00) | 11.00 | 12.00 | 25.00 | |
| Bowl, 5½" Cream Soup | 600.00 | 600.00 | | |
| *Bowl, 7½" Salad (Ruffled 75.00) | 10.00 | 12.00 | 45.00 | |
| Bowl, 8" Covered Vegetable | 25.00 | 32.50 | 37.50 (no cover) | |
| Bowl, 9" Oval Vegetable | 10.00 | 12.00 | | |
| Butter Dish and Cover | 70.00 | 75.00 | | |
| Butter Dish Bottom | 17.50 | 20.00 | | |
| Butter Dish Top | 52.50 | 55.00 | | |
| Canister Set: Coffee, Tea, Cereal Sugar, 5¼" Tall, Each | | | | 27.50 |
| Candlesticks, 4" Pr. | 50.00 | 65.00 | | |
| Candy Jar and Cover | 27.50 | 32.50 | | |
| Creamer, Flat (Cremax $50.00) | 9.00 | 10.00 | 60.00 | |
| Coaster, 3¼" | 7.50 | 8.00 | | |
| Comport, 9" | 500.00 | 600.00 | | |
| ***Cup | 7.50 | 8.50 | | |
| Dresser Set (As Shown) | | 950.00 | | |
| Frog for Vase (Also Crystal $500.00) | | 600.00 | | |
| Ice Tub, 3½" High Oval | 550.00 | 600.00 | | |
| Lamp | 225.00 | 225.00 | | |
| Pitcher, 5½", 23 or 24 oz. | | 475.00 | | |
| Pitcher, 8", 32 oz. Footed Cone | 20.00 | 25.00 | | |
| Pitcher, 10¼", 48 oz. Lemonade | 145.00 | 170.00 | | |
| Plate, 6" Sherbet | 3.50 | 4.00 | | |
| Plate, 8" Salad | 7.00 | 7.50 | | |
| **Plate, 9" Dinner | 11.00 | 12.50 | 100.00 | |
| Plate, 9" Grill | | 100.00 | | |
| Platter (Like Cherry Blossom) | 45.00 | | | |
| Platter, 10¾" Oval | 11.00 | 12.50 | 100.00 | |
| Refrigerator Dish and Cover, 5" Square | | 50.00 | | 15.00 |
| ***Relish Dish, 2-Part Oval | 10.00 | 11.00 | | |
| Salt and Pepper, 4" Footed Pair | 35.00 | 40.00 | | |
| Salt and Pepper, 6" Flat | 37.50 | | | |
| ***Saucer | 6.00 | 6.50 | | |
| Sherbet | 10.00 | 12.00 | 75.00 | |
| Sugar (Cremax $50.00) | 7.50 | 8.50 | 50.00 (open) | |
| Sugar/Candy Cover | 9.50 | 12.50 | | |
| Tray, 6" Square, Closed Handles | 9.50 | 12.00 | | |
| Tumbler, 4½", 9 oz. Flat | | 160.00 | | |
| Tumbler, 3½", 3 oz. Footed | | 90.00 | | |
| Tumbler, 4", 5 oz. Footed Juice | 12.00 | 15.00 | | |
| Tumbler, 4¾", 7 oz. Footed Water | 12.00 | 15.00 | 125.00 | |
| Tumbler, 5¼", 9 oz. Footed Lemonade | 31.50 | 33.50 | | |
| Vase, 3 Legged Rose Bowl | | 400.00 | | |
| Vase, 3 Legged Flared (Also in Crystal) | | 400.00 | | |
| Vase, 6⅞" Tall (8 Sided) | | 365.00 | | |

*Cremax $110.00
**These have now been found in amber and red.
***This has been found in yellow.

# FLORAL AND DIAMOND BAND   U.S. GLASS COMPANY, Late 1920's

Colors:   Pink, green; some iridescent, black and crystal.

A strong demand for luncheon plates and sugar lids in this pattern has pushed the prices for these items to unparalleled heights. There is more demand for the green than there has been in the past, but pink collectors still let their voices be heard. This is one of the few patterns without cups and saucers in which price increases have occurred. The latest collectors have not let the lack of cups and saucers bother them as it did previous collectors.

The smaller creamer and sugar keep turning up in black amethyst, but no other pieces in black have been reported.

Iridized pieces are still claimed by Carnival glass collectors as a pattern called "Mayflower". This makes these more valuable since two different groups of glass collectors are seeking the same items. You should be aware of mould roughness along the seams. This is significant to those of you who are perfectionists about your glass and do not want flaws. The pattern is reminiscent of early pattern glass because of this roughness and ponderous design.

In the old advertisements below, notice that two ads call this pattern, "Diamond and Floral" and the other calls it our "Floral and Diamond".

| | Pink | Green | | | Pink | Green |
|---|---|---|---|---|---|---|
| Bowl, 4½" Berry | 5.00 | 6.00 | | *Pitcher, 8", 42 oz. | 70.00 | 80.00 |
| Bowl, 5¾" Handled Nappy | 7.00 | 7.00 | | Plate, 8" Luncheon | 17.50 | 15.00 |
| Bowl, 8" Large Berry | 9.50 | 10.00 | | Sherbet | 5.00 | 6.00 |
| * Butter Dish and Cover | 80.00 | 85.00 | | Sugar, Small | 7.00 | 8.00 |
| Butter Dish Bottom | 45.00 | 52.50 | | Sugar, 5¼" | 10.00 | 10.00 |
| Butter Dish Top | 35.00 | 32.50 | | Sugar Lid | 35.00 | 40.00 |
| Compote, 5½" Tall | 9.50 | 10.00 | | Tumbler, 4" Water | 11.50 | 13.00 |
| Creamer, Small | 7.00 | 8.00 | | Tumbler, 5" Iced Tea | 15.00 | 18.00 |
| Creamer, 4¾" | 12.00 | 15.00 | | | | |

*Iridescent—$125.00
 Crystal—$100.00

**Seven-Piece Berry Set**
You'll really be most satisfied with the purchase of this set. It's very attractive, and affords a fitting and stylish addition to your present pieces. In green pressed glass, with diamond and floral design. Large bowl, 8 inches in diameter, and six sauce dishes to match, 4½ inches in diameter.
35N6838—Weight, packed, 7 pounds. Per set......**68c**

**Seven-Piece          Water Set**
Made from green pressed glass, with a floral and diamond design. You'll find that the sparkling scintillating pitcher and glasses are a set you'll be mighty proud to own when serving cold drinks. 3-pint pitcher. Six 8-ounce tumblers.
35N6837—Weight, packed, 12 pounds. Per set.**$1.18**

**Five-Piece Table Set**

Heavy pressed glass in light green, with pressed diamond and floral design. Creamer, covered sugar bowl and covered butter dish. Weight, packed, 9 pounds.
35N6836.........**65c**

**Please refer to Foreword for pricing information**

74

# FLORENTINE NO. 1, "OLD FLORENTINE", "POPPY NO. 1"

## HAZEL ATLAS GLASS COMPANY, 1932-1935

Colors:   Pink, green, crystal, yellow and cobalt.

Novice collectors still write me about the discovery of pieces in both of the Florentines that are not listed. All of this has come from confusing the two patterns; and unfortunately, there are no new pieces to report. Remembering the difference between the two is easier if you know that Florentine No. 1 was first advertised as Florentine Hexagonal and Florentine No. 2 was Florentine Round. Any pieces having serrated (bumpy) edges, be they footed or flat, are Florentine No. 1.

The lady who owns one of the two known cobalt blue pitchers was in Denver this year at the Rocky Mountain Depression Glass Society show. Very few of the cobalt pieces were made. A creamer and sugar are pictured. The 5" berry bowl is the most commonly found item in cobalt and although a few cups have surfaced, I have yet to hear of a saucer.

Speaking of the Denver show, I was able to purchase the only known pink Florentine No. 1 lemonade tumbler (shaped like Floral) which I have shown in earlier books. It was originally one of those early Washington Court House flea market finds from the *good old days*.

There have been a multitude of fired-on color pieces surfacing. Every color from blue to orange has been found. In fact, a whole set of the decorated red and yellow banded pieces (as illustrated by a plate in the picture) was found on the West coast. I did not rush out to complete my set since one piece is enough for me. It is novel though.

I need to point out that the 3¼" footed tumbler actually holds 4 oz. instead of the 3 oz. that has always been listed. This tumbler is shown on the left next to the pink shaker. It actually looks more like an egg cup than a tumbler and several collectors have been referring to it as such. So far, it has only been found in green and crystal.

The pink butter dish still remains more plentiful than collectors for it, but the yellow remains elusive. The bottom of these butters needs to be checked closely. There is usually damage around the serrated edges.

| | Crystal, Green | Yellow | Pink | Blue |
|---|---|---|---|---|
| Ash Tray, 5½" | 17.50 | 25.00 | 24.00 | |
| Bowl, 5" Berry | 8.00 | 12.00 | 8.50 | 13.00 |
| Bowl, 6" Cereal | 15.00 | 16.00 | 12.50 | |
| Bowl, 8½" Large Berry | 12.50 | 22.00 | 22.50 | |
| Bowl, 9½" Oval Vegetable & Cover | 35.00 | 37.50 | 37.50 | |
| Butter Dish and Cover | 100.00 | 140.00 | 110.00 | |
| Butter Dish Bottom | 40.00 | 70.00 | 50.00 | |
| Butter Dish Top | 60.00 | 70.00 | 60.00 | |
| Coaster/Ash Tray, 3¾" | 14.00 | 16.00 | 20.00 | |
| Creamer | 7.50 | 10.00 | 12.00 | |
| Creamer, Ruffled | 25.00 | | 25.00 | 45.00 |
| Cup | 6.00 | 8.00 | 6.50 | 65.00 |
| Pitcher, 6½", 36 oz. Footed | 32.50 | 40.00 | 37.50 | 600.00 |
| Pitcher, 7½", 48 oz. Flat, Ice Lip or None | 40.00 | 145.00 | 90.00 | |
| Plate, 6" Sherbet | 3.00 | 4.50 | 3.50 | |
| Plate, 8½" Salad | 5.50 | 9.50 | 9.00 | |
| Plate, 10" Dinner | 10.00 | 17.50 | 18.00 | |
| Plate, 10" Grill | 8.00 | 11.00 | 11.00 | |
| Platter, 11½" Oval | 10.00 | 16.00 | 15.00 | |
| Salt and Pepper, Footed | 30.00 | 45.00 | 45.00 | |
| Saucer | 2.00 | 3.50 | 3.50 | |
| Sherbet, 3 oz. Footed | 6.00 | 8.50 | 7.50 | |
| Sugar | 7.50 | 10.00 | 10.00 | |
| Sugar Cover | 11.00 | 15.00 | 12.00 | |
| Sugar, Ruffled | 22.50 | | 23.00 | 42.00 |
| Tumbler, 3¼", 4 oz. Footed | 10.00 | | | |
| Tumbler, 3¾", 5 oz. Footed Juice | 10.00 | 16.00 | 15.00 | |
| Tumbler, 4¾", 10 oz. Footed Water | 17.00 | 15.00 | 15.00 | |
| Tumbler, 5¼", 12 oz. Footed Iced Tea | 20.00 | 20.00 | 20.00 | |
| Tumbler, 5¼", 9 oz. Lemonade (Like Floral) | | | 50.00 | |

**Please refer to Foreword for pricing information**

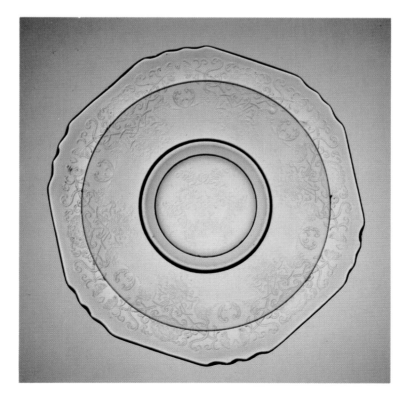

# FLORENTINE NO. 2, "POPPY NO. 2" HAZEL ATLAS GLASS COMPANY
## 1934-1937

Colors:   Pink, green, crystal, some cobalt, amber and ice blue.

Be sure to read the differences between the Florentines under Florentine No. 1 if you are having difficulty distinguishing between these patterns.

A new discovery in green is the grill plate with an indent. You might assume this indent would be for the cup, but it is for the cream soup. Were it not for a boxed set of four of these, I might have made the wrong assumption as to what went on the indent. How difficult these are to find remains to be seen; but since discovery of these last year, there have been no further reports.

Fired-on red, blue and other colors keep turning up and do not seem to excite collectors as they first did. Note the red saucer in the foreground. More ecstatically received are discoveries in amber. There has never been enough found to put together a set, but with several size tumblers having been discovered, how far behind can a pitcher be?

Note that the pink sherbet in the top picture is shaped differently than the green one on the right. This sherbet was found at a flea market in Mexico years ago and is shaped like Madrid's sherbets. It has the Florentine design on it! That puts a Hazel Atlas pattern on a Federal Glass Company mould. (And previously discussed under Florentine No. 1 was the Hazel Atlas pattern on a Jeannette Glass Company shape!) You wonder why authors have trouble getting glass listed by patterns. I suspect some sub-contracting went on in those days. For instance, in the 50's, when another company received a large order they could not fill by deadline, my Dad's company helped make the headlights and then put the other company's logo on the face. I'm sure this happened back in the 1930's with glass making.

The candy dish lids are difficult to find; so enterprising retailers have been selling the bottom as mayonnaise dishes. There is no such mayonnaise dish in Florentine; so be aware of that.

The tops to the covered oval vegetable bowl and the tops to the butter dishes are interchangeable in the Florentines. This is good if you have a bottom and are looking for a top since there should be more tops available. That is true for all except the pink in which there is no Florentine No.2.

| | Crystal, Green | Pink | Yellow | Blue | | Crystal, Green | Pink | Yellow | Blue |
|---|---|---|---|---|---|---|---|---|---|
| Bowl, 4½" Berry | 9.00 | 9.00 | 13.50 | | Pitcher, 7½", 48 oz. | 40.00 | 97.50 | 140.00 | |
| Bowl, 4¾" Cream Soup | 10.00 | 9.00 | 15.00 | | Pitcher, 8", 76 oz. | | 197.50 | 300.00 | |
| Bowl, 5" Cream Soup, or | | | | | Plate, 6" Sherbet | 2.50 | | 4.00 | |
| Ruffled Nut | | 9.50 | | 30.00 | Plate, 6¼" with Indent | 13.50 | | 22.50 | |
| Bowl, 5½" | 25.00 | | 27.50 | | Plate, 8½" Salad | 6.00 | 6.00 | 7.00 | |
| Bowl, 6" Cereal | 18.00 | | 25.00 | | Plate, 10" Dinner | 10.00 | 12.00 | 12.00 | |
| Bowl, 7½" Shallow | | | 50.00 | | Plate, 10¼" Grill | 6.50 | | 8.00 | |
| Bowl, 8" Large Berry | 15.00 | 17.00 | 19.00 | | Plate, 10¼", Grill w/Cup Ring | 15.00 | | | |
| Bowl, 9" Oval Vegetable and | | | | | Platter, 11" Oval | 10.00 | 11.00 | 11.00 | |
| Cover | 35.00 | | 45.00 | | Platter, 11½" for Gravyboat | | | 30.00 | |
| Bowl, 9" Flat | 17.50 | | | | Relish Dish, 10", 3 Part or Plain | 12.00 | 15.00 | 16.00 | |
| Butter Dish and | | | | | ** Salt and Pepper, Pr. | 35.00 | | 40.00 | |
| Cover | 85.00 | | 125.00 | | Saucer (Amber 15.00) | 2.50 | | 3.50 | |
| Butter Dish Bottom | 25.00 | | 45.00 | | Sherbet, Footed (Amber 39.50) | 6.00 | | 7.50 | |
| Butter Dish Top | 60.00 | | 80.00 | | Sugar | 6.00 | | 8.50 | |
| Candlesticks, 2¾" Pr. | 35.00 | | 45.00 | | Sugar Cover | 10.00 | | 14.50 | |
| Candy Dish and Cover | 85.00 | 100.00 | 125.00 | | Tray, Condiment for Shakers, | | | | |
| Coaster, 3¼" | 9.00 | 13.50 | 16.50 | | Creamer and Sugar (Round) | | | 52.50 | |
| Coaster/Ash Tray, 3¾" | 12.50 | | 15.00 | | Tumbler, 3½", 5 oz. Juice | 9.00 | 6.00 | 17.00 | |
| Coaster/Ash Tray, 5½" | 15.00 | | 27.50 | | Tumbler, 3½", 6 oz. Blown | 8.50 | | | |
| Comport, 3½" Ruffled | 15.00 | 8.00 | | 45.00 | *** Tumbler, 4", 9 oz. Water | 10.00 | 7.00 | 16.00 | 52.50 |
| Creamer | 6.50 | | 8.50 | | **** Tumbler, 5", 12 oz. Iced Tea | 22.00 | | 32.50 | |
| Cup (Amber 40.00) | 5.50 | | 7.00 | | Tumbler, 3¼", 5 oz. Footed | 10.00 | | 11.00 | |
| Custard Cup or Jello | 45.00 | | 65.00 | | Tumbler, 4", 5 oz. Footed | 10.00 | | 11.00 | |
| Gravy Boat | | | 35.00 | | Tumbler, 4½", 9 oz. Footed | 17.50 | | 22.50 | |
| Pitcher, 6¼", 24 oz. Cone-Footed | | | 90.00 | | Vase or Parfait, 6" | 25.00 | | 45.00 | |
| *Pitcher, 7½", 28 oz. Cone-Footed | 20.00 | | 22.00 | | | | | | |

*Blue—$400.00
**Fired-On Orange or Blue, Pr.—$35.00
***Amber—$50.00
****Amber—$65.00

**Please refer to Foreword for pricing information**

# FLOWER GARDEN WITH BUTTERFLIES, "BUTTERFLIES AND ROSES", U.S. GLASS COMPANY, Late 1920's

Colors: Pink, green, blue-green, canary yellow, crystal, amber and black.

I first mentioned the Flower Garden "pretenders" in one of my earlier books, and I am getting a lot of questions now about these. The most commonly mistaken pieces are the trivets in two sizes (7" and 10") which were found during the Depression era as mixing bowl covers on U.S. Glass bowls. These are identified by lots of flowers similar to Flower Garden but with nary a butterfly in sight. The other is a semi-circular footed dresser tray which originally held wedge-shaped perfume bottles that fit inside this tray. This tray is easily recognized by the dancing girl on it in two different places. It has no butterfly on it. It is not Flower Garden w/butterflies.

Prices for this pattern have driven away many new collectors. It's almost the realm of "I wish I could afford it", instead of "I wish I could find some of it." As the price of this has increased dramatically, more and more collections are being broken up and the supply has more than equalled the demand on many pieces. Cups, saucers, creamer and sugars have recently been more in evidence at the shows I attended than at any time I can remember.

Once again, I would like to thank Frank and Sherry McClain for the photographs of black and the miscellaneous colors. Frank has decided against becoming a professional photographer and he has these pictures of his collection to thank for that decision!

You will find several new listings. No other tumblers have been found to take their place alongside the crystal one shown in front of the flat candy in amber.

If anyone knows where to find an atomizer such as the one shown on the green perfume, let me know; we now have a blue one missing the bulb and top.

|  | Amber Crystal | Pink Green Blue-Green | Blue Canary Yellow |
|---|---|---|---|
| Ash Tray, Match-Pack Holders | 175.00 | 185.00 | 195.00 |
| Candlesticks, 4" Pr. | 40.00 | 50.00 | 75.00 |
| Candlesticks, 8" Pr. | 75.00 | 85.00 | 110.00 |
| Candy w/Cover, 6", Flat | 125.00 | 150.00 | |
| Candy w/Cover, 7½" Cone-Shaped | 75.00 | 100.00 | 150.00 |
| Candy w/Cover, Heart-Shaped | | 375.00 | 500.00 |
| *Cologne Bottle w/Stopper, 7½" | | 140.00 | 200.00 |
| Comport, 2⅞" h. | | 20.00 | 25.00 |
| Comport, 3" h. fits 10" Plate | 17.50 | 20.00 | 25.00 |
| Comport, 4¼" h. x 4¾" w. | | | 45.00 |
| Comport, 4¾" h. x 10¼" w. | 45.00 | 60.00 | 75.00 |
| Comport, 5⅞" h. x 11" w. | 50.00 | | 85.00 |
| Comport, 7¼" h. x 8¼" w. | 55.00 | 75.00 | |
| Creamer | | 65.00 | |
| Cup | | 50.00 | |
| Mayonnaise, footed 4¾" h. x 6¼" w., w/7" Plate & Spoon | 65.00 | 75.00 | 110.00 |
| Plate, 7" | 15.00 | 20.00 | 25.00 |
| Plate, 8", Two Styles | 13.50 | 16.50 | 22.50 |
| Plate, 10" | | 32.50 | 42.50 |
| Plate, 10", Indent for 3" Comport | 30.00 | 35.00 | 40.00 |
| Powder Jar, 3½", Flat | | 45.00 | |
| Powder Jar, Footed, 6¼" h. | 65.00 | 82.50 | 125.00 |
| Powder Jar, Footed, 7½" h. | 75.00 | 95.00 | 150.00 |
| Sandwich Server, Center Handle | 50.00 | 65.00 | 75.00 |
| Saucer | | 20.00 | |
| Sugar | | 60.00 | |
| Tray, 5½" x 10", Oval | 47.50 | | |
| Tray, 11¾" x 7¾", Rectangular | 47.50 | 57.50 | 77.50 |
| Tumbler, 7½ oz. | 100.00 | | |
| Vase, 6¼" | 67.50 | 87.50 | 107.50 |
| Vase, 10½" | | 100.00 | 150.00 |

*Stopper, if not broken off, ½ price of bottle

**Please refer to Foreword for pricing information**

# FLOWER GARDEN WITH BUTTERFLIES, "BUTTERFLIES AND ROSES", (Con't.)

PRICE LIST FOR BLACK ITEMS ONLY

| | |
|---|---:|
| Bon Bon w/Cover, 6⅝″ diameter | 250.00 |
| Bowl, 7¼″, w/Cover, "flying saucer" | 350.00 |
| Bowl, 8½″, Console, w/Base | 150.00 |
| Bowl, 9″ Rolled Edge, w/Base | 200.00 |
| Bowl, 11″ Footed Orange | 225.00 |
| Bowl, 12″ Rolled Edge Console w/Base | 200.00 |
| Candlestick, 6″ w/6½″ Candle, Pr. | 325.00 |
| Candlestick, 8″, Pr. | 225.00 |
| Cheese and Cracker, Footed, 5⅜″h. x 10″ w. | 325.00 |
| Comport and Cover, 2¾″ h. (Fits 10″ Indented Plate) | 200.00 |
| Cigarette Box & Cover, 4⅜″ long | 125.00 |
| Comport, Tourraine, 4¼″h. x 10″w. | 225.00 |
| Comport, Footed, 5⅝″h. x 10″w. | 225.00 |
| Comport, Footed, 7″h. | 175.00 |
| Plate, 10″, Indented | 100.00 |
| Sandwich Server, Center-Handled | 100.00 |
| Vase, 6¼″, Dahlia, Cupped | 135.00 |
| Vase, 8″, Dahlia, Cupped | 200.00 |
| Vase, 9″, Wall Hanging | 300.00 |
| Vase, 10″, 2 Handled | 225.00 |
| Vase, 10½″, Dahlia, Cupped | 250.00 |

**Please refer to Foreword for pricing information**

# FOREST GREEN    ANCHOR HOCKING GLASS COMPANY CORPORATION, 1950-1957

Color:    Forest green.

Attempting to find the elusive platter has driven several collectors into a frenzy! Why such a late pattern has pieces that are so difficult to find has always been a mystery. It is understandable in early patterns that have had breakage through usage, but a pattern only thirty years old should be more plentiful than it is. All of the bowls need to be checked closely for usage marks. The one complaint that several collectors have mentioned is that dealers sometimes do not scrutinize the later patterns as well as they do the earlier ones.

The plentiful ball vases were packed with mosquito repellent candles as were their counterparts in Royal Ruby.

The rounded cup in the right foreground is a punch cup. The regular cup is square to fit the square saucer. The punch bowl sells particularly well during the Christmas season. Due to its comparatively young age, many of these are found in original boxes which adds only a little to the value. Most collectors do not display boxed sets as such; so far, the boxes only add to the historical value and not much to the financial value of the bowl.

There are no footed creamer and sugars—just the square flat ones shown!

| | Green | | Green |
|---|---|---|---|
| Ash Tray | 3.00 | Plate, 8⅜" Luncheon | 4.00 |
| Batter Bowl | 10.00 | Plate, 10" Dinner | 8.50 |
| Bowl, 4¾" Dessert | 4.00 | Platter, Rectangular | 18.00 |
| Bowl, 5¼" Deep | 5.00 | Punch Bowl w/Stand | 22.50 |
| Bowl, 6" Soup | 8.00 | Punch Cup | 1.75 |
| Bowl, 7⅜" Salad | 7.50 | Saucer | 1.00 |
| Creamer, Flat | 4.50 | Sugar, Flat | 4.50 |
| Cup | 2.50 | Tumbler, 5 oz. | 2.00 |
| Mixing Bowl Set, 3 Piece | 22.00 | Tumbler, 10 oz. | 4.00 |
| Pitcher, 22 oz. | 12.50 | Vase, 4" Ivy | 3.00 |
| Pitcher, 3 qt. Round | 20.00 | Vase, 6⅜" | 3.50 |
| Plate, 6¾" Salad | 2.00 | Vase, 9" | 5.00 |

# FORTUNE   HOCKING GLASS COMPANY, 1937-1938

Colors:    Pink and crystal.

Fortune has not found favor with many collectors in the last few years. I suspect that this small set would be better used as an accessory pattern in conjunction with other pink patterns if it were more readily available. As it is, the candy dish is one of the few pieces that "item" collectors seek. It would have been a big help to have had a creamer and sugar, also.

Bowls are the most frequently found pieces; cups, saucers and plates will take a while to find. Another problem in trying to collect Fortune is that many dealers do not carry this small pattern to Depression Glass shows. The space for Fortune, which has few collectors, is usually used to set up a pattern that many people collect.

There are very few pieces found in crystal and I am not sure that a set could even be put together in that color. It is difficult enough to find the pink.

| | Pink, Crystal | | Pink, Crystal |
|---|---|---|---|
| Bowl, 4" Berry | 3.00 | Cup | 3.00 |
| Bowl, 4½" Dessert | 3.50 | Plate, 6" Sherbet | 2.00 |
| Bowl, 4½" Handled | 3.50 | Plate, 8" Luncheon | 5.00 |
| Bowl, 5¼" Rolled Edge | 4.50 | Saucer | 2.00 |
| Bowl, 7¾" Salad or Large Berry | 8.00 | Tumbler, 3½", 5 oz. Juice | 3.50 |
| Candy Dish and Cover, Flat | 15.00 | Tumbler, 4", 9 oz. Water | 4.50 |

**Please refer to Foreword for pricing information**

# FRUITS  HAZEL ATLAS AND OTHER GLASS COMPANIES, 1931-1933

Colors:    Pink, green, some crystal, and iridized.

The pitcher and both sizes of berry bowls are the pieces to find in Fruits. The pitcher has only been found in green and crystal. I have had several reports over the years of a pink one, but not one has ever materialized.

Tumblers are easier to find than the pitchers, but the green 12 oz. iced tea found in North Carolina years ago is a different story. This tumbler remains a solitary figure in this pattern. Experience has shown that when one of an item is found, usually more will follow. Collectors of Fruits are all awaiting that eventuality.

Remember that the iridized Fruits tumblers are not Carnival glass as many times they are erroneously labeled. The tumbler with "pears only" is the one most often found iridized, but you may find others. That is what makes this pattern interesting. You never know what may turn up!

| | Green | Pink | | Green | Pink |
|---|---|---|---|---|---|
| Bowl, 5″ Berry | 12.50 | 10.50 | Sherbet | 6.00 | 5.50 |
| Bowl, 8″ Berry | 35.00 | 30.00 | Tumbler, 3½″ Juice | 7.50 | 7.00 |
| Cup | 4.50 | 4.00 | Tumbler, 4″ (1 Fruit) | 8.00 | 7.50 |
| Pitcher, 7″ Flat Bottom | 42.50 | | Tumbler, 4″ (Combination | | |
| Plate, 8″ Luncheon | 4.00 | 4.00 | of Fruits) | 11.00 | 8.00 |
| Saucer | 2.50 | 2.50 | Tumbler, 5″, 12 oz. | 40.00 | 25.00 |

# HARP  JEANNETTE GLASS COMPANY, 1954-1957

Colors:    Crystal, crystal with gold trim, some shell pink and ice blue.

Would you believe a collector of Harp cake stands? There is one and he has made some interesting studies and has several ideas to report. I will give you all the details when room permits.

There is still a great demand for cups, saucers and plates in this pattern. Antique dealers with little knowledge of Depression Glass have pushed up the price of cake stands. I have seen the stand priced as high as $35.00 at a couple of the so-called "exclusive" antique shows. Of course, the label on the stand usually reads "pattern" or "early American pressed glass". Years ago, I would try to inform these dealers. I have learned that it is nearly always a waste of time. So now I just know differently and pass on by.

| | Crystal | | Crystal |
|---|---|---|---|
| Ash Tray/Coaster | 3.50 | Plate, 7″ | 4.00 |
| Coaster | 2.00 | Saucer | 2.00 |
| Cup | 5.50 | Tray, 2-Handled Rectangular | 20.00 |
| *Cake Stand, 9″ | 16.50 | Vase, 6″ | 10.00 |

*Ice blue or shell pink—$17.50

# GEORGIAN, "LOVEBIRDS" FEDERAL GLASS COMPANY, 1931-1936

Colors: Green and crystal.

Georgian is a pattern that became so collected in the middle 1970's (because of the Peach State Depression Club) that the supply today still suffers. There have been a few quantities discovered since that time, but the demand still exceeds the supply. There never will be enough tumblers or bowls found to please everyone.

Speaking of those items, I need to point out a few things to beginning collectors. Georgian is nicknamed "Lovebirds" by collectors because the two birds sitting together on their perch look very friendly. This causes some confusion because of the other bird pattern—"Parrot". The "Parrot" pattern is usually square shaped and has parrots and palm trees on the pieces. Georgian has birds and baskets alternating on mostly round pieces. The exception in Georgian are the tumblers. Amazingly, there are no birds on the tumblers to this pattern—only BASKETS! Knowing this sometimes will give you a chance to buy this rarely seen tumbler at a bargain price.

The bowls are another matter. The deep 6" one is the hardest to find. It is shown behind the creamer and sugar on the left. The large berry and the oval vegetable, behind the butter dish, are equally hard to find; but both turn up more frequently than the deep bowl. The oval vegetable and platter tend to be damaged on the closed handles; and the other bowls were used heavily, so they tend to be scratched and worn most of the time. Remember, damaged glass is not as collectible as mint; and paying premium prices for it is a mistake. However, if you use the pattern and need serving bowls, the vegetables served will hide the scratches. If the glass is an investment, go for mint condition.

There are two styles of dinner plates. One has only the center design and no birds; the fully designed plates are more in demand. There is a price discrepancy.

There are also two sizes of sugar and creamers pictured in the foreground. The taller (4") sugar has a lid that is found infrequently. The lids are not interchangeable; so make sure that the lid fits properly on the large sugar.

A collector in Georgia has what appears to be a creamer that did not have its spout added when it was made. It is being called a "mug". It's unusual but thin for a mug.

There is a walnut lazy susan (cold cuts server) in this pattern just as there is in Madrid. There are slots cut out to hold seven hot plates. Six plates circle a center one. Most of these have been found in Eastern Kentucky which may mean that they were a premium in that area.

|  | Green |  | Green |
|---|---|---|---|
| Bowl, 4½" Berry | 5.00 | Plate, 6" Sherbet | 3.00 |
| Bowl, 5¾" Cereal | 14.00 | Plate, 8" Luncheon | 5.50 |
| Bowl, 6½" Deep | 47.50 | Plate, 9¼" Dinner | 18.00 |
| Bowl, 7½" Large Berry | 40.00 | Plate, 9¼" Center Design Only | 16.00 |
| Bowl, 9" Oval Vegetable | 45.00 | Platter, 11½" Closed-Handled | 45.00 |
| Butter Dish and Cover | 67.50 | Saucer | 2.00 |
| Butter Dish Bottom | 42.50 | Sherbet | 8.00 |
| Butter Dish Top | 25.00 | Sugar, 3", Footed | 7.50 |
| Cold Cuts Server, 18½" Wood with |  | Sugar, 4", Footed | 8.50 |
|    Seven 5" Openings for 5" Coasters | 500.00 | Sugar Cover for 3" | 22.50 |
| Creamer, 3", Footed | 8.50 | Sugar Cover for 4" | 60.00 |
| Creamer, 4", Footed | 10.00 | Tumbler, 4", 9 oz. Flat | 35.00 |
| Cup | 7.50 | Tumbler, 5¼", 12 oz. Flat | 67.50 |
| *Hot Plate, 5" Center Design | 32.50 |  |  |

*Crystal—$18.50

# HERITAGE   FEDERAL GLASS COMPANY, Late 1930's - 1960's

Colors:   Crystal, some pink, blue, green and cobalt.

Heritage has seen a lot of collecting activity since the last book two years ago. The sugar, creamer and 8½" berry bowl have really given new collectors headaches because they are being found so infrequently. In fact, the only 8½" berry I came up with for the book was the green one I found in 1974!

The aforementioned bowl and six smaller green berry bowls were found in southern Ohio on a research trip. To date, not another green bowl has surfaced. There have been a few blue and pink ones found since then. In fact, a cobalt blue and a "smoke" colored crystal have also turned up—both in Texas. Pink seems to be found in California, since the lasts two reports have come from there.

Frankly, I have been amazed by the demand I have seen for this smaller pattern and from the letters and calls I have received about where to find the pattern. I expect to hear about the colored pieces, but the crystal is HOT! I guess my statement from the last book was taken to heart by collectors. Anyway, dealers, take note and stock it!

|  | Crystal | Pink | Blue Green |
|---|---|---|---|
| Bowl, 5" Berry | 4.50 | 25.00 | 35.00 |
| Bowl, 8½" Large Berry | 18.00 | 60.00 | 95.00 |
| Bowl, 10½" Fruit | 10.00 | | |
| Cup | 4.00 | | |
| Creamer, Footed | 15.00 | | |
| Plate, 8" Luncheon | 4.50 | | |
| Plate, 9¼" Dinner | 6.50 | | |
| Plate, 12" Sandwich | 8.50 | | |
| Saucer | 1.75 | | |
| Sugar, Open-Footed | 10.00 | | |

# HEX OPTIC, "HONEYCOMB"   JEANNETTE GLASS COMPANY, 1928-1932

Colors:   Pink, green and iridesent in 1950's.

Hex Optic kitchenware keeps this pattern in the forefront of collector's minds. Until the advent of my *Kitchenware* book in 1981, this pattern was obscure. Collecting kitchenware made Hex Optic noticed because it combined both the elements of dinnerware and kitchenware in one pattern; no other pattern does that as well.

Not only are the collectors from both these fields searching for several items; but add to that collectors of reamers who are looking for the bucket reamer and you get even more complications! Hex Optic never knew it would be so popular.

The rectangular butter dish, stacking refrigerator set, and the sugar shaker now have collectors from two fields of collecting looking for them. It is the sugar shaker and butter dish that are proving to be the most elusive and have taken the biggest price hikes.

Iridized tumblers, oil lamps and pitchers were all made during Jeannette's iridized craze of the 1950's. I have never been able to find when the teal colored tumblers were made, but a guess would be in the late 1930's when the company was making that color in other patterns.

|  | Pink, Green |  | Pink, Green |
|---|---|---|---|
| Bowl, 4¼" Ruffled Berry | 2.50 | Plate, 6" Sherbet | 1.50 |
| Bowl, 7½" Large Berry | 5.00 | Plate, 8" Luncheon | 4.50 |
| Bowl, 7¼" Mixing | 10.00 | Platter, 11" Round | 7.00 |
| Bowl, 8¼" Mixing | 14.00 | Refrigerator Dish, 4" x 4" | 7.00 |
| Bowl, 9" Mixing | 15.00 | Refrigerator Stack Set, 3 Pc. | 35.00 |
| Bowl, 10" Mixing | 18.00 | Salt and Pepper, Pr. | 17.50 |
| Bucket Reamer | 40.00 | Saucer | 1.50 |
| Butter Dish and Cover, Rectangular 1 lb. Size | 55.00 | Sugar, 2 Styles of Handles | 4.00 |
| Creamer, 2 Style Handles | 4.00 | Sugar Shaker | 85.00 |
| Cup, 2 Style Handles | 3.00 | Sherbet, 5 oz. Footed | 3.50 |
| Ice Bucket, Metal Handle | 12.50 | Tumbler, 3¾", 9 oz. | 3.50 |
| Pitcher, 5", 32 oz. Sunflower Motif in Bottom | 15.00 | Tumbler, 4¾", 7 oz. Footed | 6.50 |
| | | Tumbler, 5¾" Footed | 4.50 |
| Pitcher, 9", 48 oz. Footed | 30.00 | Tumbler, 7" Footed | 7.50 |
| | | Whiskey, 2", 1 oz. | 5.00 |

**Please refer to Foreword for pricing information**

# HOBNAIL  HOCKING GLASS COMPANY, 1934-1936

Colors:    Crystal, crystal w/red trim and pink.

The Hobnail shown here is that made only by Hocking. Almost all glass-making companies of this time period had a hobnail of some description. Many collectors combine all the hobnails together, which is fine, if you realize that this listing is only Hocking's. Maybe that will save me fifty or so letters asking why I did not list some of the pieces that you have in your collection.

All the pieces here are from Hocking's catalogue. If you have an earlier book, you may find a listing for an 18 oz. tea which is what my copy of microfilm from Hocking seems to say. It has been shown that this was only 13 oz! The 18 oz. belongs to the milk pitcher.

This pattern is collected mostly in crystal since so few pieces in pink were made. There are five if you count the dual purpose saucer/sherbet plate as two different pieces. If you can find a 5th edition book, there is a picture of a pink pitcher and tumbler set that can be used very nicely with this set.

The fired-on red trimmed pieces are more in demand than the plainer, untrimmed pieces; however, not much of the red trimmed is available at any price. Some dealers are beginning to carry this smaller pattern to shows since so many collectors are starting to ask for it.

|  | Pink | Crystal |
|---|---|---|
| Bowl, 5½″ Cereal | | 2.50 |
| Bowl, 7″ Salad | | 3.75 |
| Cup | 3.00 | 3.00 |
| Creamer, Footed | | 2.50 |
| Decanter and Stopper, 32 oz. | | 17.50 |
| Goblet, 10 oz. Water | | 4.50 |
| Goblet, 13 oz. Iced Tea | | 5.00 |
| Pitcher, 18 oz. Milk | | 13.00 |
| Pitcher, 67 oz. | | 20.00 |
| Plate, 6″ Sherbet | 1.50 | 1.00 |
| Plate, 8½″ Luncheon | 2.00 | 2.00 |
| Saucer (Sherbet Plate in Pink) | 1.50 | 1.00 |
| Sherbet | 2.50 | 2.00 |
| Sugar, Footed | | 2.50 |
| Tumbler, 5 oz. Juice | | 3.00 |
| Tumbler, 9 oz., 10 oz. Water | | 4.50 |
| Tumbler, 15 oz. Iced Tea | | 6.00 |
| Tumbler, 3 oz. Footed Wine | | 5.00 |
| Tumbler, 5 oz. Footed Cordial | | 4.50 |
| Whiskey, 1½″ oz. | | 4.00 |

**Please refer to Foreword for pricing information**

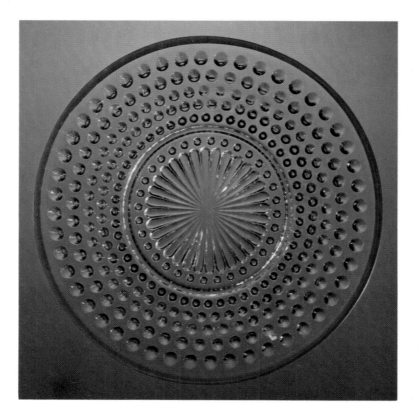

# HOLIDAY, "BUTTONS AND BOWS"   JEANNETTE GLASS COMPANY, 1947-1949

Colors:   Pink, iridescent; some shell pink opaque and crystal.

I found out that Holiday pattern "took a trip" so to speak. If you have wondered as I have, why a pattern made in the late 1940's has so many difficult-to-find pieces, then the mystery may have finally been solved. Last summer I met a serviceman who had just returned from the Phillippines after being stationed there. He had bought so many Holiday iced teas there that it astounded me! No wonder we can't find these in the United States.

It seems that the footed iced teas were sent to the Phillippines as premiums for purchasing a well-known chocolate bar and servicemen could eat (and barter) chocolate bars! Evidently, they were sent in boxes of six. The footed juices and flat soups were also in evidence. There is something going on in the Phillippines, as I had never sent a book there until recently; and now several have been shipped air mail. (I sent a book to Russia, too, and often wondered if they found Depression Glass there). I do know it is found in the Phillippines, since I saw some that had been brought from there!

Now, the stories of glass being used as ballast on ships is making more and more sense. I often wondered about that ballast story; but it has been repeated to me three times from widely ranging sources so there must be some truth to it. It is a shame that sea water destroys glass. MERMAIDS must have set some mighty colorful tables! They say the ballast was often dumped overboard rather than unloaded in port.

You should know that there are two completely different styles of cups and saucers. Some cup and saucers have rayed bottoms and others are plain. These can not be mixed since the cup ring sizes are different. You need to remember that if you purchase the cup and saucers separately. A good rule of thumb in this pattern is to buy the cup and saucers together.

The iridized platter with six footed juices was sold in the middle 1950's; I have also had a report that this set was a premium in a grocery chain in the midwest.

The problem to watch for is that points that protrude on many of the pieces in this pattern have a tendency to get nicked and chunked. The amount of damaged pieces found in this pattern indicate to me that it was used for everyday dishes and not stored in the china cabinet to be admired.

| | Pink | | Pink |
|---|---|---|---|
| Bowl, 5⅛" Berry | 7.00 | Pitcher, 6¾", 52 oz. | 25.00 |
| Bowl, 7¾" Soup | 27.50 | Plate, 6" Sherbet | 3.00 |
| Bowl, 8½" Large Berry | 14.50 | Plate, 9" Dinner | 9.50 |
| Bowl, 9½" Oval Vegetable | 12.00 | Plate, 13¾" Chop | 65.00 |
| Bowl, 10¾" Console | 70.00 | Platter, 11⅜" Oval | 9.00 |
| Butter Dish and Cover | 30.00 | Sandwich Tray, 10½" | 9.00 |
| Butter Dish Bottom | 10.00 | Saucer, 2 Styles | 3.00 |
| Butter Dish Top | 20.00 | Sherbet | 5.00 |
| Cake Plate, 10½", 3 Legged | 62.50 | Sugar | 6.00 |
| Candlesticks, 3" Pr. | 55.00 | Sugar Cover | 8.50 |
| Creamer, Footed | 6.50 | Tumbler, 4", 10 oz. Flat | 15.00 |
| Cup, Two Sizes | 5.00 | Tumbler, 4" Footed | 25.00 |
| Pitcher, 4¾", 16 oz. Milk | 45.00 | Tumbler, 6" Footed | 65.00 |

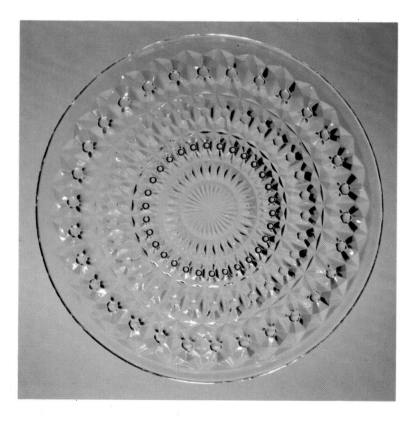

95

# HOMESPUN, "FINE RIB"   JEANNETTE GLASS COMPANY, 1939-1940

Colors:   Pink and crystal.

Homespun tumblers have all but disappeared. That is all except the omnipresent 4", 5 oz, footed juice which must have been the most heavily produced Jeannette tumbler of all time. I pointed out that there are two styles of Homespun footed tumblers in the last book. (One has a clear band of glass around the top and the other has lines that run to the top edge.) Now, I need to report that there are two styles of flat water tumblers. The more common straight sided 9 oz. is 3⅜" tall; whereas, the harder-to-find, flared top water is 4" tall. How have these small differences escaped us all these years?

Again, the tea pot lid to the child's set made the trip to the photography session alone. I remedied that situation when we got back and picked up the bottom for the next session.

It seems that the only crystal available in Homespun is the child's set which has no tea pot. All of the crystal we have been calling Homespun for years is really of Canadian manufacture. The name of this Canadian pattern is Sagany. So if you have some pieces that you think might be crystal Homespun, check again.This pattern has little squares instead of fine lines. It has all the waffling in the bottom and tops along with the same knobs. There the similarity stops when compared closely.

There is NO sugar lid! There is a Jeannette pink and green powder jar that looks similar to Homespun and the lid to this jar will fit the sugar. Fitting and belonging are two different categories. Catalogues plainly show there is no lid and Homespun was never made in green.

|  | Pink, Crystal |  | Pink, Crystal |
|---|---|---|---|
| Bowl, 4½", Closed Handles | 4.50 | Platter, 13", Closed Handles | 8.50 |
| Bowl, 5" Cereal | 12.50 | Saucer | 2.00 |
| Bowl, 8¼" Large Berry | 10.00 | Sherbet, Low Flat | 6.50 |
| Butter Dish and Cover | 40.00 | Sugar, Footed | 6.00 |
| Coaster/Ash Tray | 5.00 | Tumbler, 3⅞", 9 oz. Straight | 10.00 |
| Creamer, Footed | 6.50 | Tumbler, 4", 9 oz. Water, Flared Top | 12.00 |
| Cup | 4.50 | Tumbler, 5¼", 13 oz. Iced Tea | 18.00 |
| Pitcher, 96 oz. | 30.00 | Tumbler, 4", 5 oz. Footed | 5.00 |
| Plate, 6" Sherbet | 2.00 | Tumbler, 6¼", 9 oz. Footed | 16.50 |
| Plate, 9¼" Dinner | 9.50 | Tumbler, 6½", 15 oz. Footed | 20.00 |

## HOMESPUN CHILD'S TEA SET

|  | Pink | Crystal |
|---|---|---|
| Cup | 22.50 | 15.00 |
| Saucer | 6.00 | 4.50 |
| Plate | 9.00 | 6.50 |
| Tea Pot | 25.00 | |
| Tea Pot Cover | 35.00 | |
| Set: 14-Pieces | 210.00 | |
| Set: 12-Pieces | | 105.00 |

# INDIANA CUSTARD, "FLOWER AND LEAF BAND"   INDIANA GLASS

## COMPANY, 1930's; 1950's

Colors:   Ivory or custard, early 1930's; white, 1950's.

A dealer who retired several years ago approached me about this pattern at a recent show. She said of all the patterns that she had collected, Indiana Custard had been the hardest to complete. Since she had collected some of the larger, more popular patterns I was curious to discuss it with her. The soup bowls are even harder to find than the sherbets and the major problem she incurred was getting all of this pattern in the same shade of beige. As particular as she was about glass, I am sure that mismatched colors caused her considerable pain.

I get a ton of mail about the white which was made in the 1950's. Everyone is wanting to sell it, but I have not met a collector of the white as yet. I see it priced at 20% to 25% of the custard color, but I have never seen it sell at any price. The cup and saucer sets are usually priced in the range of $3.00. It could be used as your everyday dishes!

If you run into a stack of cup and saucers or sherbets in your travels, do not let them scare you away if they are priced too cheaply. I just received a letter from someone who saw twelve of each and since they were only $2.00 each, he was afraid that they were reproductions!

|  | French Ivory |  | French Ivory |
|---|---|---|---|
| Bowl, 4⅞" Berry | 6.50 | Plate, 5¾" Bread and Butter | 4.50 |
| Bowl, 5¾" Cereal | 15.00 | Plate, 7½" Salad | 8.50 |
| Bowl, 7½" Flat Soup | 25.00 | Plate, 8⅞" Luncheon | 8.50 |
| Bowl, 8¾" Large Berry | 20.00 | Plate, 9¾" Dinner | 13.50 |
| Bowl, 9½" Oval Vegetable | 20.00 | Platter, 11½" Oval | 22.50 |
| Butter Dish and Cover | 52.50 | Saucer | 6.00 |
| Cup | 30.00 | Sherbet | 67.50 |
| Creamer | 12.50 | Sugar | 8.50 |
|  |  | Sugar Cover | 15.00 |

**Please refer to Foreword for pricing information**

# IRIS, "IRIS AND HERRINGBONE"  JEANNETTE GLASS COMPANY, 1928-1932;

## 1950's; 1970's

Colors:  Crystal, iridescent; some pink; recently bi-colored red/yellow and blue/green combinations and white.

Iris collectors abound and this is becoming one of the hottest collectibles in the Depression Glass field. I believe that it has become one of the top five collected patterns, and this is up from about tenth of a few years ago. I could not believe collectors would pay $25.00 to $30.00 for a demitasse cup and saucer a few years ago. Now $75.00 is the norm and they are still selling. Years ago, I sold iridiized demitasse sets for $50.00 and now they are approaching $150.00. It is the saucer that is the hard piece to find. I strongly suggest that you do not buy the cups by themselves unless they are at giveaway prices. Many of the demitasse sets were sold with a glass cup on a copper saucer; so the supply of glass saucers is at a premium. See the price listed for each!

Iris is a pattern that has also been found in the Phillippines. See Holiday for a more detailed story. I only mention that here because there was a flat candy in the set found there. It did not have the feel or look of American-made glass and since it sold at the show, I did not have a chance to get a photograph of it to study. The 104 degree weather outside and my asthma problems compounded to make that show one of the few I have little recollection of today. I wish I knew more about that piece, but I do not. If you own it, write me about it.

I do not know who did the decorating jobs on the items shown in the picture, but you will find many pieces decorated as these are. The decorated pieces are much harder to sell than the plain ones. I guess collectors feel it would be difficult to complete a decorated set. The satinized (frosted) pieces with painted flowers are virtually ignored by collectors. One of the reaons that the 8" plates may be so hard to find is that so many of them were frosted.

The nut set with cracker and picks (which is made from a 11" ruffled fruit bowl) can also be found as a fruit set with knives. Many times these are found at very reasonable prices. I get more letters about these items and the lamp shades than for any other Iris pieces. The lamp shades come in other colors besides the blue shown here. I have seen them in beige, tan, white, pink and green.

Both the wines and the water goblets in iridized have plain bottoms—no rays as on crystal. There are two styles of crystal bases on the tumblers and goblets. Some have an iris flower among the rayed bottom while others do not.

There is no way to tell the iridized pieces that were issued in the 1970's from those of the 1950's. The stronger color is not an indication of any thing more than a better spraying job done during the iridizing process!

The white vases and the multi-colored red/green or other bi-colored vases are of recent vintage. The bottom to the candy was sold as a vase or flower pot in a bi-colored decoration also. Some of these got out of the factory in crystal. They are easily distinguished along with these later vases because the bottoms are plain and not ribbed as in the older versions. REMEMBER, only the plain bottom vases and candy bottoms are NEWER! Not everything with a plain bottom is new. Readers have a tendency to take my words on particular items and transfer it to other pieces. IT DOES NOT WORK THAT WAY!

| | Crystal | Iridescent | | Crystal | Iridescent | Pink, Green |
|---|---|---|---|---|---|---|
| Bowl, 4½" Berry, Beaded | | | Fruit or Nut Set | 30.00 | | |
| Edge | 27.50 | 6.50 | Goblet, 4" Wine | | 16.50 | |
| Bowl, 5" Ruffled Sauce | 6.00 | 5.50 | Goblet, 4¼", 3 oz., Cocktail | 16.00 | | |
| Bowl, 5" Cereal | 32.50 | | Goblet, 4½" Wine | 12.50 | | |
| Bowl, 7½" Soup | 80.00 | 25.00 | Goblet, 5¾", 4 oz. | 16.50 | | |
| Bowl, 8" Berry, Beaded | | | Goblet, 5¾", 8 oz. | 16.00 | 35.00 | |
| Edge | 52.50 | 10.00 | Lampshade | 30.00 | | |
| *Bowl, 9½" Salad | 8.50 | 8.00 | Pitcher, 9½" Footed | 20.00 | 27.50 | |
| Bowl, 11" Ruffled Fruit | 8.50 | 6.00 | Plate, 5½" Sherbet | 7.50 | 6.00 | |
| Bowl, 11" Fruit, Straight | | | Plate, 8" Luncheon | 35.00 | | |
| Edge | 32.50 | | Plate, 9" Dinner | 30.00 | 19.50 | |
| Butter Dish and Cover | 27.50 | 27.50 | Plate, 11¾" Sandwich | 12.00 | 11.00 | |
| Butter Dish Bottom | 5.00 | 7.50 | Saucer | 5.00 | 4.00 | |
| Butter Dish Top | 22.50 | 22.50 | Sherbet, 2½" Footed | 15.00 | 10.00 | |
| Candlesticks, Pr. | 17.50 | 22.50 | Sherbet, 4" Footed | 12.00 | | |
| Candy Jar and Cover | 70.00 | | Sugar | 6.00 | 6.00 | |
| Coaster | 32.50 | | Sugar Cover | 6.50 | 6.00 | |
| Creamer, Footed | 7.00 | 8.00 | Tumbler, 4" Flat | 47.50 | | |
| Cup | 8.50 | 7.50 | Tumbler, 6" Footed | 12.00 | 12.00 | |
| **Demitasse Cup | 20.00 | 65.00 | Tumbler, 7" Footed | 15.00 | | |
| **Demitasse Saucer | 55.00 | 75.00 | Vase, 9" | 15.00 | 14.00 | 50.00 |

*Pink—$50.00        **Ruby, Blue, Amethyst priced as Iridescent

**Please refer to Foreword for pricing information**

# JUBILEE    LANCASTER GLASS COMPANY, Early 1930's

Colors:    Yellow, pink.

Listing Jubilee as a pattern in my 5th Edition turned out to be one of the smartest things I ever did or the dumbest—depending upon which point of view you wish to pursue. I have never seen a pattern cause so much controversy over flower petal count. A dealer and collector almost came to blows at a recent show because of disagreement as to what constitutes Jubilee and what does not. I personally feel that this is a pattern that needs to be seen to be bought because mail order can cause a major headache if the principals involved do not agree on what constitutes Jubilee.

The TRUE pattern has 12 petals to the flower and is open in the center. There are usually sharp points on the petals, but some are rounded. There are NO small petals in between each of the larger petals. It is true that Lancaster made a multitude of patterns similar to Jubilee, but only one they named JUBILEE; so, if you are willing to accept these look-alikes in your sets, then collecting for you will be easier. However, if you are a purist or an advertiser of Jubilee, then you had better know how to distinguish this pattern from all the pretenders or else be prepared for returned glass.

The list of new pieces includes a couple of three-footed bowls which measure 8″ and 11″ respectively. There have been reports of other pieces, but I have only seen these! One of the fascinating reports I received was on cordials. As a cordial collector, I hope that report is true and that I can add one to my collection.

I am receiving few reports of pink Jubilee, although a couple of collectors insist they have complete sets. I have only seen the sugar thus far!

There has been a rapid price escalation on the 12½ oz. goblets. In reality, these are footed tumblers rather than goblets, but who am I to argue with tradition.

I list the tall sherbet as a champagne also. I get a lot of letters from collectors who say I have omitted the champagnes from my lists. Some companies listed these items as high sherbets during prohibition. It probably was a little difficult to sell a champagne glass when drinking was prohibited by the law of the land. That might have been construed as un-American!

The serving pieces in Jubilee are still the most difficult to find and the mayonnaise is the most avidly sought piece. I still have been unable to find a mate to my single candlestick.

| | Yellow | | Yellow |
|---|---|---|---|
| Bowl, 8″, 3 Footed, 5⅛″ High | 125.00 | Mayonnaise & Plate | 110.00 |
| | | w/Original Ladle | 125.00 |
| Bowl, 9″ Handled Fruit | 45.00 | Plate, 7″ Salad | 6.50 |
| Bowl, 11″, 3 Footed | 125.00 | Plate, 8¾″ Luncheon | 8.50 |
| Candlestick, Pr. | 65.00 | Plate, 13″ Sandwich | 25.00 |
| Cheese & Cracker Set | 65.00 | Saucer, 2 Styles | 3.00 |
| Creamer | 16.50 | Sherbet/Champagne, 4¾″ | 25.00 |
| Cup | 10.00 | Sugar | 16.00 |
| Goblet, 5″, 6 oz. | 35.00 | Tray, 11″, 2-Handled Cake | 27.50 |
| Goblet, 6″, 10 oz. | 25.00 | Tray, Center-Handled Sandwich | 45.00 |
| Goblet, 6⅛″, 12½ oz. | 65.00 | | |

**Please refer to Foreword for pricing information**

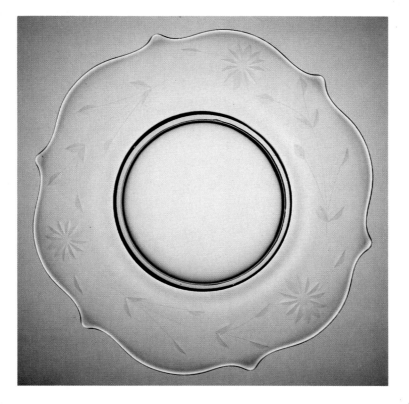

101

# LACE EDGE, "OPEN LACE"   HOCKING GLASS COMPANY, 1935-1938

Colors:   Pink, some crystal.

The abundance of Lace Edge look-alikes continues to plague new collectors and even some of the older ones. If the object of inquiry is not pink or crystal, I will guarantee that it is not Lace Edge. That eliminates the yellow and green so commonly found that is mistaken for Lace Edge. Now comes the problem with pink! The pieces that are similar to Lace Edge are usually much better quality glass. If you strike the lace and get a nice ringing sound, it definitely is not our pattern which will give a dull thud when struck. No one ever accused Lace Edge of being finely made glassware.

I have decided to keep the new picture taken for this book even with a glaring mistake shown. That is a NEWLY-MADE small candy in the foreground on the left! I was on my way to another photography session for the *Rare* book and left some of the glass behind to be pictured in my absence. The lid to the flower bowl which converts this bowl to a ribbed candy was placed on the cereal bowl making a "new" small candy. That lid and flower frog both actually fit the ribbed bottom bowl making it a dual-purpose piece (candy and flower bowl).

The frosted vase still commands a very small price compared to the clear one; that is why you get to see the frosted one in the picture. The candlesticks and console bowl are the other pieces that you can find frosted. This frosted effect is called satinized and is obtained by dipping the piece in camphoric acid. Collectors have never accepted this practice and the prices remain very low.

Several more of the 9″ comports shown in the pattern shot have been found in the Cincinnati area in the last year. The demand for these has dropped due to several being found and the avid collectors all having one by now. That happens! After the people who will pay any price to obtain rare pieces have found what they need, the next one found may be difficult to sell at a comparable price.

The butter bottom and the 7¾″ salad bowl are the same. It is the ribbed 7¾″ bowl which collectors are scurrying to find. Recently, I saw a collector who was ecstatic to find a butter top on the ribbed bottom. That made his day! The price on the large 9½″ ribbed or plain bowl is not different as it is on the smaller one. There seems to be plenty of both styles of the larger bowl.

Be sure to notice the cup in which the rays only go up part way. This has created problems with the Queen Mary cup ever since another author made that mistake in identification. Also, the wide rays on the tumbler only go up a little over halfway, and the Coronation tumblers have very small ribs that go up more than halfway.

| | Pink* | | Pink* |
|---|---|---|---|
| **Bowl, 6⅜″ Cereal | 12.50 | Fish Bowl, 1 gal. 8 oz. | |
| Bowl, 7¾″ Ribbed | 35.00 | (Crystal Only) | 20.00 |
| Bowl, 7¾″ Salad | 15.00 | Flower Bowl, Crystal Frog | 17.50 |
| Bowl, 8¼″ (Crystal) | 10.00 | Plate, 7¼″ Salad | 14.00 |
| Bowl, 9½″ Plain or Ribbed | 13.50 | Plate, 8¾″ Luncheon | 12.50 |
| ***Bowl, 10½″, 3 Legs, (Frosted, $25.00) | 135.00 | Plate, 10½″ Dinner | 18.50 |
| Butter Dish or Bon Bon | | Plate, 10½″ Grill | 12.50 |
| with Cover | 45.00 | Plate, 10½″, 3-Part Relish | 20.00 |
| Butter Dish Bottom | 15.00 | Plate, 13″, 4-Part Solid Lace | 18.50 |
| Butter Dish Top | 30.00 | Platter, 12¾″ | 19.00 |
| ***Candlesticks, Pr. (Frosted $40.00) | 135.00 | Platter, 12¾″, 5-Part | 18.00 |
| Candy Jar and Cover, Ribbed | 32.50 | Relish Dish, 7½″, 3-Part Deep | 45.00 |
| Comport, 7″ | 16.00 | Saucer | 7.50 |
| Comport, 7″ and Cover, Footed | 30.00 | ***Sherbet, Footed | 50.00 |
| Comport, 9″ | 525.00 | Sugar | 15.00 |
| Cookie Jar and Cover | 45.00 | Tumbler, 3½″, 5 oz. Flat | 8.00 |
| Creamer | 16.00 | Tumbler, 4½″, 9 oz. Flat | 10.00 |
| Cup | 16.50 | Tumbler, 5″, 10½ oz. Footed | 45.00 |
| | | Vase, 7″, (Frosted $45.00) | 245.00 |

*Satin or frosted items 50% lower in price
**Officially listed as cereal or cream soup
***Price is for absolute mint condition

**Please refer to Foreword for pricing information**

103

# LACED EDGE, "KATY BLUE"   IMPERIAL GLASS COMPANY, Early 1930's

Colors:   Blue w/opalescent edge; green w/opalescent edge.

The blue Laced Edge is the most desirable to own, but I have had a more difficult time in finding the green for pictures. Of course, collectors have let me search for the green without interference; but still I have not been successful.

It is amazing how many people are collecting this pattern that has limited availability. While in Denver a few weeks ago, I saw a very large set sell to a very happy dealer. Both the seller and the buyer seemed happy! I was surprised to see it sell so fast at the $1,500.00 price.

The serving pieces are still the pieces to find. There must have been more luncheon sets made than any other items. You can find cups, saucers, creamers, sugars, and plates with searching; but it takes a little luck to find the other pieces to go with these basics.

I received many positive comments from what I said in the 7th Edition about price "fixing" on Depression Glass. I do want to emphasize one idea that is true in all forms of advertising in the antique business. The ADVERTISED price is not necessarily the SELLING price!

| | | | |
|---|---|---|---|
| Bowl, 4½" Fruit | 14.00 | Plate, 8" Salad | 15.00 |
| Bowl, 5" | 17.50 | Plate, 10" Dinner | 27.50 |
| Bowl, 5½" | 17.50 | Plate, 12" Luncheon (Per | |
| Bowl, 7" Soup | 20.00 | Catalogue Description) | 35.00 |
| Bowl, 9" Vegetable | 40.00 | Platter, 13" | 55.00 |
| Bowl, 11" Divided Oval | 40.00 | Saucer | 7.50 |
| Bowl, 11" Oval | 45.00 | Sugar | 18.00 |
| Cup | 17.50 | Tidbit, 2/8" & 10" Plates | 55.00 |
| Creamer | 19.00 | Tumbler, 9 oz. | 27.50 |
| Mayonnaise, 3-Piece | 65.00 | Vase, 5½" | 40.00 |
| Plate, 6½" Bread & Butter | 9.50 | | |

# LAKE COMO   HOCKING GLASS COMPANY, 1934-1937

Color:   White with blue scene.

Although Lake Como is such a small pattern when considering the number of pieces available, there is probably no pattern more avidly sought by its collectors. I have talked to many other "would be" collectors who wished they could find some Lake Como, but they have been thwarted in their attempt to find it. I had difficulty in locating the soups and still have been unable to find a platter with the design intact. That is another difficulty facing these collectors. Many pieces have faded blue designs. If that were not enough, there are two distinct shades of blue to contend with when you find pieces.

Note the soup bowl which has the design embossed on the side and which is not filled in with blue. This soup is almost as large as the dinner plate. You could put a lot of soup beans with cornbread in that one! Today, you may never get a chance to try since the soups are hard to find at any price.

I am finally able to show you the regular cup. I have had a harder time finding these than the larger St. Denis style. Other collectors say I am wrong, but I can only report my experiences. The shakers remain the most readily available item, but they are being bought as soon as they make their appearance at shows.

| | White | | White |
|---|---|---|---|
| Bowl, 6" Cereal | 12.00 | Plate, 9¼" Dinner | 12.50 |
| Bowl, 9¾" Vegetable | 20.00 | Platter, 11" | 22.50 |
| Bowl, Flat Soup | 50.00 | Salt & Pepper, Pr. | 25.00 |
| Creamer, Footed | 12.00 | Saucer | 5.00 |
| Cup, Regular | 15.00 | Saucer, St. Denis | 5.00 |
| Cup, St. Denis | 12.00 | Sugar, Footed | 11.00 |
| Plate, 7¼" Salad | 7.50 | | |

**Please refer to Foreword for pricing information**

# LAUREL   McKEE GLASS COMPANY, 1930's

Colors:   French ivory, Jade green, white opal and Poudre blue.

Laurel children's sets still remain the most popular part of this pattern with the Scotty dog decal being more popular than ever. I heard that the SCOTTY DOG COLLECTORS had bid some high prices in auctions for pieces with that little dog on it! Look out Depression Glass collectors. You've got competition from another field of collecting!

Laurel collectors of blue have difficulty finding that color. There have been a few more reports of the commemorative plate shown below which has Jeannette McKee's picture embossed on it. These were made to commemorate a fifty-year celebration (1888-1938) held the week of Aug. 28-Sept. 5.

Tumblers, shakers with strong patterns, candlesticks and the three-legged bowls have remained elusive in all colors. Remember the cheese bottom is the 7½" salad plate.

Notice the 12 oz. iced tea on the left. I have no explanation as to why they all seem to have that brownish discoloration around the top. I would like to know.

| | White Opal, Jade Green | French Ivory | Poudre Blue |
|---|---|---|---|
| Bowl, 5" Berry | 4.00 | 5.00 | 10.00 |
| Bowl, 6" Cereal | 5.00 | 6.00 | 15.00 |
| Bowl, 6", Three Legs | 10.00 | 8.00 | |
| Bowl, 8" Soup | | 20.00 | |
| Bowl, 9" Large Berry | 12.00 | 15.00 | 25.00 |
| Bowl, 9¾", Oval Vegetable | 15.00 | 15.00 | 30.00 |
| Bowl, 10½", Three Legs | 25.00 | 27.50 | 45.00 |
| Bowl, 11" | 22.00 | 27.50 | 45.00 |
| Candlestick, 4" Pr. | 22.50 | 25.00 | |
| Cheese Dish and Cover | 40.00 | 50.00 | |
| Creamer, Short | 7.50 | 9.00 | |
| Creamer, Tall | 9.00 | 10.00 | 20.00 |
| Cup | 6.00 | 6.00 | 15.00 |
| Plate, 6" Sherbet | 2.50 | 3.50 | 5.00 |
| Plate, 7½" Salad | 8.00 | 8.00 | 10.00 |
| Plate, 9⅛" Dinner | 7.50 | 7.50 | 12.50 |
| Plate, 9⅛" Grill | 6.50 | 7.50 | |
| Platter, 10¾" Oval | 15.00 | 20.00 | 27.50 |
| Salt and Pepper | 45.00 | 35.00 | |
| Saucer | 2.00 | 2.50 | 5.00 |
| Sherbet | 6.50 | 9.50 | |
| Sugar, Short | 6.50 | 7.50 | |
| Sugar, Tall | 8.50 | 9.50 | 20.00 |
| Tumbler, 4½", 9 oz. Flat | 35.00 | 25.00 | |
| Tumbler, 5", 12 oz. Flat | | 35.00 | |

## CHILDREN'S LAUREL TEA SET

| | Plain | Decorated Rims | Scotty Dog Decal | Green |
|---|---|---|---|---|
| Creamer | 20.00 | 32.50 | 50.00 | 32.50 |
| Cup | 15.00 | 20.00 | 35.00 | 20.00 |
| Plate | 7.50 | 12.50 | 25.00 | 12.50 |
| Saucer | 5.50 | 7.50 | 45.00 | 7.50 |
| Sugar | 20.00 | 32.50 | 50.00 | 32.50 |
| 14-Piece Set | 150.00 | 225.00 | 400.00 | 225.00 |

**Please refer to Foreword for pricing information**

# LINCOLN INN   FENTON GLASS COMPANY, Late 1920's

Colors:   Red, cobalt, light blue, amethyst, black, green, pink, crystal, amber, jade (opaque).

If I were a sherbet collector, Lincoln Inn would give me the most fun! With the numerous colors found in Lincoln Inn, there would be a small shelf of sherbets in this pattern alone! There are several colors in which you could collect a set, but crystal is the only one that I have seen readily available. Red and cobalt blue are the most desirable colors, and, therefore, the most costly.

Serving pieces are the most difficult to find. Bowls, in particular, are scarce. Perhaps they represent limited production runs. Many collectors have only attempted to find the abundant stemware and stopped there. I have had some luck in finding pitchers in recent years, but that has been my only GOOD luck in finding Lincoln Inn.

I promised to show you the blue pitcher last time, and here it is with the only known flat tumbler to match! I am not sure the photgraph will show it, but that blue tumbler in front of the jade goblet is almost egg-shaped at the top. I have never seen a Depression era tumbler as badly formed. Obviously, the quality inspector for that day at the glass factory was "out to lunch". Of course, it may have been an experimental piece since no others have ever been reported.

The salt and pepper shakers have also turned up in most colors. These are quickly grabbed by shaker collectors as well as Lincoln Inn devotees. Shaker collectors are not as abundant as they once were, but those remaining keep in hot pursuit of any scarce ones that are found. Lincoln Inn shakers fit that category!

Lincoln Inn plates can also be found with a fruit design in the center according to a 1930's catalogue.

Several years ago, Fenton remade the pitcher in a iridized dark carnival color. If you run into that, be aware—it's recently manufactured.

| | Blue, Red | All Other Colors | | Blue, Red | All Other Colors |
|---|---|---|---|---|---|
| Ash Tray | 15.00 | 10.00 | Nut Dish, Footed | 15.00 | 10.00 |
| Bon Bon, Handled Square | 12.50 | 10.00 | Pitcher, 7¼", 46 oz. | 750.00 | 500.00 |
| Bon Bon, Handled Oval | 12.50 | 10.00 | Plate, 6" | 6.00 | 3.00 |
| Bowl, 5" Fruit | 9.50 | 7.00 | Plate, 8" | 10.00 | 6.00 |
| Bowl, 6" Cereal | 10.00 | 6.50 | Plate, 9¼" | 12.50 | 10.00 |
| Bowl, 6" Crimped | 11.00 | 7.00 | Plate, 12" | 17.50 | 10.00 |
| Bowl, Handled Olive | 12.00 | 7.00 | *Salt/Pepper, Pr. | 150.00 | 110.00 |
| Bowl, Finger | 15.00 | 10.00 | Saucer | 3.00 | 2.00 |
| Bowl, 9", Shallow | | 15.00 | Sherbet, 4½", Cone Shape | | 10.00 |
| Bowl, 9¼" Footed | 25.00 | 15.00 | Sherbet, 4¾" | 15.00 | 10.00 |
| Bowl, 10½" Footed | 35.00 | 25.00 | Sugar | 16.50 | 11.50 |
| Candy Dish, Footed Oval | 17.50 | 10.00 | Tumbler, 4 oz. Flat Juice | 15.00 | 7.50 |
| Comport | 20.00 | 12.00 | Tumbler, 5 oz. Footed | 15.00 | 8.50 |
| Creamer | 17.50 | 12.00 | Tumbler, 7 oz. Footed | 15.00 | 8.50 |
| Cup | 12.50 | 7.50 | Tumbler, 9 oz. Footed | 15.00 | 12.00 |
| Goblet, Water | 20.00 | 12.00 | Tumbler, 12 oz. Footed | 25.00 | 15.00 |
| Goblet, Wine | 25.00 | 15.00 | Vase, 12" Footed | 95.00 | 65.00 |

*Black $150.00

# LORAIN, "BASKET", No. 615 INDIANA GLASS COMPANY, 1929-1932

Colors:    Green, yellow; some crystal.

The availability of Lorain has surprised me recently. I saw a very large amount at a show in Denver. A dealer reminded me that I had purchased a large number of cereals there in 1979. They were priced at $6.00 each back then! I did remember the price! In fact the quality of glassware in some of the larger western towns is astounding. There is more in Denver, Seattle and Eugene than I had thought possible! Admittedly, more ELEGANT glass is found; but there is Depression Glass, also.

The collecting of Lorain is once again on the increase. More collectors of yellow are found than those who collect the green; but prices of each color are slowly beginning to rise. If you get left out at today's price, do not blame me as I am warning you now!

I bought a six-piece set recently and appraised an estate in which there was a twelve-place setting. Both of these sets pointed out the necessity of checking the inside rims of the flat pieces. There is a lot of mould roughness to be found on Lorain. The 8" deep berry has reached a point in price that some collectors have vowed to leave it alone. It was hard to find when it sold for $6.00! I guarantee that there are twenty of the smaller salad bowls for every one of the large berries today. I have seen only one at shows in the last year.

I need to remind new collectors that the white and green avocado colored sherbets which have a Lace Edge border are a later issue and should be treated as such. These have always been assumed to be an Indiana product; but new evidence shows that the white ones were made in the late 1950's and early 1960's by Anchor Hocking.

| | Crystal, Green | Yellow | | Crystal, Green | Yellow |
|---|---|---|---|---|---|
| Bowl, 6" Cereal | 25.00 | 45.00 | Plate, 10¼" Dinner | 27.50 | 40.00 |
| Bowl, 7¼" Salad | 30.00 | 45.00 | Platter, 11½" | 17.50 | 30.00 |
| Bowl, 8" Deep Berry | 65.00 | 110.00 | Relish, 8", 4-Part | 13.50 | 22.50 |
| Bowl, 9¾" Oval Vegetable | 27.50 | 37.50 | Saucer | 3.50 | 4.50 |
| Creamer, Footed | 11.00 | 16.00 | Sherbet, Footed | 15.00 | 25.00 |
| Cup | 8.50 | 11.50 | Snack Tray, Crystal/Trim | 15.00 | |
| Plate, 5½" Sherbet | 5.50 | 7.50 | Sugar, Footed | 10.00 | 15.00 |
| Plate, 7¾" Salad | 7.50 | 11.50 | Tumbler, 4¾", 9 oz. Footed | 15.00 | 19.00 |
| Plate, 8⅜" Luncheon | 12.50 | 20.00 | | | |

111

# MADRID  FEDERAL GLASS COMPANY, 1932-1939; INDIANA GLASS COMPANY, 1980's

Colors:  Green, pink, amber, crystal, "Madonna" blue. *(See Reproduction Section)*

Madrid still causes problems for collectors—especially those who are just starting. One of the problems occurred back in 1976 when Federal Glass Company decided to reissue Madrid for the Bicentennial under the name "Recollection" glassware. Fine; it was dated 1976; but it WAS issued in the older color of amber instead of another color. Everyone was informed and many collectors assumed it would be collectible later. However, Indiana bought the moulds when Federal went bankrupt and there has been trouble for collectors ever since. First of all, the dates were removed and crystal was made. This hurt collecting since the old crystal butter was selling for several hundred dollars and the new could be bought for $4.99.

Next, Indiana made pink and although it was lighter pink than the old, prices on the old pink went down. Now Indiana has tried to reproduce the blue. They failed to get the color right—thankfully. Unfortunately, the new blue is prettier than the old. Even I have to admit that! Look at the pink Madrid pieces shown in the REPRODUCTION SECTION in the back. So far the blue is being made in these same pieces!

The gravy boat and platter shown in front of the cookie jar in amber were found at a yard sale in Iowa a couple of years ago for 25 cents. That is not a typo! Almost all gravy boat and platters have been found in that area of the country. What kind of premium item were they? Two more walnut lazy susans have been found. One was found in Connecticut which is a long way from Eastern Kentucky where they are usually found. You can see the lazy susan pictured in the 5th Edition.

| | Amber | Pink | Green | Blue | | Amber | Pink | Green | Blue |
|---|---|---|---|---|---|---|---|---|---|
| Ash Tray, 6" Square | 150.00 | | 100.00 | | Pitcher, 8½", 80 oz. Ice Lip | 50.00 | | 185.00 | |
| Bowl, 4¾" Cream Soup | 10.00 | | | | Plate, 6" Sherbet | 2.50 | 3.00 | 3.00 | 6.50 |
| Bowl, 5" Sauce | 5.00 | 5.50 | 6.00 | 10.00 | Plate, 7½" Salad | 8.00 | 8.00 | 7.50 | 15.00 |
| Bowl, 7" Soup | 9.50 | | 11.00 | 20.00 | Plate, 8⅞" Luncheon | 5.50 | 6.00 | 7.50 | 15.00 |
| Bowl, 8" Salad | 11.50 | | 15.00 | 35.00 | Plate, 10½" Dinner | 25.00 | | 26.00 | 55.00 |
| Bowl, 9⅜" Large Berry | 14.50 | 17.50 | | | Plate, 10½" Grill | 8.00 | | 13.50 | |
| Bowl, 9½" Deep Salad | 22.00 | | | | Plate, 10¼" Relish | 8.50 | 8.50 | 12.50 | |
| Bowl, 10" Oval Vegetable | 12.50 | 12.00 | 13.50 | 25.00 | Plate, 11¼" Round Cake | 10.00 | 8.50 | | |
| *Bowl, 11" Low Console | 11.50 | 8.00 | | | Platter, 11½" Oval | 10.00 | 9.00 | 12.50 | 17.50 |
| Butter Dish and Cover | 52.50 | | 70.00 | | Salt/Pepper, 3½" Footed, Pr. | 57.50 | | 77.50 | 115.00 |
| Butter Dish Bottom | 22.50 | | 32.50 | | Salt/Pepper, 3½" Flat, Pr. | 37.50 | | 60.00 | |
| Butter Dish Top | 30.00 | | 37.50 | | Saucer | 2.50 | 3.00 | 3.50 | 5.00 |
| *Candlesticks, 2¼" Pr. | 15.00 | 13.50 | | | Sherbet, Two Styles | 6.50 | | 7.50 | 9.50 |
| Cookie Jar and Cover | 32.50 | 25.00 | | | Sugar | 6.50 | | 7.50 | 10.00 |
| Creamer, Footed | 6.00 | | 8.00 | 12.00 | Sugar Cover | 25.00 | | 30.00 | 125.00 |
| Cup | 5.00 | 6.00 | 6.50 | 11.00 | Tumbler, 3⅞", 5 oz. | 12.50 | | 30.00 | 30.00 |
| Gravy Boat and Platter | 1000.00 | | | | Tumbler, 4¼", 9 oz. | 11.00 | 11.00 | 17.50 | 20.00 |
| Hot Dish Coaster | 27.50 | | 27.50 | | Tumbler, 5½", 12 oz. 2 | | | | |
| Hot Dish Coaster w/Indent | 30.00 | | 27.50 | | Styles | 17.00 | | 25.00 | 30.00 |
| Jam Dish, 7" | 17.50 | | 13.50 | 25.00 | Tumbler, 4", 5 oz. Footed | 20.00 | | 35.00 | |
| Jello Mold, 2⅛" High | 9.00 | | | | Tumbler, 5½", 10 oz. Footed | 20.00 | | 30.00 | |
| **Pitcher, 5½", 36 oz. Juice | 30.00 | | | | Wooden Lazy Susan, 7 Hot | | | | |
| Pitcher, 8", 60 oz. Square | 37.50 | 32.50 | 110.00 | 125.00 | Dish Coasters | 500.00 | | | |
| Pitcher, 8½", 80 oz. | 50.00 | | 185.00 | | | | | | |

  *Iridescent priced slightly higher
 **Crystal—$150.00

# MANHATTAN, "HORIZONTAL RIBBED"  ANCHOR HOCKING GLASS COMPANY, 1938-1941

Colors:   Crystal, pink; some green, ruby and iridized.

The big news in Manhattan is PARK AVENUE. Unfortunately, I am speaking of the glassware line and not New York City. Anchor Hocking is issuing the Park Avenue line which "re-creates the Glamour Era of 1938 when Anchor Hocking first introduced a classic" according to the *Inspiration '87* catalogue issued by the company. I can only report what is being made as I have not seen anything except the catalogue.

Care appears to have been taken by the company to make the line only similar to the original Manhattan, but the exciting news is that it is being made in a light blue color called "Sapphire" as well as the crystal. All of the pieces, such as tumblers and the vase, have had the ball feet removed in this new line so there should be no problem in confusing the new, with the old.

The following items are set for the line, but do not be surprised if there are additional pieces later; 10 oz. rocks tumbler, 9.5 oz. all-purpose goblet, 12 oz. beverage tumbler, 16 oz. iced tea, 13 oz. footed dessert, 6" small bowl, 10" serving bowl, 8" snack plate, 13" platter (round), 6" ash tray (round), salt and pepper (round), 9¾" vase, 2 pc. 13" footed cake plate with 11¼" domed cover. That is the news to report, but I am sure that many of you will see the Park Avenue before you see this book.

The pink Manhattan cup, saucer and dinner plate do exist as you can see by the cup shown here. I have seen the plate, and the former cup's owner at one time had the saucer and sold it separately.

As of today, the cereal bowl and square ash tray are the hardest pieces to find. Many collectors are adding additional pieces to this pattern that were made by other companies. A case in point is the covered candy dish shown on the left in the top picture and the little wine next to the decanter or water bottle. This bottle was made by Hocking, but it was not a part of the original Manhattan line. It sells for about $15.00. The other two pieces are L.E. Smith and priced below. In the bottom picture is a double candlestick that sells for $10.00 from the same company. Years ago collectors would not mix pieces that looked similar, but today's collectors are not as discriminating. In fact, mixing patterns is almost in vogue now; and I have seen it done brilliantly. Some people are very creative!

Note the sauce dish in the metal holder which is notched to hold a spoon. You will find many pieces of glass that have metallic additions. These metal pieces were made by some other company to fit the glass probably as a special promotion by a store or as a premium for purchasing other items.

| | Crystal | Pink | | Crystal | Pink |
|---|---|---|---|---|---|
| Ashtray, 4" Round | 8.00 | | ***Relish Tray, 14", 4-Part | 15.00 | 15.00 |
| Ashtray, 4½" Square | 15.00 | | Relish Tray, 14" With Inserts | 30.00 | 35.00 |
| Bowl, 4½" Sauce, Handles | 5.00 | 6.00 | **Relish Tray Insert | 3.50 | 4.00 |
| Bowl, 5⅜" Berry w/Handles | 8.00 | 7.00 | Pitcher, 42 oz. | 15.00 | 30.00 |
| Bowl, 5½" Cereal | 13.50 | | Pitcher, 80 oz. Tilted | 22.00 | 35.00 |
| Bowl, 7½" Large Berry | 8.50 | 8.50 | Plate, 6" Sherbet or Saucer | 4.00 | 25.00 |
| Bowl, 8", Closed Handles | 13.00 | 17.50 | Plate, 8½" Salad | 7.50 | |
| Bowl, 9" Salad | 12.00 | 15.00 | Plate, 10¼" Dinner | 10.00 | 50.00 |
| Bowl, 9½" Fruit | 17.50 | 20.00 | Plate, 14" Sandwich | 10.00 | 10.00 |
| Candlesticks, 4½" (Square) | | | Salt/Pepper, 2" Pr. (Square) | 17.50 | 30.00 |
| Pr. | 12.00 | | Saucer/Sherbet Plate | 4.00 | 25.00 |
| Candy Dish, 3 Legs | | 7.50 | Sherbet | 6.50 | 6.00 |
| *Candy Dish and Cover | 25.00 | | Sugar, Oval | 7.00 | 6.00 |
| Coaster, 3½" | 5.00 | | ***Tumbler, 10 oz. Footed | 10.00 | 10.00 |
| Comport, 5¾" | 15.00 | 15.00 | Vase, 8" | 11.50 | |
| Creamer, Oval | 7.00 | 7.00 | *Wine, 3½" | 5.00 | |
| Cup | 11.00 | 95.00 | | | |

*"Look-Alike"
**Ruby—$3.50
***Green or iridized—$7.00

# MAYFAIR  FEDERAL GLASS COMPANY, 1934

Colors:  Crystal, amber, green

There has been a little more activity in collecting Federal's Mayfair of late. This has come about for several reasons. New collectors have been searching for patterns which can be found at shows without mortaging the homestead. There had been a lull in collecting Mayfair and several collectors told me they had received good prices when buying this pattern in quantity. That will get you hooked if nothing else will. A bargain today may be a prize tomorrow. The amber is the most highly collected color, and it is also the color most often found. This is a crystal pattern that can really be displayed well with colored accessories—if you can find enough crystal to display.

The sugar bowls have always caused problems for beginners. The footed object without handles that looks like a sherbet is the sugar. I once bought a six-piece set that had a creamer and six "sherbets", but no sugar (according the owner). I was delighted to get six sugars until I tried to sell them! That was back in the "Dark Ages" of collecting when no one wanted a creamer or a sugar separately. We have come a long way from the first to this, our *eighth* journey through the Depression Glass world. (By the way, don't pass by any of those spiral bound first books! In good shape they're selling for $85.00-$100.00 now!)

The reason Mayfair is so limited resides in the fact that Hocking had patented the name "Mayfair" which caused Federal to redesign their Mayfair moulds into what became the ROSEMARY pattern. The green items pictured here (as well as one cup, cream soup and sugar in amber) represent what is called the "transitional period" or the glass made between what was Mayfair and what became Rosemary. Note these transitional pieces have arching in the bottom of each piece rather than the waffle design and there is no waffling between the top arches. If you will turn to the Rosemary photo for reference, you will see that the glass under the arches is perfectly plain. Most collectors consider the TRANSITIONAL pieces with this Mayfair pattern rather than the Rosemary since they more closely resemble Mayfair. I suspect that after examining the reworking of the moulds, someone decided that the changes made were not complete enough and they were reworked again.

So far the cream soups have only been found in the transitional pattern of Mayfair; and no crystal has been found in anything except the pure Mayfair.

|  | Amber | Crystal | Green |
|---|---|---|---|
| Bowl, 5″ Sauce | 5.00 | 4.00 | 6.00 |
| Bowl, 5″ Cream Soup | 13.50 | 9.00 | 13.50 |
| Bowl, 6″ Cereal | 13.00 | 7.50 | 15.00 |
| Bowl, 10″ Oval Vegetable | 15.00 | 12.00 | 17.50 |
| Creamer, Footed | 10.00 | 9.50 | 12.50 |
| Cup | 6.50 | 3.50 | 6.50 |
| Plate, 6¾″ Salad | 4.50 | 3.00 | 6.00 |
| Plate, 9½″ Dinner | 10.00 | 7.00 | 10.00 |
| Plate, 9½″ Grill | 9.00 | 7.00 | 9.00 |
| Platter, 12″ Oval | 20.00 | 15.00 | 20.00 |
| Saucer | 2.00 | 1.25 | 2.00 |
| Sugar, Footed | 10.00 | 9.00 | 11.50 |
| Tumbler, 4½″, 9 oz. | 17.50 | 10.00 | 20.00 |

**Please refer to Foreword for pricing information**

# MAYFAIR, "OPEN ROSE"   HOCKING GLASS COMPANY, 1931-1937

Colors:   Ice blue, pink; some green, yellow, crystal.    *(See Reproduction Section)*

The Mayfair footed shaker now has a new home in Texas. It moved from California where it had resided after leaving Kentucky in 1981. It is still the only one known! All reports of other sightings have been fruitless.

Readers always want to know how to find yellow and green Mayfair. You have to look for it in the right areas! The last two flea markets I have attended (Burlington, Ky. and Washington Court House, Ohio) produced two yellow pieces; a cookie jar and a four-part relish. The cookie jar was no bargain, but the relish was bought for $8.00. Luck helps, but years of hard work and experience come into play also. I know, you do not believe going to flea markets is work. Well, I got up at 4:15 A.M. to drive 80 miles by 6:00 to wade in mud over my shoes to find the cookie jar. That may sound like fun and it used to be, but there are many fruitless trips in between that do not produce any desired results. At least I didn't get my vehicle mired as some people did that soaking dawn.

No other pieces in Mayfair have been reproduced except the cookie jar and the whiskey. See REPRODUC-TION SECTION in back of the book for further details. I suggest you subscribe to a monthly paper such as the DAZE (address in back) to keep up with developments between books.

Some pieces of Mayfair were "satinized" or dipped in camphoric acid to give a dull, soft finish. These pieces were usually handpainted with flowers. Some people feel these are beautiful, but most collectors avoid them and the price is 30% less than the regular issues if they sell at all.

Crystal Mayfair abounds with the shakers and juice pitcher selling about half of the prices of the pink. The most commonly found piece is a five-part relish which sells in the $15.00 range. This relish in pink is RARE.

Few of the odd-sized stemware have surfaced since that large find in Hocking's hometown about ten years ago. Some day it will happen again.

Blue Mayfair continues to be one of my bestsellers in the shop. The only problem is finding it to sell. Pink Mayfair is the pattern most commonly owned by those who do not know what Depression glass is! I have more pieces of Mayfair brought into shows to be identified than any other pattern. The cookie jar is the piece I see most often. It must have been a premium item in most of the country!

Unfortunately, the reports of a yellow console bowl were exaggerated, but green and pink do exist as shown here! The frosted pink console was found at a small flea market in Ohio for less than twenty dollars. Bargains do exist! You have to be willing to search and search to reap the rewards!

Note the two shades of blue juice pitches. The one in front is closer to the "Madonna" blue of Federal Glass rather than Hocking's blue. Very little of this shade of blue has been found; so that is a very unusual pitcher.

| | Pink* | Blue | Green | Yellow |
|---|---|---|---|---|
| Bowl, 5" Cream Soup | 34.00 | | | |
| Bowl, 5½" Cereal | 16.00 | 35.00 | 55.00 | 55.00 |
| Bowl, 7" Vegetable | 16.00 | 35.00 | 90.00 | 90.00 |
| Bowl, 9", 3⅛" High, 3 Leg Console | 3,000.00 | | 3,000.00 | |
| Bowl, 9½" Oval Vegetable | 17.50 | 39.00 | 85.00 | 90.00 |
| Bowl, 10" Vegetable | 16.00 | 40.00 | | 90.00 |
| Bowl, 10" Same Covered | 67.50 | 77.50 | | 350.00 |
| Bowl, 11¾" Low Flat | 35.00 | 45.00 | 22.00 | 95.00 |
| Bowl, 12" Deep Scalloped Fruit | 37.50 | 52.50 | 25.00 | 115.00 |
| Butter Dish and Cover or 7" Covered Vegetable | 42.50 | 220.00 | 1,000.00 | 1,000.00 |
| Butter Bottom With Indent | | | | 250.00 |
| Butter Dish Top | 30.00 | 185.00 | 900.00 | 750.00 |
| Cake Plate, 10" Footed | 18.00 | 40.00 | 75.00 | |
| Candy Dish and Cover | 37.50 | 140.00 | 400.00 | 275.00 |
| Celery Dish, 9" Divided | | | 110.00 | 110.00 |

*Frosted or satin finish items slightly lower

**Please refer to Foreword for pricing information**

# MAYFAIR, "OPEN ROSE" (Cont.)

| | Pink* | Blue | Green | Yellow |
|---|---|---|---|---|
| Celery Dish, 10" | 22.00 | 30.00 | 87.50 | 87.50 |
| ** Celery Dish, 10" Divided | 120.00 | | | |
| Cookie Jar and Lid | 32.50 | 160.00 | 500.00 | 650.00 |
| Creamer, Footed | 15.00 | 47.50 | 150.00 | 150.00 |
| Cup | 13.00 | 35.00 | 125.00 | 125.00 |
| Decanter and Stopper, 32 oz. | 105.00 | | | |
| Goblet, 3¾", 1 oz. Liqueur | 375.00 | | 350.00 | |
| Goblet, 4", 2½ oz. | 150.00 | | | |
| Goblet, 4", 3½ oz. Cocktail | 57.50 | | 300.00 | |
| Goblet, 4½", 3 oz. Wine | 57.50 | | 300.00 | |
| Goblet, 5¼", 4½ oz. Claret | 500.00 | | 400.00 | |
| Goblet, 5¾", 9 oz. Water | 45.00 | | 300.00 | |
| Goblet, 7¼", 9 oz. Thin | 115.00 | 110.00 | | |
| Pitcher, 6", 37 oz. | 32.00 | 92.50 | 375.00 | 375.00 |
| Pitcher, 8", 60 oz. | 35.00 | 105.00 | 325.00 | 325.00 |
| Pitcher, 8½", 80 oz. | 62.50 | 130.00 | 400.00 | 400.00 |
| Plate, 5¾" (Often Substituted as Saucer) | 8.00 | 13.50 | 67.50 | 67.50 |
| Plate, 6½" Round Sherbet | 9.00 | | | |
| Plate, 6½" Round, Off-Center Indent | 19.50 | 18.00 | 90.00 | |
| Plate, 8½" Luncheon | 16.00 | 26.00 | 57.50 | 57.50 |
| Plate, 9½" Dinner | 36.00 | 45.00 | 100.00 | 100.00 |
| Plate, 9½" Grill | 25.00 | 25.00 | 55.00 | 55.00 |
| Plate, 11½" Handled Grill | | | | 80.00 |
| Plate, 12" Cake w/Handles | 26.00 | 40.00 | 26.00 | |
| ** Platter, 12" Oval, Open Handles | 15.00 | 35.00 | 117.50 | 117.50 |
| Platter, 12½" Oval, 8" Wide, Closed Handles | | | 175.00 | 175.00 |
| Relish, 8⅜", 4-part | 17.50 | 35.00 | 100.00 | 100.00 |
| Relish, 8⅜" Non-Partitioned | 95.00 | | 175.00 | 175.00 |
| Salt and Pepper, Flat Pr. | 42.50 | 185.00 | 900.00 | 650.00 |
| Salt and Pepper, Footed | 3500.00 | | | |
| Sandwich Server, Center Handle | 27.50 | 45.00 | 22.50 | 90.00 |
| Saucer (Cup Ring) | 21.00 | | | 125.00 |
| Saucer (See 5¾" Plate) | | | | |
| Sherbet, 2¼" Flat | 105.00 | 65.00 | | |
| Sherbet, 3" Footed | 12.00 | | | |
| Sherbet, 4¾" Footed | 55.00 | 50.00 | 127.50 | 127.50 |
| Sugar, Footed | 17.50 | 47.50 | 150.00 | 150.00 |
| Sugar Lid | 1250.00 | | 900.00 | 1000.00 |
| Tumbler, 3½", 5 oz. Juice | 30.00 | 75.00 | | |
| Tumbler, 4¼", 9 oz. Water | 22.00 | 65.00 | | |
| Tumbler, 4¾", 11 oz. Water | 105.00 | 85.00 | 157.50 | 157.50 |
| Tumbler, 5¼", 13½ oz. Iced Tea | 33.00 | 110.00 | | |
| Tumbler, 3¼", 3 oz. Footed Juice | 55.00 | | | |
| Tumbler, 5¼", 10 oz. Footed | 27.50 | 87.50 | | 157.50 |
| Tumbler, 6½", 15 oz. Ftd. Iced Tea | 27.50 | 100.00 | 177.50 | |
| Vase (Sweet Pea) | 105.00 | 70.00 | 175.00 | |
| Whiskey, 2¼", 1½ oz. | 50.00 | | | |

*Frosted or satin finish items slightly lower
**Divided Crystal—$12.50

**Please refer to Foreword for pricing information**

# MISS AMERICA (DIAMOND PATTERN) HOCKING GLASS COMPANY, 1935-1937

Colors: Crystal, pink; some green, ice blue and red. *(See Reproduction Section)*

Miss America is a pattern that has been heavily collected even though a few of the pieces have been reproduced over the years. If nothing else, this pattern proves that copies of a highly collected pattern will not destroy the value of the original. Refer to the REPRODUCTION SECTION in the back for a complete listing of these pieces and the ways to differenciate between the old and the new.

The only other problem that occurs with Miss America is confusion with English Hobnail. There is a detailed explanation of the differences on page 58 under that pattern.

There have been few discoveries of new pieces in pink over the last few years, but there have been some other interesting colors found. Red commands the most attention, but I am partial to the light blue that is similar in color to that of English Hobnail. I told you of a new style of sherbet in blue last time and now, a new celery has been found! The normal celery is 10½" long and stands approximately 1⅛" deep. The newly discovered piece is 12¼" long and only stands ¾" deep. Both are 6½" wide. Since I mentioned the sherbets, I should point out that there are two styles of these being found. One is slightly flared at the top and is a prettier shade of pink. That is bad terminology, but I hate to describe colors. People see colors differently. To me, it is a truer pink more reminiscent of better quality glassware.

There are also two styles of shakers. One style is skinny as it goes toward the base while the other gets fatter. The major problem is that the shakers have been reproduced by at least two glass companies! So now there are reproduction differences also! Needless to say, the shakers are the most difficult item to buy today. *Buy from a reputable dealer is my only suggestion!*

The footed juice remains the most difficult goblet to find. In fact the water goblets seem to be suffering from an overabundant supply at the present. The wines are still hard to find, but not nearly as hard as that juice!

As soon as I mentioned that candy jars were sufficient for the demand in the last book, we sold out our inventory and I have only found a couple more. That shows you that the law of supply and demand does play a role in our collecting! Another man's trash is our treasure and vice versa. It took a while to sell what we had; but as soon as we were out, we got bombarded with requests.

Very few pieces of the Jade-ite Miss America have been seen, but there is little demand for it. I have not received any other reports on pieces like the sprayed-on amethyst represented by the goblet in the bottom picture. Maybe no one else will admit to having anything so ugly. It doesn't eat anything so it's cheaper than a pet. The only other piece of Miss America in existence that is worse than this is the gold-painted candy dish that Austin Hartsock has carried to shows so long that he can now claim it as a dependent on his income tax.

| | Crystal | Pink | Green | Red | | Crystal | Pink | Green | Red |
|---|---|---|---|---|---|---|---|---|---|
| Bowl, 4½" Berry | | | 7.00 | | Pitcher, 8", 65 oz. | 40.00 | 85.00 | | |
| *Bowl, 6¼" Berry | 6.00 | 12.50 | 10.00 | | Pitcher, 8½", 65 oz. w/Ice | | | | |
| Bowl, 8" Curved in at Top | 30.00 | 47.50 | | 325.00 | Lip | 57.50 | 95.00 | | |
| Bowl, 8¾" Straight Deep | | | | | ***Plate, 5¾" Sherbet | 3.00 | 5.00 | 5.00 | |
| Fruit | 22.50 | 40.00 | | | Plate, 6¾" | | | 6.00 | |
| Bowl, 10" Oval Vegetable | 10.00 | 16.50 | | | Plate, 8½" Salad | 5.00 | 14.00 | 8.00 | 60.00 |
| **Butter Dish and Cover | 190.00 | 375.00 | | | ****Plate, 10¼" Dinner | 10.00 | 17.00 | | |
| Butter Dish Bottom | 6.00 | 12.50 | | | Plate, 10¼" Grill | 7.50 | 15.00 | | |
| Butter Dish Top | 184.00 | 362.50 | | | Platter, 12¼" Oval | 10.00 | 16.00 | | |
| Cake Plate, 12" Footed | 16.50 | 27.50 | | | Relish, 8¾", 4 Part | 7.50 | 13.50 | | |
| Candy Jar and Cover, | | | | | Relish, 11¾" Round Divided | 14.00 | 350.00 | | |
| 11½" | 45.00 | 95.00 | | | Salt and Pepper, Pr. | 22.50 | 42.50 | 275.00 | |
| Celery Dish, 10½" | | | | | Saucer | 2.50 | 4.00 | | |
| Oblong | 7.50 | 15.00 | | | ***Sherbet | 6.50 | 10.00 | | |
| Coaster, 5¾" | 12.50 | 18.50 | | | Sugar | 6.00 | 12.50 | | 135.00 |
| Comport, 5" | 11.00 | 16.00 | | | ****Tumbler, 4", 5 oz. Juice | 12.50 | 35.00 | | |
| Creamer, Footed | 6.50 | 12.50 | | 135.00 | Tumbler, 4½", 10 oz. | | | | |
| Cup | 7.50 | 16.00 | 8.00 | | Water | 12.00 | 19.00 | 13.50 | |
| Goblet, 3¾", 3 oz. Wine | 16.00 | 50.00 | | 175.00 | Tumbler, 5¾", 14 oz. | | | | |
| Goblet, 4¾", 5 oz. Juice | 20.00 | 60.00 | | 175.00 | Iced Tea | 20.00 | 45.00 | | |
| Goblet, 5½", 10 oz. Water | 17.50 | 35.00 | | 160.00 | | | | | |

*Also has appeared in Cobalt Blue—$125.00
**Absolute mint price
***Also in Ice Blue—$35.00
****Also in Ice Blue—$80.00

**Please refer to Foreword for pricing information**

# MODERNTONE, "SAILBOAT" MODERNTONE, & "LITTLE HOSTESS PARTY DISHES", HAZEL ATLAS GLASS COMPANY, 1934-1942; Late 1940's - Early 1950's

Colors: Amethyst, cobalt blue; some crystal, pink and platonite fired-on colors.

I have had more than one dealer laugh at me for buying these fired-on pieces for pictures, but we have sold all the duplicates without much trouble! I know that there is no fortune to be made selling Platonite, but some collectors like these gaily decorated pieces. Is there any platter color other than yellow?

"Ships" decorations were added to Moderntone blanks. Avid is the best way to describe these collectors. Don't get between them and a bowl or cheese dish they want. You might get trampled!

Remember that the tumblers shown and priced were not officially listed as Moderntone, but they were advertised at the same time (1938) in newspaper ads.

Thanks again to Sherry McClain for the picture of amethyst Moderntone shown below. You can see all sizes of tumblers available.

Moderntone children's sets are prime collectibles now! It is the tea pot **WITH LID** that is missing from many sets.

| | Cobalt | Amethyst | Platonite Fired On Colors | | Cobalt | Amethyst | Platonite Fired On Colors |
|---|---|---|---|---|---|---|---|
| *Ash Tray, 7¾", Match Holder in Center | 95.00 | | | Plate, 5⅞" Sherbet | 3.50 | 3.00 | |
| Bowl, 4¾" Cream Soup | 13.00 | 11.00 | 4.50 | Plate, 6¾" Salad | 6.50 | 5.00 | |
| Bowl, 5" Berry | 13.50 | 6.50 | 3.50 | Plate, 7¾" Luncheon | 6.00 | 6.00 | 4.50 |
| Bowl, 5" Cream Soup, Ruffled | 17.50 | 14.00 | | Plate, 8⅞" Dinner | 9.50 | 7.50 | |
| Bowl, 6½" Cereal | 40.00 | 30.00 | 5.00 | Plate, 10½" Sandwich | 22.00 | 16.00 | |
| Bowl, 7½" Soup | 50.00 | 40.00 | | Platter, 11" Oval | 22.50 | 16.00 | 7.50 |
| Bowl, 8¾" Large Berry | 25.00 | 20.00 | 6.50 | Platter, 12" Oval | 35.00 | 25.00 | |
| Butter Dish with Metal Cover | 60.00 | | | Salt and Pepper, Pr. | 27.50 | 27.50 | 12.50 |
| Cheese Dish, 7" with Metal Lid | 175.00 | | | Saucer | 2.00 | 2.00 | 1.00 |
| Creamer | 8.00 | 6.00 | 4.00 | Sherbet | 8.50 | 7.50 | 3.50 |
| Cup | 7.50 | 6.00 | 3.00 | Sugar | 7.50 | 6.50 | 4.00 |
| Cup (Handle-less) or Custard | | | | Sugar Lid in Metal | 22.00 | | |
| | | | | Tumbler, 5 oz. | 17.50 | 14.00 | |
| *Pink — $60.00 | | | | Tumbler, 9 oz. | 16.00 | 16.00 | 6.00 |
| | | | | Tumbler, 12 oz. | 50.00 | 40.00 | |
| | | | | Whiskey, 1½ oz. | 15.00 | | |

## LITTLE HOSTESS PARTY SET

| | Pastel | Dark | | Pastel | Dark |
|---|---|---|---|---|---|
| Cup, 1¾" | 2.50 | 3.25 | Sugar, 1¾" | 3.00 | 4.00 |
| Saucer, 3⅞" | 1.00 | 2.00 | Teapot and Lid, 3½" | | 30.00 |
| Plate, 5¼" | 2.00 | 3.00 | Set, 14 Piece | 30.00 | |
| Creamer, 1¾" | 3.00 | 4.00 | Set, 16 Piece | | 65.00 |

# MOONDROPS   NEW MARTINSVILLE GLASS COMPANY, 1932-1940

Colors: Amber, pink, green, cobalt, ice blue, red, amethyst, crystal, dark green, light green, jadite, smoke, black.

Moondrops activity is limited to the red or blue or unusual pieces in the other colors. There are collectors of amber, amethyst and other colors; but they are few in comparison to those who pursue red or blue. The footed powder shown below caused a stir among collectors as it had not been seen before. I recently found a bud vase in amethyst.

| | Blue/Red | Other Colors | | Blue/Red | Other Colors |
|---|---|---|---|---|---|
| Ash Tray | 30.00 | 14.00 | Goblet, 5⅛", 3 oz. Metal Stem Wine | 12.00 | 8.50 |
| Bowl, 5¼" Berry | 10.00 | 5.00 | Goblet, 5½", 4 oz. Metal Stem Wine | 13.50 | 8.50 |
| Bowl, 6¾" Soup | 12.00 | 10.00 | Goblet, 6¼", 9 oz. Metal Stem Water | 17.50 | 13.50 |
| Bowl, 7½" Pickle | 16.00 | 11.00 | Gravy Boat | 95.00 | 65.00 |
| Bowl, 8⅜" Footed, Concave Top | 25.00 | 15.00 | Mug, 5⅛", 12 oz. | 27.50 | 17.50 |
| Bowl, 8½" 3-Footed Divided Relish | 20.00 | 12.00 | Perfume Bottle, "Rocket" | 75.00 | 35.00 |
| Bowl, 9½" 3 Legged Ruffled | 25.00 | 15.00 | Pitcher, 6⅞", 22 oz. Small | 135.00 | 75.00 |
| Bowl, 9¾" Oval Vegetable | 25.00 | 20.00 | Pitcher, 8⅛", 32 oz. Medium | 150.00 | 100.00 |
| Bowl, 9¾" Covered Casserole | 97.50 | 65.00 | Pitcher, 8", 50 oz. Large, with Lip | 155.00 | 40.00 |
| Bowl, 9¾" 2-Handled Oval | 45.00 | 30.00 | Pitcher, 8⅛", 53 oz. Large, No Lip | 150.00 | 115.00 |
| Bowl, 11½" Boat-Shaped Celery | 25.00 | 20.00 | Plate, 5⅞" | 7.00 | 5.00 |
| Bowl, 12" Round 3 Footed Console | 40.00 | 25.00 | Plate, 6⅛" Sherbet | 5.00 | 3.00 |
| Bowl, 13" Console with "Wings" | 60.00 | 35.00 | Plate, 6" Round, Off-Center Sherbet Indent | 9.00 | 7.00 |
| Butter Dish and Cover | 360.00 | 225.00 | Plate, 7⅛" Salad | 9.00 | 7.00 |
| Butter Dish Bottom | 40.00 | 35.00 | Plate, 8½" Luncheon | 11.00 | 9.50 |
| Butter Dish Top | 320.00 | 190.00 | Plate, 9½" Dinner | 15.00 | 12.00 |
| Candles, 2" Ruffled Pr. | 25.00 | 17.50 | Plate, 14" Round Sandwich | 25.00 | 13.50 |
| Candles, 4½" Sherbet Style Pr. | 22.50 | 15.00 | Plate, 14" 2-Handled Sandwich | 27.50 | 20.00 |
| Candlesticks, 5" "Wings" Pr. | 55.00 | 35.00 | Platter, 12" Oval | 20.00 | 15.00 |
| Candlesticks, 5¼" Triple Light Pr. | 75.00 | 45.00 | Powder Jar, 3 Footed | 95.00 | 75.00 |
| Candlesticks, 8½" Metal Stem Pr. | 32.50 | 25.00 | Saucer | 3.50 | 3.00 |
| Candy Dish, 8" Ruffled | 25.00 | 15.00 | Sherbet, 2⅝" | 10.00 | 7.50 |
| Cocktail Shaker, with or without | | | Sherbet, 4½" | 20.00 | 12.50 |
| Handle, Metal Top | 30.00 | 20.00 | Sugar, 2¾" | 9.00 | 7.00 |
| Comport, 4" | 17.50 | 10.00 | Sugar, 4" | 11.50 | 7.00 |
| Comport, 11½" | 40.00 | 25.00 | Tumbler, 2¾", 2 oz. Shot | 10.00 | 6.50 |
| Creamer, 2¾" Miniature | 10.00 | 7.50 | Tumbler, 2¾", 2 oz. Handled Shot | 12.50 | 7.50 |
| Creamer, 3¾" Regular | 12.00 | 7.50 | Tumbler, 3¼", 3 oz. Footed Juice | 12.50 | 8.00 |
| Cup | 9.00 | 7.50 | Tumbler, 3⅝", 5 oz. | 10.00 | 6.00 |
| Decanter, 7¾" Small | 50.00 | 32.50 | Tumbler, 4⅜", 7 oz. | 11.00 | 7.50 |
| Decanter, 8½" Medium | 57.50 | 32.50 | Tumbler, 4⅜", 8 oz. | 12.00 | 8.50 |
| Decanter, 11¼" Large | 67.50 | 37.50 | Tumbler, 4⅞", 9 oz. Handled | 20.00 | 12.00 |
| Decanter, 10¼" "Rocket" | 155.00 | 60.00 | Tumbler, 4⅞", 9 oz. | 13.50 | 10.00 |
| Goblet, 2⅞", ¾ oz. Liquor | 20.00 | 15.00 | Tumbler, 5⅛", 12 oz. | 18.00 | 11.50 |
| Goblet, 4", 4 oz. Wine | 15.00 | 10.00 | Tray, 7½", For Mini Sugar/Creamer | 25.00 | 16.00 |
| Goblet, 4¾", "Rocket" Wine | 40.00 | 25.00 | Vase, 7¾" Flat, Ruffled Top | 45.00 | 35.00 |
| Goblet, 4¾", 5 oz. | 17.00 | 11.00 | Vase, 8½" "Rocket" Bud | 120.00 | 95.00 |
| | | | Vase, 9¼" "Rocket" Style | 135.00 | 75.00 |

# MOONSTONE ANCHOR HOCKING GLASS CORPORATION, 1941-1946

Colors:   Crystal with opalescent hobnails, some green.

Moonstone did not experience the same skyrocketing prices from being placed on the cover that Manhattan did on the previous book. Of course, Manhattan is now being reissued in a similar form; so maybe it is just as well that Moonstone did not go wild! There are several reasons that it did not and I suspect that it had to do with there being an adequate supply—more than for any other reason. Time will tell what will happen to the Petalware featured on this book, but there is not a large supply of the decorated!

The red, fired-on candy shown below has been reported in other colors; and there are other pieces of red Moonstone. Evidently, these colors were run for special promotions or as premium items for some retail establishment.

The four pieces shown on the bottom right all have Moonstone labels attached to them and were purchased out of a home in Lancaster, the hometown of Anchor Hocking. There is speculation that the opalized effect was called Moonstone rather than the pattern. Note that the Bubble bowl and Lace Edge sherbet, as we know them, both have Moonstone labels.

Most questions I receive on this pattern concern items not listed. Almost all of the inquiries focus on glassware made by other companies who made hobnail patterns. Most of the questionable pieces are ones made by the Fenton Glass Company instead of Anchor Hocking. Many collectors of Moonstone mix pieces of Fenton with their sets in order to have such pieces as pitchers, shakers, cologne bottles and water goblets. Realize that the color is similar, but the hobs are more sharply defined on the Fenton pieces.

The picture with the odd pieces below is courtesy of Anchor Hocking, using glass from their morgue.

|  | Opalescent Hobnail |
|---|---|
| Bowl, 5½″ Berry | 9.00 |
| Bowl, 5½″ Crimped Dessert | 6.00 |
| Bowl, 6½″ Crimped Handled | 7.00 |
| Bowl, 7¾″ Flat | 8.00 |
| Bowl, 7¾″ Divided Relish | 7.50 |
| Bowl, 9½″ Crimped | 12.50 |
| Bowl, Cloverleaf | 8.50 |
| Candleholder, Pr. | 15.00 |
| Candy Jar and Cover, 6″ | 17.50 |
| Cigarette Jar and Cover | 15.00 |
| Creamer | 6.00 |
| Cup | 6.00 |
| Goblet, 10 oz. | 15.00 |
| Heart Bonbon, One Handle | 8.50 |
| Plate, 6¼″ Sherbet | 2.50 |
| Plate, 8″ Luncheon | 8.50 |
| Plate, 10″ Sandwich | 16.00 |
| Puff Box and Cover, 4¾″ Round | 16.00 |
| Saucer (Same as Sherbet Plate) | 2.50 |
| Sherbet, Footed | 6.00 |
| Sugar, Footed | 6.00 |
| Vase, 5½″ Bud | 8.50 |

**Please refer to Foreword for pricing information**

# MOROCCAN AMETHYST HAZEL WARE, DIVISION OF CONTINENTAL CAN, 1960's

Color: Amethyst.

I have received a lot of support from new collectors by adding this 1960's pattern to my Depression Glass book and a little static from the "old school" collectors. I will try to please everyone next year with a new concept in my books. New pieces to look for include a vase (listed below) which I purchased too late to be shown.

The name Moroccan Amethyst refers to the COLOR and there are several styles and shapes included in this pattern. It is difficult to know for sure if a particular piece is Moroccan Amethyst unless it still has a sticker attached announcing that it is, until you see a lot of pieces. You will probably find additional pieces to those listed; so please keep me informed.

As I said when I included this pattern, I feel a lot older than my forty three years seeing the glassware in my Depression Glass book that we got for wedding gifts in 1964!

| | Amethyst | | Amethyst |
|---|---|---|---|
| Ash Tray, 6⅞", Triangular | 5.00 | Plate, 12", Sandwich | 6.00 |
| Bowl, 4¾", Fruit | 3.50 | Saucer | .75 |
| Bowl, 5¾", Cereal | 4.50 | Tumbler, Juice, 2½", 4 oz. | 3.50 |
| Candy w/Lid | 17.50 | Tumbler, Old Fashion, 3¼", 8 oz. | 6.00 |
| Cocktail Shaker, 32 oz. | 15.00 | Tumbler, Water, 4½", 11 oz. | 5.50 |
| Cup | 3.00 | Tumbler, Iced Tea, 16 oz. | 8.00 |
| Plate, 7¼", Salad | 2.00 | Vase, 9" Ruffled | 27.50 |
| Plate, 9⅜", Dinner | 4.00 | | |

# MT. PLEASANT, "DOUBLE SHIELD" L.E. SMITH GLASS COMPANY, 1920's-1934

Colors: Black amethyst, amethyst, cobalt blue, crystal, pink, green.

New pieces are the "norm" in Mt. Pleasant since I have never been able to find a catalogue listing for this pattern. Keep the letters and pictures coming on Mt. Pleasant as some day, hopefully, we will get the list complete! Meanwhile, the blue is rapidly out-distancing the black in popularity and availability. There are many collectors of black glass that have Mt. Pleasant in their collections without realizing what it is. These collectors collect it because it is black, not for its being Mt. Pleasant. I received a letter from a lady in Texas who had discovered in her 400-piece collection of black that over 50 were Mt. Pleasant! She was happy to learn that a book showed some of her collection!

I received one picture of two different sized "leaf" plates, but the writer forgot to include the measurements. You might be on the lookout for this new one. I do not know if it is smaller or larger than the 8" one listed. I could not tell which one was 8" in the picture. I suspect we are looking for a 7" or 9".

I used to say this was glass that was too good to have been given away as premiums, but time and memories of collectors have proven that wrong. It was used as promotional items in western New York as well as hardware stores in Kansas and Nebraska in the early 1930's. These states should provide good hunting grounds for Mt. Pleasant!

| | Pink, Green | Black Amethyst, Amethyst, Cobalt | | Pink Green | Black Amethyst Cobalt |
|---|---|---|---|---|---|
| Bon Bon, Rolled-Up Handles, 7" | 12.50 | 17.50 | Cup | 5.00 | 8.50 |
| Bowl, 4" Opening, Rose | 15.00 | 20.00 | Leaf, 8" | | 11.00 |
| Bowl, 4", Square Footed Fruit | 10.00 | 15.00 | Mayonnaise, 5½", 3 Footed | 12.50 | 20.00 |
| Bowl, 6", 2-Handled, Square | 9.00 | 12.50 | Mint, 6", Center Handle | 10.00 | 15.00 |
| Bowl, 7", 3 Footed, Rolled Out Edge | 12.50 | 16.50 | Plate, 7", 2-Handled, Scalloped | 6.50 | 10.00 |
| Bowl, 8", Scalloped, 2-Handled | 15.00 | 20.00 | Plate, 8", Scalloped or Square | 7.50 | 11.00 |
| Bowl, 8", Square, 2-Handled | 15.00 | 20.00 | Plate, 8", 2-Handled | 7.50 | 13.50 |
| Bowl, 9", Scalloped, 1¾" Deep, Footed | | 25.00 | Plate 8¼", Square w/Indent for Cup | | 13.00 |
| Bowl, 9¼", Square Footed Fruit | 15.00 | 25.00 | Plate, 9", Grill | | 8.50 |
| Bowl, 10", Scalloped Fruit | | 28.00 | Plate, 10½", Cake, 2-Handled | 13.50 | 20.00 |
| Bowl, 10", 2-Handled, Turned-Up Edge | | 25.00 | Plate, 12", 2-Handled | 15.00 | 25.00 |
| Candlestick, Single, Pr. | 15.00 | 20.00 | Salt and Pepper, 2 Styles | 20.00 | 32.50 |
| Candlestick, Double, Pr. | 20.00 | 32.00 | Sandwich Server, Center-Handled | | 30.00 |
| Creamer | 15.00 | 12.50 | Sherbet | 6.50 | 12.50 |
| Cup (Waffle-Like Crystal) | 3.50 | | Sugar | 15.00 | 12.50 |
| | | | Vase, 7¼" | | 20.00 |

# NEW CENTURY, and incorrectly, "LYDIA RAY" HAZEL ATLAS GLASS COMPANY, 1930-1935

Colors: Green; some crystal, pink, amethyst and cobalt.

I have shown all five colors that can be found in New Century although the green is what most collectors seek. The pink, amethyst and cobalt blue are mostly found in the pitcher and tumbler sets. I keep getting letters telling me of discoveries of cobalt cups with no saucers. I have been unable to find either.

I have had three letters telling me that they too had found powder jars made from the sugar lid and a sherbet. Maybe they were sold that way, but I rather doubt it.

Some confusion still exists over the name of New Century. Another author called OVIDE by the name New Century. This pattern was given the name New Century by the factory. Be aware of that problem when ordering by mail!

| | Green, Crystal | Pink, Cobalt Amethyst | | Green, Crystal | Pink, Cobalt, Amethyst |
|---|---|---|---|---|---|
| Ash Tray/Coaster, 5⅜" | 25.00 | | Plate, 7⅛" Breakfast | 5.50 | |
| Bowl, 4½" Berry | 5.00 | | Plate, 8½" Salad | 6.00 | |
| Bowl, 4¾" Cream Soup | 9.00 | | Plate, 10" Dinner | 10.00 | |
| Bowl, 8" Large Berry | 12.00 | | Plate, 10" Grill | 8.00 | |
| Bowl, 9" Covered Casserole | 45.00 | | Platter, 11" Oval | 11.00 | |
| Butter Dish and Cover | 47.50 | | Salt and Pepper, Pr. | 27.50 | |
| Cup | 5.00 | 15.00 | Saucer | 2.00 | 5.00 |
| Creamer | 6.00 | | Sherbet, 3" | 6.00 | |
| Decanter and Stopper | 40.00 | | Sugar | 5.00 | |
| Goblet, 2½ oz. Wine | 14.00 | | Sugar Cover | 9.00 | |
| Goblet, 3¼ oz. Cocktail | 13.00 | | Tumbler, 3½", 5 oz. | 8.00 | 7.50 |
| Pitcher, 7¾", 60 oz. with or without Ice Lip | 27.50 | 25.00 | Tumbler, 4¼", 9 oz. | 10.00 | 7.50 |
| | | | Tumbler, 5", 10 oz. | 10.00 | 10.00 |
| Pitcher, 8", 80 oz. with or without Ice Lip | 30.00 | 35.00 | Tumbler, 5¼", 12 oz. | 15.00 | 12.00 |
| Plate, 6" Sherbet | 2.25 | | Tumbler, 4", 5 oz. Footed | 10.00 | |
| | | | Tumbler, 4⅞", 9 oz. Footed | 12.50 | |
| | | | Whiskey, 2½", 1½ oz. | 12.00 | |

# NEWPORT, "HAIRPIN" HAZEL ATLAS GLASS COMPANY, 1936-1940

Colors: Cobalt blue, amethyst; some pink, "Platonite" white and fired-on colors.

Several sets of pink Newport have been reported since the last book. Maybe more seeds were sold than I thought. It seems that a set of pink Newport was given away for buying seeds from a catalogue (if you missed that information before). I have found a few pieces of pink scattered about the country, but never any quantity at one time. That is probably just as well as there is little collector demand for anything except the blue and amethyst.

The cereal bowls continue to drive collectors "bananas" (which would be fine for the cereal but difficult for the collectors). You will note several price increases including the aforementioned cereals, the large sandwich plate and the cream soups. Amethyst is harder to find than the blue. However, there are more collectors searching for the blue which accounts for collectors thinking it is rarer. Remember, items that are scarce can be caused from short supplies in manufacturing OR from demand.

White Petalware collectors have been known to use white Newport shakers with their pattern since there are no Petalware shakers.

| | *Cobalt | Amethyst | | *Cobalt | Amethyst |
|---|---|---|---|---|---|
| Bowl, 4¼" Berry | 10.00 | 9.00 | Plate, 11½" Sandwich | 22.50 | 20.00 |
| Bowl, 4¾" Cream Soup | 12.00 | 11.00 | Platter, 11¾" Oval | 25.00 | 22.50 |
| Bowl, 5¼" Cereal | 22.00 | 16.00 | Salt and Pepper | 35.00 | 32.50 |
| Bowl, 8¼" Large Berry | 28.00 | 25.00 | Saucer | 2.50 | 2.50 |
| Cup | 7.50 | 6.50 | Sherbet | 9.00 | 8.50 |
| Creamer | 9.50 | 8.00 | Sugar | 9.50 | 8.00 |
| Plate, 6" Sherbet | 3.50 | 3.00 | Tumbler, 4½", 9 oz. | 22.50 | 20.00 |
| Plate, 8½" Luncheon | 7.50 | 7.50 | | | |

*White 50% of Cobalt price.

**Please refer to Foreword for pricing information**

## "NORA BIRD", PADEN CITY GLASS COMPANY, LINE 1300, 1929-1930's

Colors: Pink, green.

Nora Bird is the collector's name for this etching on Paden City's #300 line blank. Pink and green are the only colors on which I have found this etching, but it would not be surprising to find it on any of Paden City's numerous colors. You can recognize this pattern by the bird starting to take flight. On the cup, saucer and a few other pieces, the bird has already taken off. You may find additional pieces; if you do, please let me know.

|  | Pink/Green |
|---|---|
| Candlestick, Pr. | 40.00 |
| Candy Dish w/Cover, 6½", 3 Part | 50.00 |
| Creamer, Round Handle | 22.00 |
| Creamer, Pointed Handle | 20.00 |
| Cup | 20.00 |
| Ice Tub, 6" | 65.00 |
| Mayonnaise and Liner | 50.00 |
| Plate, 8" | 15.00 |
| Saucer | 10.00 |
| Sugar, Round, Handle | 22.00 |
| Sugar, Pointed Handle | 20.00 |
| Tumbler, 3" | 22.00 |
| Tumbler, 4" | 27.50 |
| Tumbler, 4¾", Footed | 32.50 |

## NORMANDIE, "BOUQUET AND LATTICE" FEDERAL GLASS COMPANY, 1933-1940

Colors: Iridescent, amber, pink, crystal.

You might notice a significant absence of a pink pitcher and tumblers in the picture. Those Normandie items (along with the dinner plates and sugar lid) have caused more than one pink collector to switch to another pattern. The price of those items mentioned are reasonable for their scarcity! That is difficult to admit, but realistic! There are other pieces in pink that are relatively easy to find; so if you are willing to collect a small set with a rather large luncheon plate as the dinner plate, I have a set for you.

In amber only the pitcher, shakers and sugar lid pose much of a threat of not being found. You can find the rest with little difficulty and without breaking the bank account.

In the iridized Normandie, you will be able to find all except the salad plates without spending your life savings. If someone says this is Carnival glass—just pass them by; you will probably not be able to convince them anyway.

| | Amber | Pink | Iridescent | | Amber | Pink | Iridescent |
|---|---|---|---|---|---|---|---|
| Bowl, 5" Berry | 4.00 | 5.00 | 4.00 | Platter, 11¾" | 11.00 | 15.00 | 10.00 |
| *Bowl, 6½" Cereal | 9.00 | 12.00 | 6.50 | Salt and Pepper, Pr. | 35.00 | 50.00 | |
| Bowl, 8½" Large Berry | 11.00 | 14.00 | 9.50 | Saucer | 1.50 | 2.00 | 1.50 |
| Bowl, 10" Oval Veg. | 12.00 | 22.00 | 12.50 | Sherbet | 5.00 | 6.50 | 6.00 |
| Creamer, Footed | 6.00 | 8.50 | 6.50 | Sugar | 5.00 | 6.00 | 5.00 |
| Cup | 5.50 | 6.50 | 5.00 | Sugar Lid | 65.00 | 100.00 | |
| Pitcher, 8", 80 oz. | 50.00 | 80.00 | | Tumbler, 4", 5 oz. | | | |
| Plate, 6" Sherbet | 2.00 | 2.00 | 2.00 | Juice | 12.50 | 32.50 | |
| Plate, 8" Salad | 6.50 | 8.00 | 40.00 | Tumbler, 4¼", 9 oz. | | | |
| Plate, 9¼" Luncheon | 5.00 | 9.00 | 7.50 | Water | 11.00 | 28.50 | |
| Plate, 11" Dinner | 15.00 | 50.00 | 12.00 | Tumbler, 5", 12 oz. | | | |
| Plate, 11" Grill | 10.00 | 12.00 | 9.00 | Iced Tea | 16.00 | 45.00 | |

*Mistaken by many as butter bottom.

**Please refer to Foreword for pricing information**

# NO. 610, "PYRAMID"   INDIANA GLASS COMPANY, 1926-1932

Colors:   Green, pink, yellow, white, crystal and black in 1974-1975 by Tiara.

Pyramid is the name by which most collectors know this pattern even though Indiana called it No. 610. The white bowl shown turned over in the foreground must have been made in the 1950's marketing foray for white glass. Several odd Indiana pieces have appeared in white from that time frame including pitchers in Sandwich and Avocado.

I still think this is one of this era's most striking patterns—but so do other collectors. The deco lines that create such a dramatic display also hold rigid points that have a tendency to be chipped. Make sure the pieces are mint *before* you pay your money.

Pitchers have always been difficult to find. The crystal is the rarest and yellow the most common. I know it is also the highest priced, but that comes from demand rather than from scarcity. Try and find a perfect pink pitcher!

Due to the high price of this pattern, a few more pieces are beginning to show up. Have you ever noticed that the higher the price gets on a item that was once moderately priced, the more available it suddenly seems to become. More people seem to be willing to part with their collection—the higher the price goes. It is called the law of supply and demand. For that reason, Depression Glass will continue to be marketable no matter how highly priced it becomes.

| | Crystal Pink | Green | Yellow | | Crystal Pink | Green | Yellow |
|---|---|---|---|---|---|---|---|
| Bowl, 4¾" Berry | 14.50 | 13.50 | 25.00 | Pitcher | 185.00 | 185.00 | 395.00 |
| Bowl, 8½" Master Berry | 20.00 | 22.50 | 45.00 | Relish Tray, 4-Part Handled | 30.00 | 37.50 | 50.00 |
| Bowl, 9½" Oval | 25.00 | 22.50 | 45.00 | Sugar | 17.50 | 17.50 | 25.00 |
| Bowl, 9½" Pickle, 5¾" Wide | 25.00 | 22.50 | 45.00 | Tray for Creamer and Sugar | 17.50 | 20.00 | 40.00 |
| Creamer | 16.50 | 16.50 | 25.00 | Tumbler, 8 oz. Footed | 20.00 | 25.00 | 42.50 |
| Ice Tub | 65.00 | 75.00 | 175.00 | Tumbler, 11 oz. Footed | 35.00 | 45.00 | 55.00 |
| Ice Tub and Lid | | | 600.00 | | | | |

---

# NO. 612, "HORSESHOE"   INDIANA GLASS COMPANY, 1930-1933

Colors:   Green, yellow, pink, crystal.

This pattern has always been called "Horseshoe" by collectors ever since I have known about Depression Glass, but I have often wondered why? The design may be reminiscent of horseshoes to glass collectors, but not to Kentuckians. We have seen a few horses and their shoes in our day!

There seems to be an increasing demand for this pattern recently. Prices were stagnating for a few years. You will find a few modest increases in price, but no big jumps as in the past. The pink candy lid has needed a bottom for a number of years. For some reason, lost in the archives of time, only the candy dish was ever made in pink. It's a shame since the pattern shows up quite well on the pink and it would have been very collectible in that color!

You can see by the plates shown that some have center designs and others do not. The plain center items sometimes confuse collectors, causing them to wonder whether the piece is No. 612 or not.

Grill plates remain as difficult to find as perfect butter dishes. Grill plates are divided plates (having raised partitions), and they were once used by many short order cooks in restaurants and grills of that era.

| | Green | Yellow | | Green | Yellow |
|---|---|---|---|---|---|
| Bowl, 4½" Berry | 16.00 | 15.00 | Plate, 6" Sherbet | 3.00 | 4.50 |
| Bowl, 6½" Cereal | 15.00 | 16.50 | Plate, 8⅜" Salad | 6.00 | 7.00 |
| Bowl, 7½" Salad | 14.00 | 16.00 | Plate, 9⅜" Luncheon | 8.00 | 8.50 |
| Bowl, 8½" Vegetable | 17.00 | 22.50 | Plate, 10⅜" Dinner | 15.00 | 16.00 |
| Bowl, 9½" Large Berry | 22.50 | 26.00 | Plate, 10⅜" grill | 27.50 | 25.00 |
| Bowl, 10½" Oval Vegetable | 15.00 | 17.50 | Plate, 11" Sandwich | 10.00 | 12.00 |
| Butter Dish and Cover | 450.00 | | Platter, 10¾" Oval | 15.00 | 15.50 |
| Butter Dish Bottom | 125.00 | | Relish, 3 Part Footed | 15.00 | 25.00 |
| Butter Dish Top | 325.00 | | Saucer | 3.00 | 3.50 |
| Candy in Metal Holder | | | Sherbet | 10.00 | 11.50 |
|   Motif on Lid—95.00 | | | Sugar, Open | 10.00 | 10.50 |
|   Also, Pink | 135.00 | | Tumbler, 4¼", 9 oz. | 75.00 | |
| Creamer, Footed | 11.50 | 12.50 | Tumbler, 4¾", 12 oz. | 85.00 | |
| Cup | 7.00 | 7.50 | Tumbler, 9 oz. Footed | 14.00 | 15.00 |
| Pitcher, 8½", 64 oz. | 200.00 | 225.00 | Tumbler, 12 oz. Footed | 75.00 | 85.00 |

**Please refer to Foreword for pricing information**

## NO. 616, "VERNON"   INDIANA GLASS COMPANY, 1930-1932

Colors:   Green, crystal, yellow.

A funny thing happened on my way to replace this picture in the book. (Every possible piece is shown here in this one; so, I don't feel I have left anything out; but this picture is an old one.) I couldn't find my box of Vernon at home which had all these pieces in it; and when I went to shows, I couldn't find any of it to buy! Either the popularity the pattern once enjoyed has waned until dealers don't bother to carry it to shows any more, or the supply has all dried up! We once had a very large set of crystal which we used for everyday dishes. I got upset at the $7.00 tumblers breaking and we "retired" the set. WHERE we "retired" the set is something of a mystery at the moment.

If someone ever turns up a pitcher to go with these tumblers, you may again see some "action" in this pattern. As it is, I'm wondering how difficult it may be to collect a set for luncheons or bridge club gatherings. Let me know how YOU fare with this pattern.

|  | Green | Crystal | Yellow |
|---|---|---|---|
| Creamer, Footed | 20.00 | 9.00 | 17.50 |
| Cup | 13.50 | 5.00 | 12.00 |
| Plate, 8" Luncheon | 6.50 | 4.00 | 6.50 |
| Plate, 11" Sandwich | 18.00 | 10.00 | 18.00 |
| Saucer | 4.50 | 2.00 | 4.50 |
| Sugar, Footed | 19.50 | 8.00 | 17.50 |
| Tumbler, 5" Footed | 25.00 | 10.00 | 22.50 |

## NO. 618, "PINEAPPLE & FLORAL"   INDIANA GLASS COMPANY, 1932-1937

Colors:   Crystal, amber; some fired-on red, green; late 1960's, avocado.

A pitcher in RED was what a midwestern dealer rushed to tell me about at the Chicago show in March. It sounded good to me but was too good to be true! The fired-on red pitcher was of the quality of the fired-on No. 618 pieces—BAD! There was a cross hatching design similar to the base of No. 618; but other than that and the horrendous color, the similarity to Pineapple and Floral ended!

The pink 7" salad bowls you are seing all over the flea markets are NEW. They are being made by Indiana and are selling for under a dollar at the local dish barn or outlet.

If you are looking for a well-made, highly polished pattern, just keep right on looking. This pattern is not for you. The mould seams on the tumblers and a few other pieces are among the worst in all Depression Glass. If not careful, you could get a nasty lip cut from using some of these tumblers.

The stands, in white or black, for the large cone-shaped vases are harder to find than the vases. I suspect that many of these remained in use at funeral homes after the glass vases were retired for more modern ones. Eventually, the stands were worn out or destroyed and the vases remained in storage.

|  | Crystal | Amber, Red |  | Crystal | Amber, Red |
|---|---|---|---|---|---|
| Ash Tray, 4½" | 13.00 | 16.00 | Plate, 11½" Indentation | 20.00 | |
| Bowl, 4¾" Berry | 20.00 | 14.00 | Plate, 11½" Sandwich | 12.50 | 13.50 |
| Bowl, 6" Cereal | 18.50 | 16.00 | Platter, 11" Closed Handles | 10.00 | 12.00 |
| Bowl, 7" Salad | 5.00 | 8.50 | Platter, Relish, 11½" | | |
| Bowl, 10" Oval Vegetable | 20.00 | 16.00 | Divided | 15.00 | |
| Comport, Diamond-Shaped | 1.50 | 6.50 | Saucer | 3.00 | 3.00 |
| Creamer, Diamond-Shaped | 6.50 | 8.50 | Sherbet, Footed | 15.00 | 15.00 |
| Cream Soup | 18.00 | 17.50 | Sugar, Diamond-Shaped | 6.50 | 8.50 |
| Cup | 7.50 | 7.00 | Tumbler, 4¼", 8 oz. | 25.00 | |
| Plate, 6" Sherbet | 3.00 | 4.00 | Tumbler, 5", 12 oz. | 30.00 | |
| Plate, 8⅜" Salad | 5.00 | 6.00 | Vase, Cone-Shaped | 25.00 | |
| *Plate, 9⅜" Dinner | 10.00 | 12.50 | Vase Holder (17.50) | | |

*Green—$22.50

**Please refer to Foreword for pricing information**

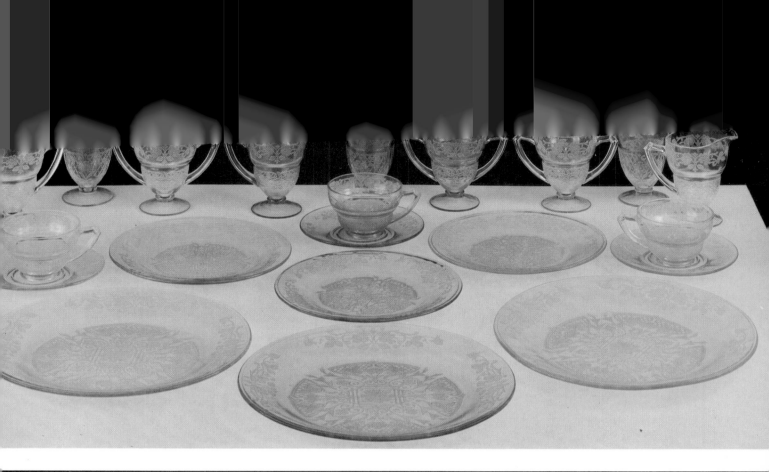

# OLD CAFE   HOCKING GLASS COMPANY, 1936-1938; 1940

Colors:   Pink, crystal, Royal Ruby.

Being easy on the pocketbook has brought Old Cafe to the attention of a few newer collectors. The price of the pitchers and dinner plate shake up some of these beginners, but I try to explain this plate would be $40.00 or $50.00 if more people collected the pattern. This is one of the few small patterns that has a dinner plate and may be one of the best reasons to start collecting Old Cafe.

I will accept the juice pitcher as Old Cafe even though it is not shown in old Hocking catalogues. I still have difficulty accepting the larger version as Old Cafe since it is found more frequently in green than pink and nothing else has ever been found in green. The pitcher was made by Hocking, so if you want a nice "go-with" piece, it's fine to collect this pitcher.

There is also a cookie jar that is a nice "go-with" piece. It is ribbed like Old Cafe, but has a cross-hatched lid. This was made as a numbered line by Hocking and not as Old Cafe.

The Royal Ruby cups are found on crystal saucers. No red saucers have been found—yet.

| | Crystal, Pink | Royal Ruby | | Crystal, Pink | Royal Ruby |
|---|---|---|---|---|---|
| Bowl, 3¾" Berry | 2.00 | 4.00 | Pitcher, 6", 36 oz. | 50.00 | |
| Bowl, 5", 1 or 2 Handles | 3.00 | | Pitcher, 80 oz. | 75.00 | |
| Bowl, 5½" Cereal | 4.00 | 8.50 | Plate, 6" Sherbet | 1.50 | |
| Bowl, 9", Closed Handles | 7.50 | 11.50 | Plate, 10" Dinner | 15.50 | |
| Candy Dish, 8" Low | 5.00 | 10.00 | Saucer | 1.50 | |
| Cup | 3.00 | 6.00 | Sherbet, Low Footed | 4.50 | |
| Lamp | 12.50 | 20.00 | Tumbler, 3" Juice | 6.50 | 7.50 |
| Olive Dish, 6" Oblong | 4.00 | | Tumbler, 4" Water | 6.00 | |
| | | | Vase, 7¼" | 9.50 | 13.50 |

# OLD ENGLISH, "THREADING"   INDIANA GLASS COMPANY

Colors:   Green, amber; some pink, crystal, forest green.

Amazingly, this pattern continues to have its devotees even without the basic necessities of plates, cups and saucers. Old English is made up of serving and occasional pieces that seem to attract those who would like to have different pieces of Depression Glass displayed as decorations. The center handled server has to be one of the hardest to find in all of Depression Glass. I have only seen three in all my travels and the Post Office did one of those in. I suppose those tire marks down the side of the package had a lot to do with the multitude of pieces inside, but it was never proven whether it was a mail truck's tires or not. That's like the box of books sent to California about which the postal person delivering said she was sorry but the box fell out of the back of the truck and it got a little damaged at that speed!

The lid to the pitcher is not shown, but it has the cloverleaf (shamrock for the Irish) as shown on the sugar and candy tops. There is a notch in this lid that allows liquid to be poured out with the top still held on (with the other hand I suppose). I guess that would save the ice if they had any!

The cheese and cracker is still shown mismatched. The pink cracker plate is the only one I have ever seen in any color and the amber compote is the only one I have seen. All of the flat pieces in old English seem to be scarce. I know collectors who enjoy finding a piece of this pattern better than anything other than breathing!

| | Pink, Green, Amber | | Pink, Green, Amber |
|---|---|---|---|
| Bowl, 4" Flat | 12.00 | Pitcher | 50.00 |
| Bowl, 9" Footed Fruit | 22.50 | Pitcher and Cover | 90.00 |
| Bowl, 9½" Flat | 25.00 | Plate, Indent for Compote | 17.50 |
| Candlesticks, 4" Pr. | 22.50 | Sandwich Server, Center Handle | 40.00 |
| Candy Dish & Cover, Flat | 40.00 | Sherbet, 2 Styles | 16.00 |
| Candy Jar with Lid | 37.50 | Sugar | 12.00 |
| Compote, 3½" Tall, 7" Across | 14.00 | Sugar Cover | 25.00 |
| Compote, Cheese For Plate | 12.50 | Tumbler, 4½" Footed | 14.00 |
| Creamer | 14.00 | Tumbler, 5½" Footed | 25.00 |
| Egg Cup (Crystal) | 6.50 | Vase, 5⅜", Fan Type, 7" | |
| Fruit Stand, 11" Footed | 32.50 | Across | 35.00 |
| Goblet, 5¾", 8 oz. | 22.50 | Vase, 12" Footed | 40.00 |

**Please refer to Foreword for pricing information**

## "ORCHID"  PADEN CITY GLASS COMPANY, Early 1930's

Colors:  Yellow, cobalt blue, green, amber, pink, red and black.

A red, 10", footed bowl which stands 4" tall has just been discovered. It may be a footed centerpiece to go with the tall candlesticks, but that is only an educated guess. It is etched on Paden City's "crow's foot" blank (#412) which is only one of several Paden City's blanks on which Orchid is found.

Most collectors seek out the red and blue colors, but yellow is also quite nice. You may find this pattern on any color produced by Paden City. I still have not seen any other plates in this pattern other than the blue shown here. The six I bought in Ohio several years ago were ignored by collectors for two years because of the price. It took a half price sale for me to be interested and then it took a lot of thought. My wife had tried to buy them several times and had offered more than I ended up paying. Sometimes "a bird in the bush. . . ." or was that "a sucker is born . . . ."

|  | All Other Colors | Red, Black Cobalt Blue |
|---|---|---|
| Bowl, 4⅞" Square | 10.00 | 22.50 |
| Bowl, 8½", 2-Handled | 22.50 | 47.50 |
| Bowl, 8¾" Square | 20.00 | 42.50 |
| Bowl, 10", Footed | 30.00 | 65.00 |
| Candlesticks, 5¾" Pr. | 30.00 | 55.00 |
| Creamer | 20.00 | 32.50 |
| Comport, 6¼" | 15.00 | 27.50 |
| Ice Bucket, 6" | 50.00 | 75.00 |
| Mayonnaise, 3 Piece | 45.00 | 65.00 |
| Plate, 8½", Square |  | 30.00 |
| Sandwich Server, Center Handled | 25.00 | 50.00 |
| Sugar | 20.00 | 32.50 |
| Vase, 10" | 40.00 | 85.00 |

## OVIDE, incorrectly dubbed "NEW CENTURY"  HAZEL ATLAS GLASS COMPANY, 1930-1935

Colors:  Green, black, white platonite trimmed with fired-on colors in 1950's.

The massive display of Ovide in this picture was the subject of several letters this year. Everyone wants to buy my Art Deco set. The problem is—it is not mine to sell. I have only one creamer and sugar which I found about ten years ago at the Three Rivers Depression Glass show in Pittsburgh. I wish more of it were available. There have been several other sets of the "flying ducks" (geese) reported; so at least, they can be found.

The trimmed pieces, with blue and black, were made as late as the 1950's and are not of the 1930's vintage. Collectors of black glass search for the "Sterling" pieces of Ovide. These are black pieces trimmed in silver— sterling silver, in fact. The word "Sterling" has been incorporated in the design.

The Ovide without designs is not selling too well at present. I suspect that it will take time before this supply is exhausted. However, numerous collectors are now considering "kitchen" sets, so Ovide might well fit that bill!

| | Black | Green | Decorated* White | | Black | Green | Decorated* White |
|---|---|---|---|---|---|---|---|
| Bowl, 4¾" Berry |  |  | 6.00 | Plate, 8" Luncheon |  | 1.50 | 6.00 |
| Bowl, 5½" Cereal |  |  | 10.00 | Plate, 9" Dinner |  |  | 7.00 |
| Bowl, 8" Large Berry |  |  | 17.50 | Platter, 11" |  |  | 12.50 |
| Candy Dish and Cover | 25.00 | 15.00 | 25.00 | Salt and Pepper, Pr. | 20.00 | 9.00 | 20.00 |
| Cocktail, Footed Fruit | 3.00 | 2.00 |  | Saucer | 2.00 | 1.25 | 4.00 |
| Creamer | 5.00 | 2.50 | 12.00 | Sherbet | 5.00 | 1.50 | 10.00 |
| Cup | 5.00 | 2.00 | 8.00 | Sugar, Open | 5.00 | 2.50 | 12.00 |
| Plate, 6" Sherbet |  | 1.00 | 5.00 | Tumbler |  |  | 15.00 |

*Art Deco Triple Price

**Please refer to Foreword for pricing information**

# OYSTER AND PEARL  ANCHOR HOCKING GLASS CORPORATION, 1938-1940

Colors:    Pink, crystal, Ruby Red, white with fired-on pink or green.

The picture tells it all! This patten has few pieces, but some of them are massive and need a lot of space to display them. The large bowl and plate make one of the finest salad sets in all of Depression Glass. If you collect Royal Ruby, you ought to put this set in your collection.

There are still few people "turned on" by the fired-on colors. Why not pick up these up to use for entertaining. None of your friends will ever have seen any thing like these and you can start them collecting by giving them the bowl. I tried that with our photographer a few years ago by giving him a candlestick of which I had two. This year the candlestick got "accidentally" returned in my camera case. I tried to expand his horizons into glassware, but was unsuccessful with fired-on Oyster and Pearl. *Maybe you will have better luck with your friends.*

We sell a lot of the relish dishes in my shop to people who want to buy a piece of Depression Glass for a friend. They make great gift items. More people are buying items with a history to give as gifts than ever before. At least older glass is not worth **less** the minute you walk out the store with it as is the case with anything new.

Somehow the 5½" handled bowl was omitted from the list last time. It's listed now. Note that the so-called heart-shaped bowl is not made in red.

| | Crystal, Pink | Royal Ruby | White With Fired-On Green Or Pink |
|---|---|---|---|
| Bowl, 5¼" Heart-Shaped, 1-Handle | 5.00 | | 5.25 |
| Bowl, 5½", One Handled | 4.00 | 9.50 | |
| Bowl, 6½" Deep-Handled | 8.00 | 15.00 | |
| Bowl, 10½" Deep Fruit | 16.00 | 32.50 | 11.00 |
| Candleholder, 3½" Pr. | 15.00 | 32.50 | 12.50 |
| Plate, 13½" Sandwich | 10.00 | 27.50 | |
| Relish Dish, 10¼" Oblong | 6.00 | | |

**Please refer to Foreword for pricing information**

145

# "PARROT", SYLVAN   FEDERAL GLASS COMPANY, 1931-1932

Colors:   Green, amber; some crystal and blue.

Parrot prices continue on an upswing. That is hard to believe since it is one of the highest priced patterns already. There is no inexpensive tumbler in Parrot; but I sold a dozen in a recent ad at the prices listed below. There were several other calls after they had all been sold; so it was not one person interested, but several.

There have been no reports of pitchers since the original discovery of 37 in an old hardware store in Ohio. Of those at least five have met with accidents, so that cache is dwindling. There are no reports of newly discovered pieces as was the case in the last two books. The hot plate shown below is shaped like Georgian-style hot plates, but the one known previously is shaped like those of Madrid with pointed edges. If you find either style, consider yourself lucky. The one pictured below may be a little rarer. Only time will tell, but the price is high for either style.

Amber Parrot has its devotees, but the price discourages beginners. Very few butter dishes, sugar lids and no pitchers have been found to date. I used to think that we would eventually find everything that was made in all patterns. Only now do I realize that there will still be new discoveries as long as there are collectors willing to "dig out" attics, basements and garages. No one can even guess at what lies awaiting discovery. Who would have ever thought of "blue" Parrot? I met the lady a few years ago who sold the sherbet pictured here. A family member had worked for Federal Glass Company and this was in his estate. How many more treasures are there?

The company name for this pattern is Sylvan which is derived from the Latin for woods. Collectors have always recognized that bird and called it "Parrot". It is hard to mistake a parrot in a palm tree!

The pointed edges and ridges on cups, sherbets, lids, etc. should be checked closely when you are purchasing this pattern. They were and still are easily damaged. DAMAGED or REPAIRED glassware should not bring MINT prices! I emphasize that here—for many sugar and butter lids have been repaired. If it has been repaired, it should be sold as such and the seller should always tell the buyer. I have no qualms with repaired glass if it is done properly and all parties are aware of the repair. My main concern is that many so-called glass grinders are just that. They grind glass, but they do not repair it. The glass would have been better off left alone. Ask to see examples of a glass grinders work before you hand over your treasures. Are edges rounded and smoothed to near mint condition, or are they left flattened and sharp? Can you feel the repair? Are chips and flakes ground away leaving noticeable dips in the surface, or is the edge reworked to insure uniformity? Can you see scratches and cracks or is it "as smooth as glass"? Unless it was a badly damaged piece, you should not notice the repair until close examination!

| | Green | Amber |
|---|---|---|
| Bowl, 5" Berry | 12.50 | 10.00 |
| Bowl, 7" Soup | 27.50 | 25.00 |
| Bowl, 8" Large Berry | 50.00 | 60.00 |
| Bowl, 10" Oval Vegetable | 35.00 | 45.00 |
| Butter Dish and Cover | 240.00 | 650.00 |
| Butter Dish Bottom | 27.50 | 200.00 |
| Butter Dish Top | 212.50 | 450.00 |
| Creamer, Footed | 20.00 | 30.00 |
| Cup | 25.00 | 25.00 |
| Hot Plate, 5", 2 Styles | 495.00 | |
| Pitcher, 8½", 80 oz. | 850.00 | |
| Plate, 5¾" Sherbet | 17.50 | 11.00 |
| Plate, 7½" Salad | 17.50 | |
| Plate, 9" Dinner | 30.00 | 25.00 |
| Plate, 10½" Round Grill | 20.00 | |
| Plate, 10½" Square Grill | | 17.50 |
| Plate, 10¼" Square | 45.00 | 45.00 |
| Platter, 11¼" Oblong | 27.50 | 45.00 |
| Salt and Pepper, Pr. | 177.50 | |
| Saucer | 8.50 | 8.50 |
| *Sherbet, Footed Cone | 16.50 | 15.00 |
| Sherbet, 4¼" High | 195.00 | |
| Sugar | 20.00 | 20.00 |

*Blue $100.00

| | Green | Amber |
|---|---|---|
| Sugar Cover | 95.00 | 300.00 |
| Tumbler, 4¼", 10 oz. | 95.00 | 95.00 |
| Tumbler, 5½", 12 oz. | 110.00 | 110.00 |
| Tumbler, 5¾" Footed Heavy | 95.00 | 105.00 |
| Tumbler, 5½", 10 oz. Footed (Madrid Mold) | | 110.00 |

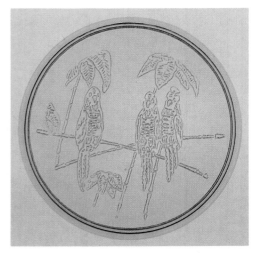

**Please refer to Foreword for pricing information**

# PATRICIAN, "SPOKE" FEDERAL GLASS COMPANY, 1933-1937

Colors: Pink, green, amber ("Golden Glo") and yellow.

Patrician amber is still the most commonly found pattern in my area. The amber was called "Golden Glo" by Federal. A few boxes of the dinner plates recently turned up and the finder said that the pattern was listed on the outside as "Golden Glo" although it looked like Patrician to him. These plates were a premium for the purchase of a ten-pound bag of a well-known flour. No wonder these are so plentiful! The interesting thing about this find is the box was labelled as "cake plates" to be given with flour. There was no cake plate as such in Patrician. These have always been called the dinner plate; it is however, one of the largest dinner plates in Depression Glass; so maybe we blew one!

Saucers still remain harder to find than cups. Many dealers will not sell you saucers separately in this pattern. In fact, most dealers will not break up cup and saucer to sell the pieces individually in any pattern. In my shop, we try to accomodate the customer when possible; but in this pattern, the saucers are not sold separately. Now, if you want a Patrician cup, that can be arranged!

The hexagonal shape of Patrician pieces has always infatuated new collectors. To this day, I remember the first pitcher and cookie jar that I saw. At that time, I did not know Madrid from Patrician, but I liked that cookie jar and I had the same feeling for the pitcher. I bought the cookie for $3.00; but I passed by the pitcher for $5.00. At that time, most pitchers were only selling for $5.00 to $7.50 and I couldn't spend that much and gamble on making a profit! I was a Kentucky school teacher at the time—enough said.

Sugar lids are often repaired, so check them closely.

There are two styles of pitchers. The crystal pitcher shown has an applied handle. The amber pitcher handle is moulded. You can see the shapes of the handles are different. The applied handle pitcher stands 8¼" high, and the moulded handle pitcher stands 8" high. Both styles hold 75 oz., but the applied handle style is harder to find in amber and green.

| | Amber, Crystal | Pink | Green | | Amber, Crystal | Pink | Green |
|---|---|---|---|---|---|---|---|
| Bowl, 4¾" Cream Soup | 11.00 | 15.00 | 16.00 | Plate, 6" Sherbet | 6.75 | 4.50 | 5.00 |
| Bowl, 5" Berry | 7.50 | 9.50 | 8.50 | Plate, 7½" Salad | 10.00 | 12.50 | 10.00 |
| Bowl, 6" Cereal | 16.00 | 17.50 | 18.00 | Plate, 9" Luncheon | 7.50 | 6.50 | 7.00 |
| Bowl, 8½" Large Berry | 30.00 | 17.50 | 20.00 | Plate, 10½" Dinner | 5.50 | 20.00 | 27.50 |
| Bowl, 10" Oval Vegetable | 20.00 | 15.00 | 18.00 | Plate, 10½" Grill | 9.00 | 9.50 | 10.00 |
| Butter Dish and Cover | 70.00 | 195.00 | 90.00 | Platter, 11½" Oval | 20.00 | 15.00 | 15.00 |
| Butter Dish Bottom | 47.50 | 150.00 | 50.00 | Salt and Pepper, Pr. | 42.50 | 70.00 | 45.00 |
| Butter Dish Top | 22.50 | 45.00 | 40.00 | Saucer | 6.00 | 5.00 | 5.00 |
| Cookie Jar and Cover | 65.00 | | 300.00 | Sherbet | 8.50 | 8.00 | 9.00 |
| Creamer, Footed | 7.00 | 8.50 | 9.50 | Sugar | 6.50 | 7.00 | 7.00 |
| Cup | 6.00 | 7.50 | 8.00 | Sugar Cover | 32.50 | 40.00 | 40.00 |
| Jam Dish | 17.50 | 20.00 | 25.00 | Tumbler, 4", 5 oz. | 22.50 | 20.00 | 25.00 |
| Pitcher, 8", 75 oz., Molded | | | | Tumbler, 4½", 9 oz. | 20.00 | 18.50 | 20.00 |
| Handle | 85.00 | 85.00 | 85.00 | Tumbler, 5½", 14 oz. | 27.50 | 22.00 | 30.00 |
| Pitcher, 8¼", 75 oz., Applied | | | | Tumbler, 5¼", 8 oz. Ftd. | 31.50 | | 37.50 |
| Handle | 90.00 | 90.00 | 90.00 | | | | |

# "PATRICK", LANCASTER GLASS COMPANY, Early 1930's

Colors: Yellow and pink.

Collectors are becoming more aware of Jubilee's brother pattern, Patrick, but not to the extent that I first figured they would. There are many similarities between the patterns, but little similarity in collecting trends. Jubilee's star shines far brighter than Patrick's.

I have found little Patrick in the pink; the cup and saucer shown were borrowed. Since the shapes are the same as those of Jubilee, it is easy to figure out that it is the floral pattern of Jubilee that is the attracting force. Patrick has its own floral bouquet, but that has not helped it obtain the followers that rushed to collect Jubilee.

Serving dishes are hard to find in Patrick. Many collectors are beginning to pick up other yellow Lancaster bowls and accessory items with the same shapes to go with both Patrick and Jubilee. They blend beautifully, so why not?

| | Yellow/ Pink | | Yellow/ Pink |
|---|---|---|---|
| Bowl, 9", Handled Fruit | 20.00 | Mayonnaise, 3 Piece | 37.50 |
| Bowl, 11", Console | 25.00 | Plate, 7" Sherbet | 5.00 |
| Candlesticks, Pr. | 35.00 | Plate, 7½" Salad | 6.00 |
| Candy Dish, 3 Footed | 32.50 | Plate, 8" Luncheon | 6.50 |
| Cheese & Cracker Set | 35.00 | Saucer | 2.00 |
| Creamer | 10.50 | Sherbet, 4¾" | 13.00 |
| Cup | 8.00 | Sugar | 10.00 |
| Goblet, 4" Cocktail | 17.50 | Tray, 11", 2-Handled | 17.50 |
| Goblet, 4¾", 6 oz. Juice | 15.00 | Tray, 11", Center Handled | 25.00 |
| Goblet, 6", 10 oz. Water | 22.00 | | |

# "PEACOCK REVERSE", LINE 412   PADEN CITY GLASS COMPANY, 1930's

Colors:   Cobalt blue, red, yellow and black.

"Peacock Reverse" can be found on at least two of Paden City's glassware lines: Line #412 commonly called "Crow's Foot" by collectors and Line #991 which is Paden City's Penny Line. That is not to say that there may not be others.

I have been stumped in finding pieces recently, but I am sure there are new pieces to be found in this pattern! So, help me look!

| All Colors | | | All Colors | |
|---|---|---|---|---|
| Bowl, 4⅞" Square | 22.00 | | Plate, 8½" Luncheon | 25.00 |
| Bowl, 8¾" Square | 50.00 | | Plate 10⅜", 2-Handled | 32.50 |
| Bowl, 8¾" Square with Handles | 57.50 | | Saucer | 12.50 |
| Candlesticks, 5¾" Square Base, | | | Sherbet, 4⅝" Tall, 3⅜" Diameter | 32.50 |
| Pr. | 72.50 | | Sherbet, 4⅞" Tall, 3⅝ Diameter | 32.50 |
| Candy Dish, 6½" Square | 65.00 | | Sugar, 2¾" Flat | 47.50 |
| Creamer, 2¾" Flat | 47.50 | | Tumbler, 4", 10 oz. Flat | 42.50 |
| Cup | 37.50 | | Vase, 10" | 75.00 |
| Plate, 5¾" Sherbet | 17.50 | | | |

# "PEACOCK & WILD ROSE",   PADEN CITY GLASS COMPANY, LINE 1300, 1930's

Colors:   Pink, green, cobalt blue, black and red.

"Another of Paden City bird lines" is the way I heard a dealer describe this pattern recently. "I can't collect them because they all look alike!" exclaimed another. A bird is a bird, but not all birds look alike. Some patterns are readily recognized, while others take some study. The more study and work you do—the richer the rewards. So study and you will know how to tell the difference in these "bird" patterns when you see them.

All of the Paden City bird lines are collectible, but the peacocks have more followers than any other etching, even NBC knows that!

| | All Colors |
|---|---|
| Bowl, 8½", Flat | 27.50 |
| Bowl, 8½", Fruit, Oval, Footed | 40.00 |
| Bowl, 8¾", Footed | 25.00 |
| Bowl, 9½", Center Handled | 30.00 |
| Bowl, 9½", Footed | 37.50 |
| Bowl, 10½", Center Handled | 32.50 |
| Bowl, 10½", Footed | 37.50 |
| Bowl, 10½", Fruit | 35.00 |
| Bowl, 11", Console | 30.00 |
| Bowl, 14", Console | 37.50 |
| Candlestick, 5", Pr. | 50.00 |
| Candy Dish w/Cover, 7" | 67.50 |
| Comport, 6¼" | 20.00 |
| Ice Bucket, 6" | 65.00 |
| Ice Tub, 4¾" | 60.00 |
| Plate, Cake, Low Foot | 30.00 |
| Relish, 3 Part | 30.00 |
| Vase, 10" | 67.50 |

**Please refer to Foreword for pricing information**

# PETALWARE  MacBETH-EVANS GLASS COMPANY, 1930-1940

Colors:  Monax, Cremax, pink, crystal, cobalt and fired-on red, blue, green and yellow.

Petalware on the cover may have surprised a few of you, but you must admit—it's pretty! The "Florette" (as the red floral pattern was called) has been idling about for years. I suspect this may change and even more collectors (especially those buying this book for the first time) will know what Petalware is before they know about any other pattern!

Of course, the "Florence Cherry" was placed in the center of one photograph purely by "accident". That plate makes a great family gift if you have the right name! Speaking of the fruits in this pattern reminds me that many collectors are looking for these pieces as wall decorations for the dining room or kitchen. There are at least eight different fruits in the set of red ribbon-decorated plates; and there's another series or two on Cremax colored plates.

For those who have not read American Sweetheart, refer there for an explanation of Cremax and Monax colors made by MacBeth-Evans. I might add here that true Cremax will glow green under a black light. If your teenager has one in his room highlighting a poster on the wall maybe he will let you borrow the light to check it out.

Lampshades like the larger one in the photo do not sell very well; but they are rather numerous. Smaller ones sell slowly with the ceiling globes being more in demand. The one pictured was bought for $9.00 not very long ago.

Monax (white) is an inexpensive pattern to collect if you are looking for a pattern to start. Decorated petalware is prettier, but more costly. Choose the plain, undecorated Monax or Cremax and you can buy a set of Depression Glass for less than you can buy a new set of today's higher priced "Inflation" dishes. You may have to invest in a beautiful table cloth in order to show these wonderful old dishes to advantage, but it will be worth it!

| | Pink, Crystal | CREMAX, MONAX | | Florette |
| | | Plain | Fired-On Decorations | |
|---|---|---|---|---|
| Bowl, 4½" Cream Soup | 4.00 | 7.50 | 8.50 | |
| Bowl, 5¾" Cereal | 3.50 | 4.50 | 6.50 | 15.00 |
| Bowl, 7" Soup | | 10.00 | 15.00 | |
| *Bowl, 9" Large Berry | 7.50 | 12.50 | 15.00 | 27.50 |
| Cup | 2.50 | 4.50 | 6.00 | 10.00 |
| **Creamer, Footed | 2.50 | 4.50 | 8.00 | 12.50 |
| Lamp Shade (many sizes) $8.00 to $15.00 | | | | |
| Mustard with Metal Cover in Cobalt Blue Only $7.50 | | | | |
| Pitcher, 80 oz. (Crystal Decorated Bands) | 20.00 | | | |
| Plate, 6" Sherbet | 1.50 | 2.00 | 4.00 | |
| Plate, 8" Salad | 1.75 | 3.00 | 6.00 | 8.50 |
| Plate, 9" Dinner | 3.50 | 3.50 | 7.50 | |
| Plate, 11" Salver | 4.00 | 6.50 | 12.00 | 17.50 |
| Plate, 12" Salver | | 6.50 | 15.00 | |
| Platter, 13" Oval | 7.50 | 12.00 | 15.00 | |
| Saucer | 1.00 | 1.50 | 2.50 | 3.00 |
| Sherbet, 4" Low Footed | | 12.50 | | |
| **Sherbet, 4½" Low Footed | 3.00 | 4.50 | 7.50 | 15.00 |
| **Sugar, Footed | 2.50 | 4.50 | 7.50 | 12.50 |
| Tidbit Servers or Lazy Susans, Several Styles 12.00 to 17.50 | | | | |
| ***Tumblers (Crystal Decorated Bands) 2.50 to 7.50 | | | | |

*Also in cobalt at 37.50
**Also in cobalt at 20.00
***Several Sizes

**Please refer to Foreword for pricing information**

## "PRETZEL", NO. 622  INDIANA GLASS COMPANY, 1930's-1970's

Colors:  Crystal, teal.

Indiana may still be making a piece or two of this pattern, but I have not been able to confirm it. The abundance of celery trays and two-handled pickles makes me wonder if they ought to be included with the leaf-shaped olive dish that I am certain they are making now.

You can be assured that the pitcher and tumblers were made in limited quantities as was the teal issue. I have not seen any teal pieces in the two years since I wrote the last book, and that has not been for lack of trying!

Very few square snack plates with indents for the cup have been found. This is not one of Indiana's more popularly collected patterns and probably will never be because it is predominately found in crystal. Crystal patterns have never found acceptance with the majority of collectors. Yet most crystal sets I've seen are very beautiful when displayed in quantity.

|  | Crystal* |
|---|---|
| Bowl, 4½″ Fruit Cup | 2.50 |
| Bowl, 7½″ Soup | 7.50 |
| Bowl, 9⅜″ Berry | 10.00 |
| Celery, 10¼″ Tray | 2.50 |
| Creamer | 4.50 |
| Cup | 3.50 |
| Olive, 7″ Leaf Shape | 2.50 |
| Pickle, 8½″, 2 Handled | 3.00 |
| Pitcher, 39 oz. | 95.00 |
| Plate, 6″ | 1.50 |
| Plate 7¼″ Square, Indent | 6.00 |
| Plate, 7¼″ Square, Indent 3-Part | 6.00 |
| Plate, 8⅜″ Salad | 3.00 |
| Plate, 9⅜″ Dinner | 4.00 |
| Plate, 11½″ Sandwich | 7.00 |
| Saucer | 1.00 |
| Sugar | 3.50 |
| Tumbler, 5 oz., 3½″ | 10.00 |
| Tumbler, 9 oz., 4½″ | 12.00 |
| Tumbler, 12 oz., 5½ | 15.00 |

* Teal Triple Price

---

# PRIMO, "PANELLED ASTER"  U.S. GLASS COMPANY, Early 1930's

Colors:  Green, yellow.

I received two letters since the last book from collectors agreeing with Cathy, my wife, that they had also seen a center-handled server in this pattern. Mind you that neither one owned one, they had just seen it. I still have not; so maybe Scotty will beam it up by the 9th book.

The pink and black coasters shown are just like the green and yellow Primo pattern. Evidently, these were made by U.S. Glass for other patterns besides Primo. No pink or black Primo has been found; or perhaps the four colors made up a bridge type set?

You will find mould roughness as a general characteristic of most seams in this pattern.

| | Yellow/Green | | Yellow/Green |
|---|---|---|---|
| Bowl, 4½″ | 6.50 | Plate, 10″ Dinner | 10.00 |
| Bowl, 7¾″ | 12.50 | Plate, 10″ Grill | 7.50 |
| Cake Plate, 10″, 3 Footed | 13.50 | Saucer | 2.00 |
| Coaster/Ash Tray | 6.00 | Sherbet | 6.50 |
| Creamer | 7.50 | Sugar | 7.50 |
| Cup | 6.50 | Tumbler, 5¾″, 9 oz. | 12.00 |
| Plate, 7½″ | 5.00 | | |

**Please refer to Foreword for pricing information**

# PRINCESS HOCKING GLASS COMPANY, 1931-1935

Colors: Green, topaz, apricot yellow, pink and blue.

Princess collectors have a multitude of bowls and tumblers to find in order to complete a set. Tumblers are hard to find in most patterns and Princess is no exception. Bowls are the most difficult to find, however. Collecting any bowl in green, pink or yellow will drive collectors to drink!

Add to the difficulty of finding yellow bowls the problem of having two distinctly different shades of yellow and it's enough to make a grown man weep! Hocking called their yellow "Topaz" and collectors have given the lighter, brighter shade of yellow this name. The darker, almost amber yellow is called honey-amber or just amber. There is less of this amber shade of yellow available and it is the least collected. Not all pieces of Princess have been found in the darker shade which adds to the dilemma for collectors of that color. The shades of yellow are so different that they do not mix well; so you need to know which shade your pieces are when buying. This is particularly tough when purchasing by phone.

Both the divided and undivided relish bowls are shown. In pink, the divided is shown on the right, and in green the undivided is shown on the right behind the cup and saucer. Some dealers have tried to call these soup bowls.

There are three rare pitchers shown. The square footed, pink and green and the yellow juice pitchers are all known in quantities of less than five. In collecting fields that can truly be considered rare! I can still remember the first time I saw the yellow juice. I was in a Lexington home delivering a book and some glass. The lady I took the yellow Princess to was mixing frozen orange juice in this pitcher. I tried to buy it then, but since she was collecting that pattern, I was unsuccessful. A few years later, she gave up collecting and I bought her glass which included the pitcher. It now resides in Louisiana—with a stopover in Kansas.

The blue turns up rarely and that is a shame. There should be more available, but so far only the cookie jar, grill plate, cup and saucer have been seen. Supposedly, there was a whole set in Texas years ago, but no one has ever seen it again. I could write a book on all these rare sets that have been seen. I would title it *Lost Gold of the Depression Era.*

|  | Green | Pink | Yellow Amber |  | Green | Pink | Yellow Amber |
|---|---|---|---|---|---|---|---|
| Ash Tray, 4½" | 55.00 | 57.50 | 75.00 | Plate, 10½" Grill, Closed Handles | 8.00 | 5.00 | 6.00 |
| Bowl, 4½" Berry | 16.50 | 12.00 | 35.00 | Plate, 11½" Handled Sandwich | 10.00 | 7.50 | 20.00 |
| Bowl, 5" Cereal or Oatmeal | 20.00 | 15.00 | 22.50 | Platter, 12" Closed Handles | 13.00 | 11.00 | 37.50 |
| Bowl, 9" Octagonal Salad | 25.00 | 18.00 | 75.00 | Relish, 7½" Divided | 17.50 | 12.50 | 50.00 |
| Bowl, 9½" Hat-Shaped | 25.00 | 14.50 | 85.00 | Relish, 7½" Plain | 60.00 |  | 100.00 |
| Bowl, 10" Oval Vegetable | 17.50 | 15.00 | 40.00 | Salt and Pepper, 4½" Pr. | 40.00 | 32.00 | 45.00 |
| Butter Dish and Cover | 60.00 | 70.00 | 500.00 | Spice Shakers, 5½" Pr. | 32.00 |  |  |
| Butter Dish Bottom | 20.00 | 20.00 | 200.00 | *** Saucer (Same as Sherbet Plate) | 5.00 | 3.50 | 3.00 |
| Butter Dish Top | 40.00 | 50.00 | 300.00 | Sherbet, Footed | 14.00 | 11.00 | 27.50 |
| Cake Stand, 10" | 15.00 | 12.00 |  | Sugar | 8.50 | 6.50 | 9.50 |
| Candy Dish and Cover | 35.00 | 37.50 |  | Sugar Cover | 12.50 | 11.50 | 12.50 |
| Coaster | 22.50 | 52.50 | 67.50 | Tumbler, 3", 5 oz. Juice | 21.00 | 17.00 | 20.00 |
| * Cookie Jar and Cover | 35.00 | 40.00 |  | Tumbler, 4", 9 oz. Water | 20.00 | 14.00 | 18.00 |
| Creamer, Oval | 10.00 | 9.00 | 10.00 | Tumbler, 5¼", 13 oz. Iced Tea | 25.00 | 16.50 | 20.00 |
| ** Cup | 9.00 | 6.50 | 7.50 | Tumbler, 4¾", 9 oz. Sq. Ftd. | 55.00 | 45.00 |  |
| Pitcher, 6", 37 oz. | 35.00 | 75.00 | 500.00 | Tumbler, 5¼", 10 oz. Footed | 22.50 | 16.00 | 16.00 |
| Pitcher, 7⅜", 24 oz. Footed | 500.00 | 400.00 |  | Tumbler, 6½", 12½ oz. Ftd. | 60.00 | 35.00 | 90.00 |
| Pitcher, 8", 60 oz. | 35.00 | 32.00 | 500.00 | Vase, 8" | 22.00 | 17.50 |  |
| *** Plate, 5½" Sherbet | 5.00 | 3.50 | 3.00 |  |  |  |  |
| Plate, 8" Salad | 9.50 | 7.00 | 8.00 |  |  |  |  |
| Plate, 9" Dinner | 19.00 | 12.00 | 12.00 |  |  |  |  |
| ** Plate, 9" Grill | 10.00 | 6.50 | 6.50 |  |  |  |  |

*Blue—$500.00
**Blue—$95.00
***Blue—$50.00

**Please refer to Foreword for pricing information**

# QUEEN MARY (PRISMATIC LINE), "VERTICAL RIBBED"

## HOCKING GLASS COMPANY, 1936-1949

Colors:    Pink, crystal; some Ruby Red.

Queen Mary is a pattern that has not caught the eye of Deco collectors the way some patterns have. Maybe vertical lines are not as acceptable as the horizontal lines. In any case, there are collectors of Queen Mary who are glad not to have the added competition of looking for pink footed tumblers and dinner plates. Those two items are beginning to be harder to find in crystal, also.

The pink cereal bowl, which is the same as the butter bottom, has disappeared from sight. Several collectors have reported that these, along with the celery or pickle dish, cannot be found in any condition—good or bad. I cannot confirm that as I have not had any collectors ask me to find them a celery, but several have asked for butter bottoms.

There are two sizes of cups to be found. The smaller cup sits on a saucer with cup ring and the larger cup comes with a typical Hocking saucer/sherbet plate that has no ident. The smaller cup seems to be the most plentiful at present.

Several pieces of Queen Mary were made in Ruby Red including the candlestick and large bowl. In the 1950's, the 3½" round ashtray was made in Forest Green and Royal Ruby.

| | Pink | Crystal | | Pink | Crystal |
|---|---|---|---|---|---|
| Ash Tray, 2" x 3¾" Oval | 3.50 | 2.00 | Coaster/Ash Tray, 4¼" Square | 4.50 | 4.50 |
| *Ash Tray, 3½" Round | | 2.00 | Comport, 5¾" | 7.50 | 5.00 |
| Bowl, 4" One Handle Or None | 3.00 | 2.50 | Creamer, Oval | 5.00 | 4.00 |
| Bowl, 5" Berry | 4.50 | 3.00 | Cup (2 sizes) | 5.00 | 4.50 |
| Bowl, 5½", Two Handles | 5.00 | 4.00 | Plate, 6" and 6⅝" | 2.50 | 2.50 |
| Bowl, 6" Cereal | 15.00 | 4.00 | Plate, 8½" Salad | 4.50 | 4.00 |
| Bowl, 7" Small | 6.00 | 5.00 | Plate, 9¾" Dinner | 20.00 | 9.00 |
| Bowl, 8¾" Large Berry | 8.50 | 7.00 | Plate, 12" Sandwich | 8.00 | 6.00 |
| Butter Dish or Preserve and | | | Plate, 14" Serving Tray | 10.00 | 9.00 |
| Cover | 80.00 | 20.00 | Relish Tray, 12", 3-Part | 9.00 | 7.00 |
| Butter Dish Bottom | 15.00 | 4.00 | Relish Tray, 14", 4-Part | 10.00 | 9.00 |
| Butter Dish Top | 65.00 | 16.00 | Salt and Pepper, Pr. | | 15.00 |
| Candy Dish and Cover | 25.00 | 15.00 | Saucer | 1.50 | 1.50 |
| **Candlesticks, 4½" Double | | | Sherbet, Footed | 4.50 | 3.50 |
| Branch, Pr. | | 12.00 | Sugar, Oval | 4.50 | 4.00 |
| Celery or Pickle Dish, 5" x 10" | 12.00 | 7.00 | Tumbler, 3½", 5 oz. Juice | 6.00 | 3.00 |
| Cigarette Jar, 2" x 3" Oval | 5.50 | 3.50 | Tumbler, 4", 9 oz. Water | 5.50 | 4.00 |
| Coaster, 3½" | 2.50 | 2.00 | Tumbler, 5", 10 oz. Footed | 20.00 | 12.50 |

*Ruby Red—$5.00; Forest Green—$3.00        **Ruby Red—$27.50

---

# RAINDROPS, "OPTIC DESIGN"    FEDERAL GLASS COMPANY 1929-1933

Colors:    Green, crystal.

Raindrops is a smaller pattern that is fun to collect. Several pieces are found easily, but others are quite rare. The sugar lid, shakers and the 7½" berry bowl are all missing in most collections of this pattern. That should tell you what is hard to find.

I still have only owned three Raindrops sugar lids in seventeen years of dealing in Depression Glass. I have sold three Mayfair sugar lids since the last book came out and they are supposedly rare. The Mayfair lids number more than Raindrops' lids, but there are thousands of collectors of Mayfair wanting a lid whereas only a few collectors are searching for Raindrops. DEMAND and not RARITY determines price. Some rare items are often overlooked because no one collects them. No matter how rare an item is, there has to be a demand before it will sell.

| | Green | | Green |
|---|---|---|---|
| Bowl, 4½" Fruit | 2.50 | Sherbet | 5.00 |
| Bowl, 6" Cereal | 4.00 | Sugar | 5.00 |
| Bowl, 7½" Berry | 20.00 | Sugar Cover | 30.00 |
| Cup | 4.00 | Tumbler, 3", 4 oz. | 3.00 |
| Creamer | 5.00 | Tumbler, 2⅛", 2 oz. | 3.00 |
| Plate, 6" Sherbet | 1.50 | Tumbler, 3⅞", 5 oz. | 5.00 |
| Plate, 8" Luncheon | 3.00 | Tumbler, 4⅛", 9½ oz. | 7.50 |
| Salt and Pepper, Pr. | 125.00 | Tumbler, 5", 10 oz. | 7.50 |
| Saucer | 1.00 | Whiskey, 1⅞", 1 oz. | 4.00 |

**Please refer to Foreword for pricing information**

# RADIANCE   NEW MARTINSVILLE GLASS COMPANY, 1936-1939

Colors:   Red, cobalt and ice blue, amber, crystal, emerald green.

Radiance is a pattern often found in antique shops and shows. This glass is better than Depression so it is allowed at the finer shows where basic Depression ware is taboo. Radiance probably belongs to the Elegant book, but it has been considered Depression for so long that it is hard to move it there.

Collectors of butter dishes, pitchers and other items can have a field day in this pattern with all the colors available. The only cause for alarm is the cost. You need a deep pocketbook to collect many pitchers or butter dishes in this pattern.

Red is the most commonly found color; but amber and light blue are available. Any of these three colors can be accumulated into a set with patience, hard work and the basic necessity—funds. Cobalt blue is another story. Very little is available at any price. This is the only pitcher and tumbler I have seen in that color.

Crystal items sell for about half of the lowest price listed with those items decorated in gold or silver selling for a little more. I have watched a silver decorated butter sit for two years for $85.00—to give you an idea. No one will pay that much for it.

The punch bowl ladles are rare. The dipper on the ladle is a Radiance cup, in case you have not seen one. Punch bowls are ball-shaped. I now have a dark green one to show you next time.

| | Red | Ice Blue, Amber | | Red | Ice Blue, Amber |
|---|---|---|---|---|---|
| Bowl, 5″, Nut, 2-Handled | 12.00 | 7.50 | Creamer | 15.00 | 10.00 |
| Bowl, 6″, Bonbon | 13.00 | 8.00 | Cruet, Indiv. | 45.00 | 30.00 |
| Bowl, 6″, Bonbon, Footed | 15.00 | 9.00 | Cup | 12.00 | 10.00 |
| Bowl, 6″, Bonbon w/Cover | 35.00 | 25.00 | Cup, Punch | 9.00 | 5.00 |
| Bowl, 7″, Relish, 2-Part | 15.00 | 10.00 | Decanter w/Stopper, Handled | 105.00 | 65.00 |
| Bowl, 7″, Pickle | 12.50 | 10.00 | Ladle for Punch Bowl | 100.00 | 75.00 |
| Bowl, 8″, Relish, 3-Part | 22.50 | 15.00 | Lamp, 12″ | 80.00 | 50.00 |
| Bowl, 10″, Celery | 15.00 | 10.00 | Mayonnaise, 3 Piece, Set | 25.00 | 12.00 |
| Bowl, 10″, Crimped | 25.00 | 15.00 | Pitcher, 64 oz. (Cobalt: | | |
| Bowl, 10″, Flared | 27.50 | 17.50 | $250.00) | 175.00 | 125.00 |
| Bowl, 12″, Crimped | 32.50 | 22.50 | Plate, 8″, Luncheon | 12.00 | 7.50 |
| Bowl, 12″, Flared | 30.00 | 20.00 | Plate, 14″, Punch Bowl Liner | 45.00 | 20.00 |
| Bowl, Punch | 135.00 | 75.00 | Salt & Pepper, Pr. | 60.00 | 37.50 |
| Butter Dish | 350.00 | 150.00 | Saucer | 5.00 | 3.50 |
| Candlestick, 8″ Pr. | 50.00 | 30.00 | Sugar | 14.00 | 9.00 |
| Candlestick, 2-lite, Pr. | 75.00 | 50.00 | Tray, Oval | 25.00 | 20.00 |
| Cheese/Cracker, (11″ Plate) | | | Tumbler, 9 oz. (Cobalt: $25.00) | 20.00 | 12.50 |
| Set | 40.00 | 22.00 | Vase, 10″, Flared | 35.00 | 22.50 |
| Comport, 5″ | 17.50 | 12.00 | Vase, 12″, Crimped | 55.00 | 40.00 |
| Comport, 6″ | 22.50 | 15.00 | | | |
| Condiment Set, 4 piece w/Tray | 200.00 | 125.00 | | | |

## "RIBBON"    HAZEL ATLAS GLASS COMPANY, Early 1930's

Colors:    Green; some black, crystal, pink.

Ribbon is a pattern that quietly sits and then sneaks up on collectors. All of a sudden they are out searching for the candy, creamer and sugar and tumblers after finding a small piece for a bargain price. It seems no one gets excited about Ribbon, until they get "wrapped" up in it. Forgive the high school pun!

The only pink pieces to be found have been shakers; and there are only a few items in black. You will not go into debt collecting Ribbon.

Note the shapes of Ribbon follow closely those of Cloverleaf and Ovide. These shapes must have found favor with Hazel Atlas customers as they used them over and over. Then, too, this may have been done to redesign old moulds and save the cost of new ones.

| | Green | Black | | Green | Black |
|---|---|---|---|---|---|
| Bowl, 4" Berry | 4.00 | | Plate, 8" Luncheon | 3.00 | 10.00 |
| Bowl, 8" Large Berry | 13.50 | 17.50 | Salt and Pepper, Pr. | 17.50 | 35.00 |
| Candy Dish and Cover | 27.50 | | Saucer | 1.50 | |
| Creamer, Footed | 8.00 | | Sherbet, Footed | 4.00 | |
| Cup | 3.50 | | Sugar, Footed | 8.00 | |
| Plate, 6¼" Sherbet | 1.50 | | Tumbler, 6", 10 oz. | 16.50 | |

## RING, "BANDED RINGS"    HOCKING GLASS COMPANY 1927-1933

Colors:    Crystal, crystal w/pink, red, blue, orange, yellow, black, silver, etc. rings; green, some pink, "Mayfair" blue, red.

I still have trouble picturing this pattern as it was advertised, "New Fiesta"; ads featured gaily skirted dancing girls with colorful sombreros and outfitted in colors of orange, yellow and green! Note the colored bands on the glass which went with the dancing girls. Collectors have always tried to match the bands of colors in order. I have cautioned against this for years as it is nigh impossible! Collectors have come around to my thinking in that respect. Go for the over-all appearance of color and let the sequence of color alone.

I might add a little comment here. I get quite a few letters about colored banded pieces that are not Ring. You can mix these with Ring if you wish, but the impressed rings have to be in the glass to be Ring. On a true Ring pattern, there are rings in the glass even without color—and some of you are missing that point. Colored rings are not all that is necessary.

Unusual colors of red and "Mayfair" blue have been found. I would not mind having a set in that blue if you find one.

| | Crystal | Crystal Decor., Green | | Crystal | Crystal Decor., Green |
|---|---|---|---|---|---|
| Bowl, 5" Berry | 2.50 | 3.50 | Sandwich Server, Center | | |
| Bowl, 7" Soup | 7.50 | 10.00 | Handle | 12.00 | 20.00 |
| Bowl, 8" Large Berry | 5.00 | 7.50 | Saucer | 1.25 | 1.50 |
| Butter Tub or Ice | | | Sherbet, Low (for 6½" | | |
| Bucket | 10.00 | 17.50 | Plate) | 4.00 | 10.00 |
| Cocktail Shaker | 10.00 | 17.50 | Sherbet, 4¾" Footed | 4.00 | 7.50 |
| **Cup | 3.00 | 3.50 | Sugar, Footed | 3.00 | 4.00 |
| Creamer, Footed | 3.50 | 4.50 | Tumbler, 3½", 5 oz. | 2.50 | 4.00 |
| Decanter and Stopper | 15.00 | 25.00 | Tumbler, 4¼", 9 oz. | 3.50 | 4.50 |
| Goblet, 7¼", | | | Tumbler, 5⅛", 12 oz. | 4.00 | 5.00 |
| 9 oz. | 6.00 | 12.50 | Tumbler, 3½" Footed | | |
| Ice Tub | 12.00 | 17.50 | Cocktail | 4.00 | 5.00 |
| Pitcher, 8", 60 oz. | 10.00 | 15.00 | Tumbler, 5½" Footed | | |
| *Pitcher, 8½", 80 oz. | 12.00 | 20.00 | Water | 4.00 | 6.00 |
| Plate, 6¼" Sherbet | 1.25 | 1.50 | Tumbler, 6½", Footed | | |
| Plate, 6½", Off-Center | | | Iced Tea | 5.00 | 9.00 |
| Ring | 1.50 | 4.50 | Vase, 8" | 12.50 | 27.50 |
| **Plate, 8" Luncheon | 1.50 | 3.00 | Whiskey, 2", 1½ oz. | 3.50 | 5.50 |
| ***Salt and Pepper, Pr., 3" | 15.00 | 25.00 | | | |

*Also found in Pink. Priced as Green.    **Red—17.50. Blue—27.50    ***Green—52.50.

**Please refer to Foreword for pricing information**

162

# ROCK CRYSTAL, "EARLY AMERICAN ROCK CRYSTAL"

## McKEE GLASS COMPANY, 1920's and 1930's in colors

Colors: Four shades of green, aquamarine, vaseline, yellow, amber, pink and satin frosted pink, red slag, dark red, red, amberina red, crystal, frosted crystal, crystal with goofus decoration, crystal with gold decoration, amethyst, milk glass, blue frosted or "Jap" blue and cobalt blue.

Since we have rather large sets in red and crystal, I can safely say that it takes both time and money to put these sets together. All of the glass shown here except the two red pitchers has been gathered piece by piece over a ten year period. The pitcher has escaped us due to price differences between the owners and what we have been willing to pay. Add to that the problem of color variation since our red is all about the same shade and the pitchers tend always to run toward the deep, almost black, red. Some day we will find just the right color and price. Half of the fun of collecting is the looking. If you found everything you were looking for, then what would you collect?

The listings here are not complete in regard to every piece made in Rock Crystal, but they should give enough representative examples to cover any variations of bowls or plates left out. There are numerous bowls, with varying edges, heights and diameters. It would take more space to list the descriptions than it would to photograph them all. Remember all bowls and plates can be found with straight or scalloped edges.

If anyone has the 12½" scalloped center bowl in red, Cathy would be willing to trade the straight edge one in on it. She has always preferred the scalloped edge bowls and plates.

Although not shown, you will find many other colors of Rock Crystal available. I have noticed a strong collector interest in amber in the South the last few years, and some activity in the green. The one thing about this pattern is that every color looks as well as the next when you put a group of it together. The pattern makes any color "look pretty"!

|  | Crystal | All Other Colors | Red |
|---|---|---|---|
| *Bon Bon, 7½" S.E. | 15.00 | 20.00 | 40.00 |
| Bowl, 4" S.E. | 8.00 | 10.00 | 20.00 |
| Bowl, 4½" S.E. | 9.00 | 10.00 | 22.50 |
| Bowl, 5" S.E. | 10.00 | 12.50 | 25.00 |
| **Bowl, 5" Finger Bowl with 7" Plate, P.E. | | | |
| Bowl, 7" Pickle or Spoon Tray | 17.50 | 22.00 | 47.50 |
| Bowl, 7" Salad S.E. | 17.50 | 22.50 | 45.00 |
| Bowl, 8" Salad S.E. | 20.00 | 22.00 | 45.00 |
| Bowl, 9" Salad S.E. | 20.00 | 23.00 | 50.00 |
| Bowl, 10½" Salad S.E. | 20.00 | 25.00 | 65.00 |
| Bowl, 11½" 2-Part Relish | 27.00 | 30.00 | 50.00 |
| Bowl, 12" Oblong Celery | 20.00 | 30.00 | 47.50 |
| ***Bowl, 12½" Footed Center Bowl | 40.00 | 75.00 | 210.00 |
| Bowl, 13" Roll Tray | 25.00 | 40.00 | |
| Bowl, 14" 6-Part Relish | 25.00 | 42.50 | |
| Butter Dish and Cover | 250.00 | | |
| Butter Dish Bottom | 140.00 | | |
| Butter Dish Top | 110.00 | | |
| ****Candelabra, 2-Lite Pr. | 35.00 | 60.00 | 175.00 |
| Candelabra, 3-Lite Pr. | 40.00 | 65.00 | 200.00 |
| Candlestick, 5½" Low Pr. | 27.50 | 45.00 | 100.00 |
| Candlestick, 8½" Tall Pr. | 60.00 | 75.00 | 185.00 |
| Candy and Cover, Round | 27.50 | 50.00 | 125.00 |
| Cake Stand, 11", 2¾" High, Footed | 20.00 | 35.00 | 85.00 |

*S.E. McKee designation for scalloped edge
**P.E. McKee designation for plain edge
***Red Slag—$300.00. Cobalt—$137.50
****Cobalt—$75.00

**Please refer to Foreword for pricing information**

| | Crystal | All Other Colors | Red |
|---|---|---|---|
| Comport, 7″ | 27.50 | 37.50 | 55.00 |
| Creamer, Flat S.E. | 20.00 | | |
| Creamer, 9 oz. Footed | 15.00 | 25.00 | 50.00 |
| Cruet and Stopper, 6 oz. Oil | 50.00 | | |
| Cup, 7 oz. | 11.00 | 20.00 | 45.00 |
| Goblet, 7½ oz., 8 oz. Low Footed | 13.50 | 22.50 | 45.00 |
| Goblet, 11 oz. Low Footed Iced Tea | 15.00 | 22.00 | 55.00 |
| Jelly, 5″ Footed S.E. | 13.50 | 20.00 | 37.50 |
| Lamp, Electric | 60.00 | 150.00 | 350.00 |
| Parfait, 3½ oz. Low Footed | 9.00 | 30.00 | 60.00 |
| Pitcher, qt. S.E. | 75.00 | 150.00 | |
| Pitcher, ½ gal., 7½″ High | 85.00 | 165.00 | |
| Pitcher, 9″ Large Covered | 125.00 | 200.00 | 500.00 |
| Pitcher, Fancy Tankard | 140.00 | 400.00 | 650.00 |
| Plate, 6″ Bread and Butter S.E. | 4.50 | 6.50 | 12.50 |
| Plate, 7½″ P.E. & S.E. | 6.50 | 9.00 | 17.50 |
| Plate, 8½″ P.E. & S.E. | 7.50 | 9.50 | 25.00 |
| Plate, 9″ S.E. | 12.50 | 17.50 | 35.00 |
| Plate, 10½″ S.E. | 13.50 | 18.50 | 40.00 |
| Plate, 11½″ S.E. | 14.50 | 20.00 | 45.00 |
| Plate, 10½″ Dinner S.E. (Large Center Design) | 40.00 | 50.00 | 110.00 |
| Punch Bowl and Stand, 14″ | 295.00 | | |
| Salt and Pepper (2 Styles) | 60.00 | 100.00 | |
| Salt Dip | 25.00 | | |
| Sandwich Server, Center-Handled | 20.00 | 35.00 | 85.00 |
| Saucer | 5.00 | 7.00 | 12.50 |
| Sherbet or Egg, 3½ oz. Footed | 12.00 | 20.00 | 50.00 |
| Spooner | 27.50 | | |
| Stemware, 1 oz. Footed Cordial | 15.00 | 35.00 | 50.00 |
| Stemware, 2 oz. Wine | 16.00 | 23.00 | 45.00 |
| Stemware, 3 oz. Wine | 16.00 | 25.00 | 45.00 |
| Stemware, 3½ oz. Footed Cocktail | 12.00 | 17.50 | 35.00 |
| Stemware, 6 oz. Footed Champagne | 12.50 | 17.50 | 28.00 |
| Stemware, 8 oz. Large Footed Goblet | 13.50 | 22.50 | 45.00 |
| Sundae, 6 oz. Low Footed | 9.50 | 15.00 | 28.00 |
| Sugar, 10 oz. Open | 11.00 | 18.00 | 30.00 |
| Sugar, Lid | 25.00 | 35.00 | 55.00 |
| Syrup with Lid | 85.00 | | |
| Tumbler, 2½ oz. Whiskey | 12.50 | 17.50 | 40.00 |
| Tumbler, 5 oz. Juice | 12.00 | 18.00 | 40.00 |
| Tumbler, 5 oz. Old Fashioned | 12.00 | 18.00 | 35.00 |
| Tumbler, 9 oz. Concave or Straight | 15.00 | 22.00 | 40.00 |
| Tumbler, 12 oz. Concave or Straight | 20.00 | 30.00 | 50.00 |
| Vase, Cornucopia | 50.00 | 75.00 | |
| Vase, 11″ Footed | 40.00 | 75.00 | 125.00 |

**Please refer to Foreword for pricing information**

# ROSE CAMEO   BELMONT TUMBLER COMPANY, 1931

Color:   Green.

No one has been able to find any information to confirm or deny that Hazel Atlas made Rose Cameo. I know that Belmont Tumbler has a 1931 patent on the pattern, but many pieces of this pattern were found by collectors digging at the Hazel Atlas factory site. Of course, a yellow Cloverleaf shaker was found at Akro Agate "digs". Probably some worker had one in his pail and tossed it out by mistake. Since a box of pieces of Rose Cameo were found, it seems unlikely that these pieces came from a lunch pail.

There are two different tumblers, but they vary only slightly. One has a more flared edge than the other. Of the bowls, the straight-sided, six-inch one is the hardest to find. It is pictured on its side behind the flared-edge tumbler. The bottom surface covers much more area than does the bottom of the curved sided bowls.

The only confusion in this pattern comes from Cameo. It is hard to remember that new collectors still get these confused at times. There is a little rose inside this cameo; but there is a dancing girl inside the cameo of the pattern called Cameo.

|  | Green |  | Green |
|---|---|---|---|
| Bowl, 4½" Berry | 4.50 | Sherbet | 8.00 |
| Bowl, 5" Cereal | 8.00 | Tumbler, 5" Footed (2 Styles) | 11.00 |
| Bowl, 6" Straight Sides | 11.00 | | |
| Plate, 7" Salad | 5.50 | | |

---

# ROSEMARY, "DUTCH ROSE"   FEDERAL GLASS COMPANY 1935-1937

Colors:   Amber, green, pink; some iridized.

If I have been asked one time this year, I have been asked fifty, "Where are the cereal bowls?" I have seen a few in amber and they were well priced! Keep looking! At $15.00 you should be able to find a few.

There is still a lack of pink tumblers. For that matter, there is a dearth of pink Rosemary except in basic pieces. Green is getting harder to find, too. Thankfully, the collector demand is for amber which is the most readily available (except for the cereals mentioned).

The sugar bowl has no handles and looks like a larger sherbet. This has created confusion for those who expect a sugar bowl to have handles on each side. After all, the creamer has its usual handle.

Rosemary pattern resulted from Federal's having to change their Mayfair pattern since Hocking already had the patent on "Mayfair". You will notice that Rosemary has plain glass at the base of its pieces except for a center rose motif. It has neither the *arches* of the "transitional" Mayfair pieces nor the *arches and waffling* of the regular Mayfair pieces.

|  | Amber | Green | Pink |  | Amber | Green | Pink |
|---|---|---|---|---|---|---|---|
| Bowl, 5" Berry | 4.00 | 5.00 | 6.50 | Plate, Dinner | 5.50 | 10.00 | 12.00 |
| Bowl, 5" Cream Soup | 8.00 | 14.00 | 13.00 | Plate, Grill | 6.00 | 10.00 | 12.00 |
| Bowl, 6" Cereal | 15.00 | 20.00 | 20.00 | Platter, 12" Oval | 9.50 | 15.00 | 14.00 |
| Bowl, 10" Oval Vegetable | 9.00 | 20.00 | 20.00 | Saucer | 2.00 | 3.50 | 2.00 |
| Creamer, Footed | 6.50 | 9.50 | 9.00 | Sugar, Footed | 6.50 | 9.50 | 9.00 |
| Cup | 4.00 | 7.00 | 4.50 | Tumbler, 4¼", 9 oz. | 17.50 | 20.00 | 25.00 |
| Plate, 6¾" Salad | 4.00 | 6.00 | 3.50 | | | | |

**Please refer to Foreword for pricing information**

# ROULETTE, "MANY WINDOWS"   HOCKING GLASS COMPANY, 1935-1939

Colors:   Green; some pink and crystal.

In my travels, I have seen more real roulette wheels than I have some of the tumblers in Roulette. Green and pink tumblers must have been used for toasts and smashed against the wall at parties because they are just not to be found today!

Basic pieces (cup, saucer, sherbet and luncheon plate) are plentiful in green. There are even more than enough pitchers to be found in both colors. Other pieces are the fly in the ointment.

With pink, there is little worry except for tumblers. Serving pieces were not made; so that search is eliminated for you. That is not so in green and crystal; the fruit bowl and sandwich plate were made.

Crystal pitchers have been found. The two that I have seen were decorated with colored stripes. One was even found in Canada. These fit the category of rare, but they are not in high demand. Roulette is a striking pattern. It is a shame there isn't more of it! I would settle for a creamer and sugar.

| | Pink, Crystal | Green |
|---|---|---|
| Bowl, 9″ Fruit | 8.50 | 10.00 |
| Cup | 3.50 | 4.25 |
| Pitcher, 8″, 64 oz. | 22.50 | 25.00 |
| Plate, 6″ Sherbet | 2.00 | 2.25 |
| Plate, 8½″ Luncheon | 4.00 | 4.00 |
| Plate, 12″ Sandwich | 7.50 | 7.50 |
| Saucer | 1.25 | 2.25 |
| Sherbet | 3.00 | 4.50 |
| Tumbler, 3¼″, 5 oz. Juice | 4.50 | 9.50 |
| Tumbler, 3¼″, 7½ oz. Old Fashioned | 8.00 | 17.50 |
| Tumbler, 4⅛″, 9 oz. Water | 10.00 | 12.50 |
| Tumbler, 5⅛″, 12 oz. Iced Tea | 10.00 | 16.50 |
| Tumbler, 5½″, 10 oz. Footed | 10.00 | 15.00 |
| Whiskey, 2½″, 1½ oz. | 6.50 | 9.00 |

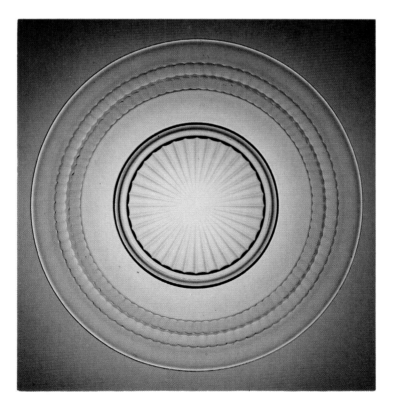

171

# "ROUND ROBIN"   MANUFACTURER UNKNOWN, Probably early 1930's

Colors:   Green, some iridescent and crystal.

There have been a few reports of domino trays in Round Robin this time! Those are the first reports for several years. I used to have people contact me about selling the one in the photograph; but I needed that one, so I was never talked out of it. I suppose I should explain why it is called a domino tray for new readers. It comes from the fact that a cream pitcher sits in the center ring and sugar cubes are placed around the tray outside of that ring. I guess we know what brand of sugar led to that name for the tray!

There does not seem to be enough iridized available to collect it in large sets, but green could be collected with only a little difficulty. Finding the domino tray would be the major problem.

The footed cups are one of the few in that style which occur in patterns in the book. Most patterns have flat cups. It is also the only pattern except Cameo that has a domino tray.

| | Green | Iridescent | | Green | Iridescent |
|---|---|---|---|---|---|
| Bowl, 4" Berry | 4.25 | 4.00 | Plate, 8" Luncheon | 2.50 | 3.00 |
| Cup, Footed | 4.00 | 5.00 | Plate, 12" Sandwich | 5.00 | 6.00 |
| Creamer, Footed | 5.00 | 5.50 | Saucer | 1.50 | 1.50 |
| Domino Tray | 25.00 | | Sherbet | 4.00 | 5.00 |
| Plate, 6" Sherbet | 1.50 | 1.50 | Sugar | 4.50 | 5.00 |

# ROXANA   HAZEL ATLAS GLASS COMPANY, 1932

Colors:   Yellow, crystal; some white.

I talked to several ladies named Roxana at the shows I have attended in the last few years and only one did not collect this pattern!

The frustrating thing about this pattern is the lack of a cup for its saucer. There is no logical explanation for this and I have given up trying to figure out why. It makes more sense to have a pattern like Bowknot with a cup and no saucer than vice versa.

The cereal bowl is pictured on a stand on the left which makes it look more like a plate than a bowl. If you collect this pattern, you need to check the scalloped edges carefully as they hide small nicks easily.

Roxana would make a nice little breakfast or salad set. Cereal with fresh strawberries would look great in the yellow bowl!

| | Yellow | White | | Yellow |
|---|---|---|---|---|
| Bowl, 4½" x 2⅜" | 6.00 | 10.00 | Plate, 6" Sherbet | 2.50 |
| Bowl, 5" Berry | 4.00 | | Saucer | 2.50 |
| Bowl, 6" Cereal | 6.50 | | Sherbet, Footed | 4.00 |
| | | | Tumbler, 4", 9 oz. | 10.00 |

**Please refer to Foreword for pricing information**

# ROYAL LACE   HAZEL ATLAS GLASS COMPANY, 1934-1941

Colors:   Cobalt blue, crystal, green, pink; some amethyst.

There has been less confusion between the straight edge and the rolled edge console bowl since we used this rolled edge console in pink for a pattern shot! There's a big difference in price between the rolled edge and the straight edge bowl (shown in blue in the photograph if you do not know the difference).

I will set up all three bowls and show them side by side in the next book. I just purchased a large collection that has all three styles, but it was too late to get them in this book.

The collection mentioned was complete except for 10 oz. tumblers and 5″ berry bowls. There were plenty of iced teas in blue but a hole where the rare size tumblers should have been. The collector was so meticulous that he never found berry bowls with inside rims good enough to suit him. The inside rims are the weak spot of this pattern; if you collect Royal Lace—be aware of that one point.

Very little green is appearing in the market; grab it when you can find it! Until collections are broken up through deaths and divorce, many pieces of glass are not being offered at any price. This is a rising market! Be prepared to pay more or do without. It is as simple as that!

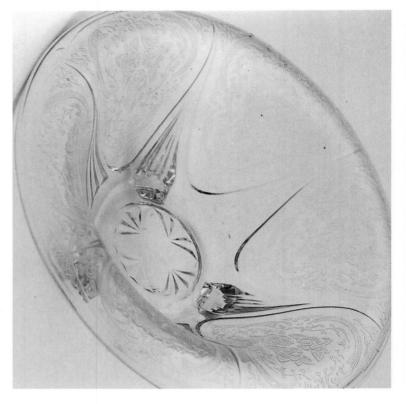

|  | Crystal | Pink | Green | Blue | Amethyst |
|---|---|---|---|---|---|
| Bowl, 4¾″ Cream Soup | 8.50 | 12.00 | 22.50 | 24.00 | |
| Bowl, 5″ Berry | 10.00 | 18.00 | 21.00 | 30.00 | |
| Bowl, 10″ Round Berry | 12.00 | 15.00 | 22.50 | 38.00 | |
| Bowl, 10″, 3 Legged Straight Edge | 13.50 | 20.00 | 30.00 | 42.50 | |
| Bowl, 10″, 3 Legged Rolled Edge | 75.00 | 27.50 | 60.00 | 195.00 | |
| Bowl, 10″, 3 Legged Ruffled Edge | 17.50 | 25.00 | 50.00 | 265.00 | |
| Bowl, 11″ Oval Vegetable | 13.00 | 18.00 | 22.00 | 37.50 | |
| Butter Dish and Cover | 55.00 | 110.00 | 225.00 | 385.00 | |
| Butter Dish Bottom | 35.00 | 70.00 | 150.00 | 250.00 | |
| Butter Dish Top | 20.00 | 40.00 | 75.00 | 135.00 | |
| Candlestick, Straight Edge Pr. | 20.00 | 27.50 | 45.00 | 75.00 | |
| Candlestick, Rolled Edge Pr. | 37.50 | 37.50 | 55.00 | 105.00 | |
| Candlestick, Ruffled Edge Pr. | 22.50 | 35.00 | 50.00 | 100.00 | |
| Cookie Jar and Cover | 25.00 | 37.50 | 52.50 | 235.00 | |
| Cream, Footed | 8.00 | 11.00 | 17.50 | 30.00 | |
| Cup | 5.50 | 9.50 | 14.00 | 23.50 | |
| Pitcher, 48 oz., Straight Sides | 32.00 | 42.00 | 80.00 | 75.00 | |
| Pitcher, 8″, 68 oz. | 40.00 | 49.50 | 85.00 | 117.50 | |
| Pitcher, 8″, 86 oz. | 42.50 | 55.00 | 100.00 | 135.00 | |
| Pitcher, 8½″, 96 oz. | 45.00 | 62.50 | 120.00 | 160.00 | |
| Plate, 6″ Sherbet | 2.50 | 3.50 | 6.00 | 8.50 | |
| Plate, 8½″ Luncheon | 5.00 | 8.00 | 10.00 | 22.50 | |
| Plate, 9⅞″ Dinner | 7.50 | 12.00 | 18.00 | 27.50 | |
| Plate, 9⅞″ Grill | 6.00 | 9.50 | 15.00 | 22.50 | |
| Platter, 13″ Oval | 12.50 | 17.50 | 25.00 | 37.50 | |
| Salt and Pepper, Pr. | 35.00 | 42.50 | 100.00 | 190.00 | |
| Saucer | 2.50 | 3.50 | 5.00 | 6.50 | |
| Sherbet, Footed | 7.00 | 9.00 | 17.50 | 27.50 | |
| Sherbet in Metal Holder | 3.50 | | | 19.50 | 27.50 |
| Sugar | 7.00 | 9.00 | 15.00 | 20.00 | |
| Sugar Lid | 13.00 | 22.50 | 30.00 | 100.00 | |
| Tumbler, 3½″, 5 oz. | 10.00 | 14.00 | 22.00 | 30.00 | |
| Tumbler, 4⅛″, 9 oz. | 8.50 | 11.00 | 20.00 | 26.00 | |
| Tumbler, 4⅞″, 10 oz. | 15.00 | 27.50 | 32.50 | 55.00 | |
| Tumbler, 5⅜″, 12 oz. | 17.50 | 27.50 | 35.00 | 45.00 | |
| Toddy or Cider Set: Includes Cookie Jar Metal Lid, Metal Tray, 8 Roly-Poly Cups and Ladle | | | | 100.00 | 120.00 |

**Please refer to Foreword for pricing information**

# ROYAL RUBY  ANCHOR HOCKING GLASS COMPANY, 1938-1960's; 1977

Colors:  Ruby red.

Royal Ruby collectors have gone wild trying to find that double card holder/cigarette box shown in the center of the picture. Since it had never been shown before, few collecors knew of its existence. I had never seen one until this one was found in Nashville, but I have now found two others. They may not be as rare as first believed; but they are not a commonly found Royal Ruby piece either.

Most of the Royal Ruby craze can be traced back to Anchor Hocking's original promotion that started in 1938. From that one promotion has grown a red glass collecting phenomena that still rages today. Not all red glass is Royal Ruby. Only glass manufactured by Anchor Hocking can be called "Royal Ruby". Unfortunately, collectors of red glass do not differentiate.

Round dinnerware items with a footed creamer and sugar are from the early lines of this pattern. I might add that the slotted sugar lid does not fit all sugar bowls. That is one lid that should be purchased only on the bowl, if you want it to fit! Evidently, the ones sold without lids had a slightly smaller diameter at the top making it impossible to put lids on these. If you purchase a lid separately, remember I told you to beware!

Three other items that are hard to find are the oval vegetable bowl, the 13¾" salad plate and the 11½" salad bowl. Two ladies almost had a fight over an oval vegetable bowl at a show in Chicago recently. Both wanted it and there was only one. One lady picked it up as the other lady looked at it and it got worse from there.

The tumbler with the metal lid has "old Reliable Tea Bags" packaged inside. There is also Anchor Hocking's "Royal Ruby" sticker on the tumbler. I suspect the tumbler was free when purchasing the tea. There is not much tea inside; so I do not know.

The pattern shot is of a citronnella candle enclosed in a Royal Ruby ball vase. These were heavily promoted in Florida and other mosquito-infested areas. Forest Green vases can be found the same way.

| | Red | | Red |
|---|---|---|---|
| Ash Tray, 4½" Square | 2.50 | Plate, 9" or 9¼" Dinner | 7.50 |
| Bowl, 4¼" Berry | 4.00 | Plate, 13¾" | 15.00 |
| Bowl, 5¼9", Popcorn | 8.00 | Punch Bowl | 17.50 |
| Bowl, 7½" Soup | 9.50 | Punch Bowl Base | 15.00 |
| Bowl, 8" Oval Vegetable | 27.50 | Punch Cup | 2.00 |
| Bowl, 8½" Large Berry | 12.50 | Saucer (Round or Square) | 1.50 |
| Bowl, 10" Deep, Popcorn | 17.50 | Sherbet, Footed | 6.50 |
| Bowl, 11½" Salad | 20.00 | Sugar, Flat | 6.00 |
| Card Holder/Cigarette Box | 35.00 | Sugar, Footed | 5.00 |
| Creamer, Flat | 6.00 | Sugar Lid | 8.00 |
| Creamer, Footed | 7.50 | Tumbler, 2½ oz. Footed Wine | 10.00 |
| Cup (Round or Square) | 3.50 | Tumbler, 3½ oz. Cocktail | 7.50 |
| Goblet, Ball Stem | 7.00 | Tumbler, 5 oz. Juice, 2 Styles | 5.00 |
| Lamp | 20.00 | Tumbler, 9 oz. Water | 5.00 |
| Pitcher, 22 oz. Tilted or Upright | 20.00 | Tumbler, 10 oz. Water | 5.00 |
| Pitcher, 3 qt. Tilted | 25.00 | Tumbler, 13 oz. Iced Tea | 9.50 |
| Pitcher, 3 qt. Upright | 30.00 | Vase, 4" Ball-Shaped | 4.50 |
| Plate, 6½" Sherbet | 2.00 | Vase, 6½" Bulbous, Tall | 7.50 |
| Plate, 7" Salad | 3.50 | Vases, Several Styles (Small) | 5.00 |
| Plate, 7¾" Luncheon | 4.00 | Vases, Several Styles (Large) | 10.00 |

**Please refer to Foreword for pricing information**

# "S" PATTERN, "STIPPLED ROSE BAND" MacBETH-EVANS GLASS COMPANY, 1930-1933

Colors: Crystal; crystal w/trims of silver, blue, green, amber; pink; some amber, green, fired-on red, Monax, and light yellow.

The pink and green "S" Pattern pitchers are rarely found. They come in the "Dogwood" style as shown. An "American Sweetheart" style crystal pitcher is shown also. These crystal pitchers are found in both styles. These pitchers are not common; so be on the lookout for them. In fact, the amber pitcher is even more difficult to find. There are few amber collectors, however, so few people are aware of this.

There are two sizes of cake plates in this pattern. The most commonly found is the 11" (which is directly opposite the Dogwood where the 11" is almost impossible to find). In the Dogwood, the 13" cake plate is the one likely to be found. In "S Pattern", the 13" cake plate is rarely seen in crystal and almost never in amber!

The red and Monax pieces of "S" Pattern make you wonder why no blue has been found since all these colors abound in its sister pattern, "American Sweetheart". I remember finding four red 8" plates in the early 1970's and sold three so fast at $50.00 that I wondered if I had goofed in pricing! I kept one for a long time and finally was able to sell it for $35.00. We thought that a whole set would be found and prices would skyrocket as they had in American Sweetheart. Live and learn, as they say.

The only red that ever turned up in quantity was a fired-on variety and that has never been an attraction in any pattern. There are two distinct shades of amber, light and dark. Collectors do not make an issue of this unless the amber goes to light yellow which is mostly ignored by all.

The crystal with a platinum trim makes an elegant setting. New collectors might note that this is an under valued set.

| | Crystal | Yellow, Amber, Crystal With Trims |
|---|---|---|
| *Bowl, 5½" Cereal | 2.50 | 3.50 |
| Bowl, 8½" Large Berry | 7.50 | 12.50 |
| *Creamer, Thick or Thin | 4.00 | 5.50 |
| *Cup, Thick or Thin | 2.50 | 3.50 |
| Pitcher, 80 oz. (Like "Dogwood") (Green or Pink 550.00) | 37.50 | 75.00 |
| Pitcher, 80 oz. (Like "American Sweetheart") | 45.00 | |
| Plate, 6" Sherbet (Monax 14.00) | 1.50 | 2.00 |
| **Plate, 8" Luncheon | 2.00 | 2.50 |
| Plate, 9¼" Dinner | 3.50 | 4.50 |
| Plate, Grill | 5.00 | 6.50 |
| Plate, 11" Heavy Cake | 30.00 | 32.50 |
| ***Plate, 13" Heavy Cake | 47.50 | 57.50 |
| *Saucer | 1.00 | 1.50 |
| Sherbet, Low Footed | 3.50 | 6.00 |
| *Sugar, Thick and Thin | 4.00 | 5.50 |
| Tumbler, 3½", 5 oz. | 2.50 | 4.50 |
| Tumbler, 4", 9 oz. (Green or Pink 57.50) | 3.50 | 5.50 |
| Tumbler, 4¾", 10 oz. | 3.50 | 6.00 |
| Tumbler, 5", 12 oz. | 7.50 | 10.00 |

*Fired-on red items will run approximately twice price of amber
**Deep Red—$40.00
***Amber—$77.50

179

# SANDWICH   HOCKING GLASS COMPANY, 1939-1964; 1977

Colors:

| | | | | | |
|---|---|---|---|---|---|
| Crystal | 1950's-1960's | Pink | 1939-1940 | Forest Green | 1950's-1960's |
| Amber | 1960's | Royal Ruby | 1939-1940 | White (opaque) | 1950's |

A Canadian collector sent me some updated information on bowl sizes for which all collectors will be grateful. Any help on correcting size discrepancies is certainly appreciated and the photos sent by Rejean Matte were fantastic—even showing the pieces beside rulers. Thank you!

Several items were shown and not listed previously; I hope that is now remedied. The biggest concern of collectors has been juice tumblers. There are two sizes: 3 oz. measuring 3⅜" and 5 oz. measuring 3⁹⁄₁₆".

Bowls are found with smooth or scalloped edges. I hope we have it all straightened out now in our listings below. If you find an error, let me know. There have been a few "whoppers" in the past; so nothing would surprise me any more. How would you like to proof-read all these numbers? It is not impossible as we do it somehow. Yet errors do occur and some travel from book to book if we are not informed.

Last book's report on punch bowl bases being sold only with the bowl and 12 cups is being confirmed. Several letters have reported finding sets with bowl and cups in original boxes. None of these 6 cup sets had bases for the bowls! Not many of the bowl sets with a 12" plate have been found. Maybe the original buyers felt the bowl was too deep to be a salad even though it was sold that way.

No lid has ever been found for the green cookie jar. The factory worker who remembered it being sold as a vase must have had a better memory than some of the others I talked with back in 1972. There have been no reproductions in this pattern except the cookie jar and that is easily spotted. The newer model has a height of 10¼", a 5½" opening and a 20" circumference at its largest part. The original stands only 9¼" tall, with a 4⅞" mouth and is only 19" in circumference at its largest part.

The larger green pitcher still remains difficult to find. You will find a big jump in price on green dinner plates and modest increases on the other harder-to-find green items (which include any pieces that were not packed in oatmeal).

I showed the green, rolled edge sherbet last time, but I should mention it again. It is 2" high and 4" wide as opposed to the normally found 2¼" high and 3⅜" wide. It was found by an Ashland, Kentucky, collector.

| | Crystal | Desert Gold | Ruby Red | Forest Green | Pink | | Crystal | Desert Gold | Forest Green |
|---|---|---|---|---|---|---|---|---|---|
| Bowl, 4⁵⁄₁₆", Smooth | | | | 2.00 | | Custard Cup Liner | 7.50 | | 1.50 |
| Bowl, 4⅞", Scalloped | 8.50 | | | | | Pitcher, 6" Juice | 42.50 | | 90.00 |
| Bowl, 4⅞" Smooth | 4.00 | 3.00 | 9.00 | | 2.50 | Pitcher, ½ gal. Ice Lip | 45.00 | | 175.00 |
| Bowl, 5¼" Scalloped | 6.00 | | 15.00 | | | Plate, 7" Dessert | 8.00 | 8.00 | |
| Bowl, 6½" Cereal | 18.00 | 9.00 | | | | Plate, 8" | 3.00 | | |
| Bowl, 6½" Smooth | 7.00 | 6.00 | | | | Plate, 9" Dinner | 11.00 | 6.00 | 47.50 |
| Bowl, 6½" Scalloped | 6.00 | | 20.00 | 27.50 | | Plate, 9" Indent | | | |
| Bowl, 7" Salad | 6.50 | | | 40.00 | | For Punch Cup | 3.00 | | |
| Bowl, 8" Smooth | | | | | | Plate, 12" Sandwich | 9.00 | 10.00 | |
| Bowl, 8" Scalloped | 6.50 | | 30.00 | 45.00 | 12.50 | Punch Bowl | 15.00 | | |
| Bowl, 8¼" Oval | 6.00 | | | | | Punch Bowl Stand | 17.50 | | |
| Bowl, 9¼" Salad | 17.50 | | | | | Punch Cup | 2.00 | | |
| Butter Dish, Low | 32.50 | | | | | Saucer | 1.00 | 3.00 | 6.00 |
| Butter Dish Bottom | 17.50 | | | | | Sherbet, Footed | 6.00 | | |
| Butter Dish Top | 15.00 | | | | | Sugar and Cover | 12.50 | | *15.00 |
| Cookie Jar and | | | | | | Tumbler, 3⅜ " 3 oz. | | | |
| Cover | 30.00 | 30.00 | | *16.00 | | Juice | 9.00 | | |
| Creamer | 4.00 | | | 17.50 | | Tumbler, 3⁹⁄₁₆" 5 oz. | | | |
| Cup, Tea or Coffee | 1.50 | 3.50 | | 13.00 | | Juice | 5.00 | | 2.75 |
| Custard Cup | 3.50 | | | 1.50 | | Tumbler, 9 oz. Water | 6.50 | | 3.25 |
| Custard Cup, Ruffled | 8.50 | | | | | Tumbler, 9 oz. Footed | 16.50 | 40.00 | |

*No Cover

# SANDWICH INDIANA GLASS COMPANY, 1920's-1980's

Colors:

| | | | | | |
|---|---|---|---|---|---|
| Crystal | Late 1920's-Today | Pink | Late 1920's-Early 1930's | Teal Blue | 1950's |
| Amber | Late 1920's-1970's | Red | 1933-1970's | Lt. Green | 1930's |

The big "news" is that Indiana has made for Tiara a butter dish which is extremely close to the old teal color made in the 1950's. It's available as a hostess gift item for selling a certain amount of Tiara glass. Because of the new Sandwich being made today by Indiana, I'm dropping crystal from my listing. It's become a collector's pariah! The list is too long to examine each piece to tell the difference between old and new. In many cases, there is little difference since the same moulds are being used. Hopefully, somebody at Indiana will wise up and stop making the old colors as I was told they would do after the "pink Avocado" fiasco in 1974. Instead of trying to entice collectors to new wares, they are stuck on trying to destroy the market for the old glassware which has been collectible for years but which may never be again. Perhaps you could start collecting Hocking Sandwich, if you like the pattern. They re-made a cookie jar, but they carefully made it different from the old which showed their awareness of collectors in the field! For those of you who have collected the crystal Indiana Sandwich or the teal butter dish and have a sizable investment involved, I can only say that time will tell as to the future collectiblity of this pattern. At present, it doesn't look too promising. The really maddening thing is that all this "new" Sandwich is being touted to prospective buyer as glass that's going to be worth a great deal in the future based on its past history--and the company is steadily destroying those very properties they're using to sell the new glass! Supreme irony!

I can vouch for six items in red Sandwich dating from 1933, i.e. cups, saucers, luncheon plates, water goblets, creamers and sugars. However, in 1969, Tiara Home Products produced red pitchers, 9 oz. goblets, cups, saucers, wines, wine decanters, 13" serving trays, creamers, sugars and salad and dinner plates. Now, if your dishes glow yellow under a black light or if you KNOW that your Aunt Sophie held her red dishes in her lap while fording the swollen stream in a buggy, then I'd say your red Sandwich pieces are old. Other than that, I know of no way to tell if they are or not. NO, I won't even say that old red glass glows under black light. I know SOME of it does because of a certain type ore they used then. However, I've seen some newer glass glow, but Tiara's 1969 red Sandwich glass does not. Presently, the only two colors remotely worth having are pink and green, and who knows but what the company will make those tomorrow!

| | Pink, Green | Teal Blue | Red | | Pink, Green | Teal Blue | Red |
|---|---|---|---|---|---|---|---|
| Ash Tray Set (Club, Spade, Heart, Diamond Shapes) | | | | Goblet, 9 oz. | 15.00 | | 40.00 |
| $3.00 each crystal | 15.00 | | | Pitcher, 68 oz. | 100.00 | | |
| Bowl, 4¼" Berry | 3.00 | | | Plate, 6" Sherbet | 2.50 | 4.50 | |
| Bowl, 6" | 3.50 | | | Plate, 7" Bread and Butter | 3.50 | | |
| Bowl, 6" 6 Sides | | 7.50 | | Plate, 8" Oval, Indent for Sherbet | 5.00 | 7.50 | |
| Bowl, 8¼" | 10.00 | | | Plate, 8⅜" Luncheon | 4.50 | | 15.00 |
| Bowl, 9" Console | 15.00 | | | Plate, 10½" Dinner | 12.50 | | |
| Bowl, 10" Console | 18.00 | | | Plate, 13" Sandwich | 12.50 | | |
| * Butter Dish and Cover, Domed | 157.50 | 150.00 | | Sandwich Server, Center Handle | 27.50 | | |
| Butter Dish Bottom | 47.50 | 40.00 | | Saucer | 2.50 | 3.50 | 5.00 |
| Butter Dish Top | 110.00 | 110.00 | | Sherbet, 3¼" | 5.00 | 6.00 | |
| Candlesticks, 3½" Pr. | 15.00 | | | Sugar, Large Open | 8.50 | | 40.00 |
| Candlesticks, 7" Pr. | 37.50 | | | Tumbler, 3 oz. Footed Cocktail | 15.00 | | |
| Creamer | 6.50 | | 40.00 | Tumbler, 8 oz. Footed Water | 12.50 | | |
| Creamer and Sugar on Diamond Shaped Tray | | 27.50 | | Tumbler, 12 oz. Footed Iced Tea | 22.50 | | |
| Cruet, 6½ oz. and Stopper | | 127.50 | | **Wine, 3", 4 oz. | 17.50 | | |
| Cup | 4.50 | 4.50 | 25.00 | | | | |
| **Decanter and Stopper | 85.00 | | | | | | |

*Beware new Teal
**Beware new Green

# SHARON, "CABBAGE ROSE"   FEDERAL GLASS COMPANY, 1935-1939

Colors:   Pink, green, amber; some crystal.   *(See Reproduction Section)*

Dealers told me Sharon was in the doldrums, but I think you can forget that! I bought a set of each color recently and ran an ad in the Daze. I was pleasantly surprised by the number of calls on several items especially in amber. Most of the calls were for the footed and the thick and thin iced teas. Many items received only one call, but these items received several. The pink thick tumblers and jam dish received a lot of action, also. The jam dish is the same as the butter bottom without the indented ledge and it stands only 1½" tall as opposed to 2" tall for the soup. Several of the green tumblers went to new homes, but the price on these slows down anyone but the seriously minded collector.

No matter how many times you describe the cheese dish, some one thinks he just bought one for less than the price of the butter. It is highly unlikely, but not impossible to find one for a bargain price today. The bottom to the cheese dish is a SALAD plate with a RAISED rim on the flat plate. The top fits inside this ring and sits flat on the plate. If the bottom is not FLAT like a plate or does not have a groove for the top to fit in, you do not have a cheese dish. The top of the cheese dish and the butter dish are the same. Jam dishes are rare and that is why they are expensive!

In some rural areas of the country, you will find many pieces of Sharon that are marked as premium items from co-ops or other agriculturally oriented centers. What is commonly seen in one area is rarely seen in others. That is one of the things that makes collecting fun.

The tumbler shown below was made to be converted into a lamp by screwing on a burner. This is the only one of these to have been found to date. This is another thing that makes collecting fun. You never know what will turn up next.

| | Amber | Pink | Green |
|---|---|---|---|
| Bowl, 5" Berry | 6.00 | 7.00 | 8.50 |
| Bowl, 5" Cream Soup | 16.50 | 29.00 | 32.50 |
| Bowl, 6" Cereal | 11.00 | 15.00 | 17.50 |
| Bowl, 7½" Flat Soup, 2" Deep | 27.50 | 27.50 | |
| Bowl, 8½" Large Berry | 4.50 | 16.00 | 22.00 |
| Bowl, 9½" Oval Vegetable | 10.00 | 16.00 | 17.50 |
| Bowl, 10½" Fruit | 15.00 | 22.00 | 24.00 |
| Butter Dish and Cover | 40.00 | 35.00 | 67.50 |
| Butter Dish Bottom | 20.00 | 17.50 | 30.00 |
| Butter Dish Top | 20.00 | 17.50 | 37.50 |
| *Cake Plate, 11½" Footed | 16.00 | 24.00 | 45.00 |
| Candy Jar and Cover | 35.00 | 33.00 | 135.00 |
| Cheese Dish and Cover | 150.00 | 575.00 | |
| Creamer, Footed | 10.00 | 11.00 | 14.00 |
| Cup | 8.00 | 9.00 | 12.00 |
| Jam Dish, 7½" | 25.00 | 100.00 | 32.50 |
| Pitcher, 80 oz. with Ice Lip | 100.00 | 95.00 | 295.00 |
| Pitcher, 80 oz. without Ice Lip | 97.50 | 90.00 | 300.00 |
| Plate, 6" Bread and Butter | 3.00 | 3.00 | 4.50 |
| **Plate, 7½" Salad | 11.00 | 16.00 | 14.00 |
| Plate, 9½" Dinner | 9.50 | 10.00 | 12.00 |
| Platter, 12½" Oval | 12.00 | 13.50 | 16.00 |
| Salt and Pepper, Pr. | 32.50 | 32.50 | 55.00 |
| Saucer | 4.00 | 5.50 | 5.50 |
| Sherbet, Footed | 9.00 | 10.00 | 22.50 |
| Sugar | 650 | 7.50 | 10.00 |
| Sugar Lid | 17.50 | 17.50 | 27.50 |
| Tumbler, 4⅛", 9 oz. Thick | 21.00 | 20.00 | 42.50 |
| Tumbler, 4⅛", 9 oz. Thin | 21.00 | 20.00 | 50.00 |
| Tumbler, 5¼", 12 oz. Thin | 28.00 | 32.50 | 80.00 |
| Tumbler, 5¼", 12 oz. Thick | 37.50 | 55.00 | 75.00 |
| **Tumbler, 6½", 15 oz. Footed | 60.00 | 32.50 | |

*Crystal—$5.00
**Crystal—$13.50

**Please refer to Foreword for pricing information**

# "SHIPS" or "SAILBOAT" also known as "SPORTSMAN SERIES" HAZEL

## ATLAS GLASS COMPANY, Late 1930's

Color:    Cobalt blue w/white and red decorations.

Ships was well received as a new pattern in the last book. There are few additions this time, but every little bit helps. There are now three plates to look for as there is one that measures 8" to go along with the dinner and bread and butter. I assume this one is a salad until I find out differently.

The shot glass was pictured on the "rare" page in one of my early books. It has come a long way in price since then. This shot measures 2¼" and holds 2 oz. of fluid. We use them to hold toothpicks in Kentucky! Nobody drinks bourbon in something that small or so I have been informed. I am the one who did not buy a Bohemian decanter for $10.00 at a garage sale because I couldn't think of the word "decanter" in order to look it up.

Be sure that the designs are good and that they are WHITE. Once they turn beige, the ship is sunk! There are a multitude of other designs on blue. You will find skiers, angel fish, windmills, dogs, polo players, and several styles of boats, but it is the sailboat that collectors enjoy. Ships comes with a variety of pieces. All other designs sell for about the same as Ships but none sell as well!

Red glasses with ships are found frequently; until a pitcher is found, however, they will not generate much excitement.

Those items that have BOTH white and red decoration on blue will sell for 20-25% more than the prices listed.

|  | Blue/white |  | Blue/white |
|---|---|---|---|
| Cup (Plain) "Moderntone" | 7.50 | Saucer | 12.50 |
| Cocktail Mixer w/Stirrer | 17.50 | Tumbler, 2 oz., 2¼" Shot Glass | 95.00 |
| Cocktail Shaker | 25.00 | Tumbler, 5 oz., 3¾", Juice | 7.50 |
| Ice Bowl | 25.00 | Tumbler, 6 oz., Roly Poly | 7.50 |
| Pitcher w/o Lip, 82 oz. | 40.00 | Tumbler, 8 oz., 3⅜", Old Fashion | 12.00 |
| Pitcher w/Lip, 86 oz. | 35.00 | Tumbler, 9 oz., 3¾", Straight Water | 10.00 |
| Plate, 5⅞", Bread & Butter | 14.00 | Tumbler, 9 oz., 4⅝", Water | 8.00 |
| Plate, 8", Salad | 17.50 | Tumbler, 10½ oz., 4⅞", Iced Tea | 10.00 |
| Plate, 9", Dinner | 20.00 | Tumbler, 12 oz., Iced Tea | 15.00 |

# SIERRA, "PINWHEEL"    JEANNETTE GLASS COMPANY, 1931-1933

Colors:    Green, pink.

Sierra is one of the few patterns that has had price increases in almost all pieces since the last book! I do not know what created this collecting surge, but it has been a boon to dealers who had this glassware in stock. Both the green and pink have been affected. Naturally the harder-to-find items have increased the most. The oval vegetable bowl, pitcher and tumblers in both colors will tug on your pocketbook. Most of the rest of the pattern can be found without difficulty and without breaking many twenty dollar bills—unless you want to consider the Adam/Sierra butter dish as a "must" item! Many pink Sierra collectors leave this butter to their rich Adam collecting friends. For a discussion of this butter, go back to Adam where it is pictured (p.7).

A table setting of Sierra always amazes collectors at shows where club members set up displays. It is not a pattern that many consider collecting until they see a group of it together. Maybe it has been the displays and word of mouth that has started this collecting bonanza; but in any case, if you have ever considered Sierra as a pattern, now is the time to go ahead and collect it before it is too late.

The cups have the serrated panels going up to the top edge becoming plain glass. I point this out as many times the wrong cup has been placed upon Sierra saucers. No, the edge is plain. Otherwise these would make great "dribble" cups for the practical joker.

|  | Pink | Green |  | Pink | Green |
|---|---|---|---|---|---|
| Bowl, 5½" Cereal | 7.00 | 8.00 | Platter, 11" Oval | 25.00 | 30.00 |
| Bowl, 8½" Large Berry | 10.00 | 15.00 | Salt and Pepper, Pr. | 27.50 | 30.00 |
| Bowl, 9¼" Oval Vegetable | 25.00 | 50.00 | Saucer | 3.50 | 4.00 |
| Butter Dish and Cover | 45.00 | 50.00 | Serving Tray, 10¼", 2 Handles | 9.00 | 10.00 |
| Creamer | 10.00 | 14.00 | Sugar | 12.50 | 12.50 |
| Cup | 7.50 | 9.00 | Sugar Cover | 10.00 | 10.00 |
| Pitcher, 6½", 32 oz. | 45.00 | 75.00 | Tumbler, 4½", 9 oz. Footed | 30.00 | 47.50 |
| Plate, 9" Dinner | 10.50 | 13.00 |  |  |  |

**Please refer to Foreword for pricing information**

# SPIRAL  HOCKING GLASS COMPANY, 1928-1930

Colors:   Green, pink.

I found out how many collectors of Spiral there are through a mistake in the 7th edition! SOMEHOW the price listing for Strawberry was also placed as the listing for Spiral! THREE MONTHS LATER, it was a non-Spiral collector who called to sell me a green Spiral pitcher for a Strawberry price who clued me to the mix-up! (An errata sheet was placed in all books shipped after the discovery was made).

The Spiral center-handled server is shown in the Twisted Optic pattern. The one shown here belongs to the Twisted Optic pattern. This was done deliberately after some collectors told me they thought it helped for comparison purposes to distinguish between the two patterns. For those who notice things carefully, the branched, squared-off handle of the Twisted Optic server in NO WAY resembles the gracefully curved Hocking-style handles shown on the cup, creamer and sugar. The handle DOES, however, closely resemble the square topped Imperial handles of the creamer and sugars shown in Twisted Optic.

Generally speaking, Hocking Spirals go to the left or with the clock and Imperial's Twisted Optic spirals go right or counterclockwise. However, Imperial's candy jar appears to go left—unless you turn it upside down; and Spiral's center-handled server goes right—unless you look through the bottom.

|  | Pink, Green |  | Pink, Green |
|---|---|---|---|
| Bowl, 4¾" Berry | 4.00 | Preserve and Cover | 20.00 |
| Bowl, 7" Mixing | 6.00 | Salt and Pepper, Pr. | 17.50 |
| Bowl, 8" Large Berry | 7.50 | Sandwich Server, Center Handle | 17.50 |
| Creamer, Flat or Footed | 5.00 | Saucer | 1.00 |
| Cup | 4.00 | Sherbet | 3.00 |
| Ice or Butter Tub | 15.00 | Sugar, Flat or Footed | 5.00 |
| Pitcher, 7⅝", 58 oz. | 22.00 | Tumbler, 3", 5 oz. Juice | 2.50 |
| Plate, 6" Sherbet | 1.00 | Tumbler, 5", 9 oz. Water | 4.50 |
| Plate, 8" Luncheon | 2.00 |  |  |

---

# STARLIGHT  HAZEL ATLAS GLASS COMPANY, 1938-1940

Colors:   Crystal, pink; some white, cobalt.

The plate in the rear of Starlight is not Delphite blue, but white. The reflection from the cobalt bowl in the background made it look that color. Maybe there would be more collectors of Starlight if it came in Delphite!

Crystal collectors have admitted that the sherbets are the hardest pieces to find after I had been saying that for years. I have not had any reports of finding other 12" bowls. This particular bowl makes a good salad bowl for the large plate. Either of the large bowls will do that quite well. This set is a great one to use for either everyday or for special occasions. I know of collectors who do both!

I have never been able to find any pieces of pink other than the closed-handle bowl even though they are supposed to exist. I am removing most pink pieces from the listing until confirmation that they exist. If you know otherwise, send pictures!

|  | Crystal, White | Pink |  | Crystal, White | Pink |
|---|---|---|---|---|---|
| Bowl, 5½" Cereal | 3.00 | 5.00 | Plate, 9" Dinner | 4.00 |  |
| * Bowl, 8½", Closed | | | Plate, 13" Sandwich | 7.50 | 7.50 |
| Handles | 4.00 | 9.00 | Relish Dish | 9.50 |  |
| Bowl, 11½" Salad | 14.00 | | Salt and Pepper, Pr. | 16.00 |  |
| Bowl, 12", 2¾" Deep | 17.50 | | Saucer | 1.00 |  |
| Plate, 6" Bread and Butter | 2.00 | | Sherbet | 7.50 |  |
| Creamer, Oval | 3.00 | | Sugar, Oval | 3.00 |  |
| Cup | 2.50 | | | | |
| Plate, 8½" Luncheon | 2.50 | | | | |

*Cobalt—$20.00

**Please refer to Foreword for pricing information**

# STRAWBERRY and "CHERRYBERRY"   U.S. GLASS COMPANY, Early 1930's

Colors:   Pink, green, crystal; some iridized.

Strawberry caused a few "red" moments in my life in the last book! How this pattern's price listing found its way under the Spiral pattern is a great mystery! Maybe it's the computer technician's famous "cosmic ray" theory. When he can't explain why random letters or jibberish appears on a page 12 lines below where I'm typing, he'll grin and proclaim, "Ah, a 'cosmic ray' probably passed by and 'confused' my computer."

"Cherryberry" is now selling for the same prices as "Strawberry" since there are so few collectors. "Cherryberry" refers to the fact that there are cherries in the pattern instead of strawberries. Neither fruits are widely found; but the Cherryberry is more rarely seen than the Strawberry.

Only the butter tops have the pattern. All bases of U.S. Glass butters are plain and therefore interchangeable with any other when the colors match. New collectors, notice how large the sugar is since it is oft times sold as a more costly spooner if the top is missing. It is the top of that sugar that is hard to find.

Strawberry items are on the right and Cherryberry items are pictured on the left of the photo.

| | Crystal, Iridescent | Pink Green | | Crystal, Iridescent | Pink Green |
|---|---|---|---|---|---|
| Bowl, 4" Berry | 5.00 | 7.00 | Olive Dish, 5" One-Handled | 6.50 | 10.00 |
| Bowl, 6¼", 2" Deep | 22.50 | 40.00 | Pickle Dish, 8¼" Oval | 7.00 | 10.00 |
| Bowl, 6½" Deep Salad | 10.00 | 15.00 | ** Pitcher, 7¾" | 150.00 | 130.00 |
| Bowl, 7½" Deep Berry | 10.00 | 14.00 | Plate, 6" Sherbet | 3.50 | 5.00 |
| * Butter Dish and Cover | 100.00 | 125.00 | Plate, 7½" Salad | 6.50 | 9.00 |
| Butter Dish Bottom | 50.00 | 52.50 | Sherbet | 5.50 | 6.50 |
| Butter Dish Top | 50.00 | 72.50 | Sugar, Small Open | 10.00 | 12.50 |
| Comport, 5¾" | 9.00 | 13.00 | Sugar Large | 12.50 | 15.00 |
| Creamer, Small | 9.00 | 12.50 | Sugar Cover | 17.50 | 30.00 |
| Creamer, 4⅝" Large | 12.50 | 17.50 | *** Tumbler, 3⅝", 9 oz. | 14.00 | 22.00 |

# SUNFLOWER   JEANNETTE GLASS COMPANY, 1930's

Colors:   Pink, green, some delphite; some opaques.

Green and pink Sunflower have both increased in price due to recent collecting demand. One of the new collectors pointed out that he was having a little difficulty in finding green cups, but no one seemed to have saucers. I took note of that and bought two small lots of green Sunflower in the next few months. Guess what! Not a saucer was in either batch of glass, but seven cups were among the pieces. I have no theory as to why. You might check what the availability of green saucers is in your area and let me know. There are a few patterns which have saucers that are harder to find than cups, but very few. Perhaps green Sunflower is one!

I have been unable to find a Delphite sugar to go with the creamer pictured or a saucer to go with the mustard colored cup. Those pieces were obviously experimental. No one would have dared made a whole set of that *beautiful* color.

There are very few trivets being found. These are 7" in diameter, three-footed, and have a slight turned-up edge. The plentiful cake plate also has three legs but is 10" in diameter and has no turned-up edge. These cake plates were packed in 20 pound bags of flour for at least four years according to a letter from a reader. It seems that she remembered having over thirty at her garage sale and couldn't sell them for ten cents because everyone else had bunches of them, also. I know that I sold several for a dollar each at a garage sale of my own in 1971. Dad just found a box of that glass which did not sell. We were amazed. The left-overs included pink American Sweetheart dinner plates, pink Cherryberry bowls, and pink Sharon cups and dinner plates— all priced for two dollars each! It makes you wonder what sold for the $400.00 I collected that week-end. That was how I supplemented my paltry teaching salary that summer!

| | Pink | Green | | Pink | Green |
|---|---|---|---|---|---|
| * Ash Tray, 5", Center Design Only | 7.00 | 7.00 | Saucer | 3.00 | 4.00 |
| Cake Plate, 10", 3 Legs | 9.00 | 9.00 | Sugar (Opaque $85.00) | 12.00 | 13.00 |
| ** Creamer (Opaque $85.00) | 12.50 | 13.50 | Tumbler, 4¾", 8 oz. Footed | 15.00 | 20..00 |
| Cup | 8.00 | 9.00 | Trivet, 7", 3 Legs, Turned Up Edge | 175.00 | 185.00 |
| Plate, 9" Dinner | 9.00 | 12.00 | | | |

*Found in ultramarine—$20.00    **Delphite—$65.00

**Please refer to Foreword for pricing information**

# SWANKY SWIGS 1930's-1950's

Swanky Swigs originally came with a Kraft Cheese product. In fact, the last one pictured still has the "Old English Sharp" cheese in it! The product was priced at 27 cents and the glass was packed in 1954 paper. I'm only scratching the surface on these. If you want to delve deeper, there are interesting articles on them in the Depression Daze newspaper, an ad for which is in the back of this book. You can still find these at bargain prices at yard sales! Pick a design you particularly like and perk up your serving of breakfast juices! The daffodils and cornflowers are favorites of customers in my shop.

**Top Picture**

| | | | | | |
|---|---|---|---|---|---|
| Top Row | Band No. 1 | | Red & Black | 3⅜" | 1.50- 2.50 |
| | | | Red & Blue | 3⅜" | 2.00- 3.00 |
| | | | Blue | 3⅜" | 2.50- 3.50 |
| | Band No. 2 | | Red & Black | 4¾" | 3.00- 4.00 |
| | | | Red & Black | 3⅜" | 2.00- 3.00 |
| | Band No. 3 | | Blue & White | 3⅜" | 2.00- 3.00 |
| | Circle & Dot: | | Blue | 4¾" | 5.00- 7.50 |
| | | | Blue | 3½" | 4.00- 5.00 |
| | | | Red, Green | 3½" | 2.50- 3.50 |
| | | | Black | 3½" | 4.00- 5.00 |
| | | | Red | 4¾" | 5.00- 7.50 |
| | Dot | | Black | 4¾" | 6.00- 8.00 |
| | | | Blue | 3½" | 4.00- 5.00 |
| 2nd Row | Star: | | Blue | 4¾" | 4.00- 5.00 |
| | | | Blue, Red, Green, Black | 3½" | 2.50- 3.50 |
| | | | Cobalt w/White Stars | 4¾" | 12.00-14.00 |
| | Centennials: | | W. Va. Cobalt | 4¾" | 14.00-16.00 |
| | | | Texas Cobalt | 4¾" | 14.00-16.00 |
| | | | Texas Blue, Black, Green | 3½" | 15.00-17.00 |
| | Checkerboard | | Blue, Red | 3½" | 15.00-17.50 |
| 3rd Row | Checkerboard | | Green | 3⅛" | 20.00-22.50 |
| | Sailboat | | Blue | 4½" | 10.00-15.00 |
| | | | Blue | 3½" | 8.00-10.00 |
| | | | Red, Green | 4½" | 10.00-12.50 |
| | | | Green, Lt. Green | 3½" | 8.00-10.00 |
| | Tulip No. 1 | | Blue, Red | 4½" | 5.00- 6.00 |
| | | | Blue, Red | 3½" | 2.50- 3.50 |
| 4th Row | Tulip No.1 | | Green | 4½" | 5.00- 6.00 |
| | | | Green, Black | 3½" | 2.50- 3.50 |
| | | | Green w/Label | 3½" | 4.00- 5.00 |
| | *Tulip No.2 | | Red, Green, Black | 3½" | 15.00-17.50 |
| | Carnival | | Blue, Red | 3½" | 2.00- 3.00 |
| | | | Green, Yellow | 3½" | 4.00- 6.00 |
| | Tulip No. 3 | | Dk. Blue, Lt. Blue | 3¾" | 1.00- 2.00 |

**Second Picture**

| | | | | | |
|---|---|---|---|---|---|
| 1st Row | Tulip No.3 | | Red, Yellow | 3¾" | 1.00- 2.00 |
| | Posey: Tulip | | Red | 4½" | 10.00-12.00 |
| | | | Red | 3½" | 2.00- 3.00 |
| | | | Red | 3¼" | 6.00- 8.00 |
| | Posey: Violet, Jonquil, Cornflower No.1 | | | 4½" | 10.00-12.00 |
| | Posey: Violet, Jonquil, Cornflower No.1 | | | 3½" | 2.00- 3.00 |
| | Cornflower No.2 | | Lt. Blue, Dk. Blue | 3½" | 1.50- 2.50 |
| 2nd Row | Cornflower No.2 | | Red, Yellow | 3½" | 1.50- 2.50 |
| | Forget-Me-Not | | Dk. Blue, Blue, Red, Yellow | 3½" | 1.00- 2.00 |
| | | | Yellow w/Label | 3½" | 3.00- 4.00 |
| | Daisy | | Red & White | 3¾" | 4.00- 5.00 |
| | Daisy | | Red, White & Green | 3¾" | 1.00- 1.50 |
| | Bustling Betsy | | Blue | 3¾" | 1.50- 2.00 |
| | | | Blue | 3¼" | 4.00- 5.00 |
| | | | Green, Orange | 3¾" | 1.50- 2.50 |
| 3rd Row | Bustling Betsy | | Yellow, Red, Brown | 3¾" | 1.50- 2.50 |
| | Antique Pattern: | | | | |
| |   Clock & Coal Scuttle | | Brown | 3¾" | 1.50- 2.50 |
| |   Lamp & Kettle | | Blue | 3¾" | 1.50- 2.50 |
| |   Coffee Grinder & Plate | | Green | 3¾" | 1.50- 2.50 |
| |   Spinning Wheel & Bellows | | Red | 3¾" | 1.50- 2.50 |
| |   Coffee Pot & Trivet | | Black | 3¾" | 1.50- 2.50 |
| |   Churn & Cradle | | Orange | 3¾" | 2.00- 3.00 |
| 4th Row | Kiddie Cup: | | | | |
| |   Squirrel & Deer | | Brown | 3¾" | 1.50- 2.50 |
| |   Bear & Pig | | Blue | 3¾" | 1.50- 2.50 |
| |   Cat & Rabbit | | Green | 3¾" | 1.50- 2.50 |
| |   Bird & Elephant | | Red | 3¾" | 1.50- 2.50 |
| |   Bird & Elephant w/Label | | | 3¾" | 3.00- 4.00 |
| |   Duck & Horse | | Black | 3¾" | 1.50- 2.50 |
| |   Dog & Rooster | | Orange | 3¾" | 2.00- 3.00 |
| |   Dog & Rooster w/Cheese | | | | 8.00-10.00 |

*West Coast lower in price

**Please refer to Foreword for pricing information**

KRAFT
PIMENTO
CHEESE SPREAD
KRAFT
Olive
Pimento
KRAFT
Old
English
KRAFT
Old English

# SWIRL, "PETAL SWIRL"   JEANNETTE GLASS COMPANY, 1937-1938

Colors:    Ultra-marine, pink, Delphite, some amber, ice-blue.

Swirl comes in several unusual colors as shown in the photograph. Only the Delphite has enough pieces to put together a small set. The amber and light blue bowls are the only pieces I have seen in those colors.

The ultra-marine is the most collected color, but as with all of Jeannette's patterns found in this color, variation in shades of color is the major problem. Much ultra-marine is greener than blue. The variation may be only slightly noticeable or distinctly detracting. The greener tint is usually avoided by most collectors; but like all things, some prefer the greener shade. This is another of the patterns that is difficult to order by mail because of color hues.

The Swirl pitcher shown in the pattern shot still remains one of three known! All of these have been found in the Pittsburgh area which is near the old factory site.

Many times the coasters are found inside small advertising tires. This overlaps another collecting field—advertising, and a specialty item field of tire collecting within that field! Thus, competition makes the coasters even harder to find!

That large quantity of candy and butter dishes has finally been absorbed by collectors and once again the price is rising on these items. In another pattern, a couple dozen butter dishes would not seem like a lot; but that many Swirl butters found in a barn in Pennsylvania created a glut for a while!

Many collectors of Swirl have discovered Jennyware which was Jeannette's kitchenware line that matches Swirl in many details including concentric circles. You can see the Jennyware pictured on page 216 of my *Kitchen Glassware of the Depression Years*.

Some plates have round edges instead of the fluted variety shown in the pattern shot; more collectors seek the fluted edge plate.

| | Pink | Ultra-marine | Delphite | | Pink | Ultra-marine | Delphite |
|---|---|---|---|---|---|---|---|
| Ash Tray, 5⅜" | 6.00 | | | Pitcher, 48 oz. Footed | | 950.00 | |
| Bowl, 5¼" Cereal | 5.50 | 8.00 | 9.00 | Plate, 6½" Sherbet | 2.50 | 3.50 | 3.00 |
| Bowl, 9" Salad | 9.50 | 15.00 | 20.00 | Plate, 7¼" | 4.50 | 7.50 | |
| Bowl, 9" Salad, Rimmed | 12.00 | 18.00 | | Plate, 8" Salad | 5.00 | 9.50 | 5.00 |
| Bowl, 10" Footed, | | | | Plate, 9¼" Dinner | 7.00 | 10.00 | 7.50 |
| Closed Handles | | 22.00 | | Plate, 10½" | | | 12.00 |
| Bowl, 10½" Footed | | | | Plate, 12½" Sandwich | 7.50 | 13.50 | |
| Console | 12.50 | 19.00 | | Platter, 12" Oval | | | 22.50 |
| Butter Dish | 130.00 | 195.00 | | Salt and Pepper, Pr. | | 27.50 | |
| Butter Dish Bottom | 25.00 | 35.00 | | Saucer | 1.50 | 2.00 | 2.00 |
| Butter Dish Top | 105.00 | 160.00 | | Sherbet, Low Footed | 6.00 | 10.00 | |
| Candleholders, Double | | | | Soup, Tab Handles | | | |
| Branch Pr. | | 22.50 | | (Lug) | 12.50 | 15.00 | |
| Candleholders, Single | | | | Sugar, Footed | 6.50 | 9.50 | 7.50 |
| Branch Pr. | | | 85.00 | Tumbler, 4", 9 oz. | 8.00 | 15.00 | |
| Candy Dish, Open, 3 | | | | Tumbler, 4⅝", 9 oz. | 11.00 | | |
| Legs | 6.00 | 8.50 | | Tumbler, 5⅛", 13 oz. | 16.00 | 45.00 | |
| Candy Dish with Cover | 55.00 | 75.00 | | Tumbler, 9 oz. Footed | 12.50 | 18.00 | |
| Coaster, 1" x 3¼" | 5.50 | 7.50 | | Vase, 6½" Footed | 11.50 | 15.00 | |
| Creamer, Footed | 6.50 | 9.50 | 7.50 | Vase, 8½" Footed | | 17.50 | |
| Cup | 4.75 | 8.25 | 6.00 | | | | |

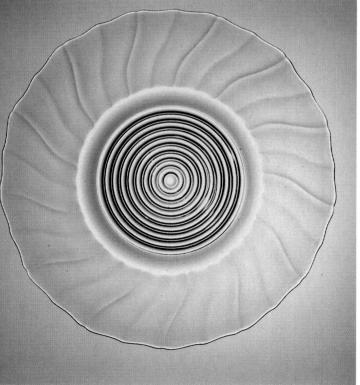

# TEA ROOM  INDIANA GLASS COMPANY, 1926-1931

Colors:    Pink, green, amber, some crystal.

How high will Tea Room prices go? If I knew, I would also give out forecasts on the stock market and make a lot more money than sitting at this computer.

It is as difficult to predict glass-buying trends as it is any others, but the Deco-look of Tea Room has stood the test of inflation; and when other patterns were only holding their own in prices, Tea Room was steadily increasing in price. There have always been some collectors of this pattern with lots of money to spend for MINT glass. That is true in all collecting fields. In early baseball cards, a mint card may bring fifty times that of a lesser grade. In Tea Room, collectors are paying premium prices for MINT pieces. All prices in this book are for mint glass, but in Tea Room this needs to be *UNDERLINED*.

Note the newly discovered creamer and sugar. They are like the pattern known as "Cracked Ice" made by Indiana, but do not have the diagonal lines of that pattern. The knobs are different than other Tea Room pieces, but the pattern is the same. A green sugar is pictured with lid and the pink creamer and sugar without lid are shown.

I spent a few days in early March driving between shows in Pittsburgh and Chicago. In a shop in Indiana that had several thousand pieces of Depression Glass (that were all priced out of the range for buying to resell), I bought a pink, flat banana dish like the one in the front of the picture. That should not be surprising except that it cost $3.00! I used it in my seminar that weekend as an example that bargains could still be found!

Few amber pieces are being found, and most that are come from the Atlanta area. One older lady remembers these were promoted by Coca-Cola. If you live in that area, you might keep your eyes open.

The center-handled servers have made some large jumps in price. They are selling at the prices listed! These are not hoped for prices, but actual selling prices. There is a difference!

Except for the pitcher and the commonly found 9″ ruffled vase, crystal sells for 50% to 60% of the lowest price listed. That 9″ vase sells for $10.00 to $12.00 on a good day.

| | Green | Pink | | Green | Pink |
|---|---|---|---|---|---|
| Bowl, Finger | 35.00 | 30.00 | * Saucer | 15.00 | 15.00 |
| Bowl, 7½″ Banana Split, Flat | 60.00 | 60.00 | Sherbet, Low Footed | 16.00 | 14.00 |
| Bowl, 7½″ Banana Split, Footed | 55.00 | 45.00 | Sherbet, Low Flared Edge | 25.00 | 20.00 |
| Bowl, 8½″ Celery | 25.00 | 20.00 | Sherbet, Tall Footed | 30.00 | 27.50 |
| Bowl, 8¾″ Deep Salad | 65.00 | 50.00 | Sugar w/Lid 3″ | 95.00 | 90.00 |
| Bowl, 9½″ Oval Vegetable | 45.00 | 40.00 | Sugar, 4″ | 12.50 | 10.00 |
| Candlestick, Low, Pr. | 35.00 | 30.00 | Sugar, 4½″ Footed | | |
| Creamer, 3¼″ | 20.00 | 20.00 | (Amber $45.00) | 14.00 | 12.00 |
| Creamer, 4″ | 12.50 | 10.00 | Sugar, Rectangular | 14.00 | 12.50 |
| Creamer, 4½″ Footed | | | Sugar, Flat with Cover | 90.00 | 80.00 |
| (Amber $45.00) | 13.50 | 12.00 | Sundae, Footed, Ruffled Top | 75.00 | 60.00 |
| Creamer, Rectangular | 14.00 | 12.50 | Tray, Center-Handled | 155.00 | 115.00 |
| Creamer & Sugar on Tray, 3½″ | 52.50 | 50.00 | Tray, Rectangular Sugar & | | |
| *Cup | 27.50 | 25.00 | Creamer | 35.00 | 30.00 |
| Goblet, 9 oz. | 60.00 | 50.00 | Tumbler, 8½ oz., Flat | 75.00 | 65.00 |
| Ice Bucket | 40.00 | 35.00 | Tumbler, 6 oz. Footed | 25.00 | 25.00 |
| Lamp, 9″ Electric | 35.00 | 30.00 | Tumbler, 9 oz. Footed | | |
| Marmalade, Notched Lid | 125.00 | 100.00 | (Amber $45.00) | 22.00 | 20.00 |
| Mustard, Covered | 95.00 | 85.00 | Tumbler, 11 oz. Footed | 32.50 | 27.50 |
| Parfait | 50.00 | 45.00 | Tumbler, 12 oz. Footed | 40.00 | 35.00 |
| **Pitcher, 64 oz. (Amber $300.00) | 100.00 | 95.00 | Vase 6″ Ruffled Edge | 85.00 | 70.00 |
| Plate, 6½″ Sherbet | 20.00 | 18.00 | Vase, 9″ Ruffled Edge | 75.00 | 60.00 |
| Plate, 8¼″, Luncheon | 25.00 | 22.50 | Vase 9″ Straight | 50.00 | 40.00 |
| Plate, 10½″, 2-Handled | 40.00 | 35.00 | Vase 11″ Ruffled Edge | 145.00 | 120.00 |
| Relish, Divided | 16.00 | 13.00 | Vase 11″ Straight | 70.00 | 65.00 |
| Salt and Pepper, Pr. | 40.00 | 37.50 | | | |

*Prices for absolute mint pieces
**Crystal—$175.00

**Please refer to Foreword for pricing information**

# THISTLE   MacBETH-EVANS, 1929-1930

Colors:   Pink, green; some yellow, crystal.

Thistle is one of the most difficult patterns to photograph. Our photographer finally learned the secret on Fire-King Oven Ware, but we are still working on getting this so the pattern shows well. Delicate patterns are always a problem. If all patterns were as bold as Miss America, we could really do justice to the glass. Those of you who have sent me pictures or have tried to photograph your glass, you know what I mean.

The mould shapes of Thistle pieces are like the thin Dogwood. It is a shame that no creamer and sugar were ever made for this pattern. Several collectors have said that they use the thin Dogwood creamer and sugar with their sets in lieu of Thistle. The *heavy* Thistle pieces being found in pink, green and blue are being made by Mosser Glass in Cambridge, Ohio. These are copies of an old pattern glass. There was never a pitcher, tumbler, creamer, sugar or butter dish made in OUR Thistle.

The 10¼″ bowl in Thistle is harder to find than those same bowls in Dogwood. The price would be much higher if there were more collectors.

|  | Pink | Green |  | Pink | Green |
|---|---|---|---|---|---|
| Bowl, 5½″ Cereal | 12.00 | 15.00 | Plate, 10¼″ Grill | 12.50 | 15.00 |
| Bowl, 10¼″ Large Fruit | 185.00 | 125.00 | Plate, 13″ Heavy Cake | 72.50 | 95.00 |
| Cup, Thin | 14.00 | 17.50 | Saucer | 7.50 | 7.50 |
| Plate, 8″ Luncheon | 8.00 | 12.50 |  |  |  |

---

# "THUMBPRINT", PEAR OPTIC   FEDERAL GLASS COMPANY, 1929-1930

Color:   Green.

Not all items shown here were made by Federal, but they all blend together well. This photograph was taken by Raymond Mills using Imogene McKinney's Thumbprint collection. She is one of the new breed collectors who does not feel limited to collecting the pieces only made for her pattern. There were many companies that made a "Thumbprint" pattern and many of these pieces blend quite nicely with Federal's Thumbprint; so take advantage of that! (She disliked my old picture of Thumbprint so intensely, she offered her collection for use!)

Thumbprint is still not one of the best selling patterns in Depression Glass, but if you enjoy the excitement of hunting, this pattern may be your cup of tea. Finding the creamer and sugar is one thing certain to challenge you.

|  | Green |  | Green |
|---|---|---|---|
| Bowl, 4¾″ Berry | 2.00 | Salt and Pepper, Pr. | 20.00 |
| Bowl, 5″ Cereal | 2.50 | Saucer | 1.00 |
| Bowl, 8″ Large Berry | 6.00 | Sherbet | 4.00 |
| Creamer, Footed | 10.00 | Sugar, Footed | 10.00 |
| Cup | 2.50 | Tumbler, 4″, 5 oz. | 3.50 |
| Plate, 6″ Sherbet | 1.25 | Tumbler, 5″, 10 oz. | 4.00 |
| Plate, 8″ Luncheon | 2.00 | Tumbler, 5½″, 12 oz. | 4.00 |
| Plate, 9¼″ Dinner | 4.50 | Whiskey, 2¼″, 1 oz. | 3.00 |

**Please refer to Foreword for pricing information**

# TWISTED OPTIC   IMPERIAL GLASS COMPANY, 1927-1930

Colors:   Pink, green, amber; some blue, canary yellow.

Today, there seems to be more collecting interest in the canary yellow (which is commonly called vaseline by collectors) and the blue than in any other colors. Green used to be the commonly collected color. Sugar and creamer collectors search for the amber in this pattern. The amber is rarely seen. I have never seen canary yellow or blue sugars and creamers. If you have a pair (or even one), drop me a line.

The green center-handled server in the middle is not Twisted Optic, but Spiral. Read the explanation for this under Spiral.

As a matter of clarification, the sandwich server listed as two handled is a serving plate with two handles.

| | *All Colors | | All Colors |
|---|---|---|---|
| Bowl, 4¾" Cream Soup | 7.00 | Plate, 8" Luncheon | 2.00 |
| Bowl, 5" Cereal | 3.00 | Preserve (Same as candy but | |
| Bowl, 7" Salad or Soup | 6.00 | with Slot in Lid) | 17.50 |
| Candlesticks, 3" Pr. | 10.00 | Sandwich Server, Center Handle | 15.00 |
| Candy Jar and Cover | 17.50 | Sandwich Server, Two Handled | 5.50 |
| Creamer | 6.00 | Saucer | 1.00 |
| Cup | 3.00 | Sherbet | 4.00 |
| Pitcher, 64 oz. | 17.50 | Sugar | 5.00 |
| Plate, 6" Sherbet | 1.50 | Tumbler, 4½", 9 oz. | 4.50 |
| Plate, 7" Salad | 2.00 | Tumbler, 5¼", 12 oz. | 6.50 |
| Plate, 7½" x 9" Oval with Indent | 4.00 | | |

*Blue, Canary Yellow 50% more

---

# U.S. SWIRL   U.S. GLASS COMPANY, Late 1920's

Colors:   Pink, green.

There are no new pieces to report, but there is a new color! I received a letter about iridized pieces. It would make sense to find pieces in iridized color since both Aunt Polly and Strawberry are found iridized. All the shapes found so far in U.S. Glass have matched the mould shapes of Aunt Polly. Maybe some blue will be found in U.S. Swirl!

I still have been unable to find a creamer in green. I saw more pink in my travels than I did green; but green seems to be the color most collected.

| | Green | Pink |
|---|---|---|
| Bowl, 4⅜", Berry | 4.50 | 5.00 |
| Bowl, 5½", 1 Handle | 8.50 | 9.00 |
| Bowl, 7⅞", Large Berry | 11.00 | 12.00 |
| Bowl, 8¼", Oval | 16.00 | 17.50 |
| Butter and Cover | 52.50 | 67.50 |
| Butter Bottom | 42.50 | 52.50 |
| Butter Top | 10.00 | 15.00 |
| Candy w/Cover, 2-Handled | 20.00 | 22.50 |
| Creamer | 10.00 | 11.00 |
| Pitcher, 8", 48 oz. | 30.00 | 30.00 |
| Plate, 6⅛", Sherbet | 1.50 | 1.75 |
| Plate, 7⅞", Salad | 4.50 | 5.00 |
| Salt and Pepper, Pr. | 32.50 | 35.00 |
| Sherbet, 3¼" | 3.50 | 4.00 |
| Sugar w/Lid | 25.00 | 25.00 |
| Tumbler, 4⅝", 12 oz. | 8.50 | 9.00 |
| Vase, 6½" | 12.50 | 13.50 |

**Please refer to Foreword for pricing information**

# "VICTORY"   DIAMOND GLASS-WARE COMPANY, 1929-1932

Colors:   Amber, pink, green; some cobalt blue; black.

I opened a large can of worms when I pictured so much cobalt blue Victory in the last book. I have been besieged by requests to sell what I have pictured. I wish I could, but then, where would I find more the next time I need to photograph?

Victory gravy boat and platters, soup bowls and goblets still are rarely found. I visited a mall in Columbus, Ohio, earlier this year which mostly had furniture displayed. Out of the thirty or so dealers, only a dozen had glass. The amazing thing was that only five or six had Depression Glass and of those—there were three sets of green Victory displayed! One was a large set of eight and the others were smaller. Out of curiosity, I talked to each dealer about the glass. Not one even knew the name of the pattern. All they knew—it was Depression Glass. It was priced out of sight!

| | Amber, Pink, Green | Black, Blue | | Amber, Pink, Green | Black, Blue |
|---|---|---|---|---|---|
| Bon Bon, 7" | 9.00 | 15.00 | Gravy Boat and Platter | 125.00 | 250.00 |
| Bowl, 6½" Cereal | 8.00 | 18.00 | Mayonnaise Set: 3½" Tall, 5½" | | |
| Bowl, 8½" Flat Soup | 12.00 | 25.00 | Across, 8½" Indented Plate | | |
| Bowl, 9" Oval Vegetable | 25.00 | 45.00 | w/Ladle | 35.00 | 65.00 |
| Bowl, 11" Rolled Edge | 20.00 | 35.00 | Plate, 6" Bread and Butter | 3.00 | 8.00 |
| Bowl, 12" Console | 27.50 | | Plate, 7" Salad | 5.50 | 10.00 |
| Bowl, 12½" Flat Edge | 22.50 | 50.00 | Plate, 8" Luncheon | 5.00 | 12.50 |
| Candlesticks, 3" Pr. | 25.00 | 65.00 | Plate, 9" Dinner | 15.00 | 22.50 |
| Cheese & Cracker Set, 12" Indented Plate & Compote | 35.00 | | Platter, 12" | 17.50 | 45.00 |
| | | | Sandwich Server, Center Handle | 20.00 | 45.00 |
| Comport, 6" Tall, 6¾" Diameter | 10.00 | | Saucer | 2.00 | 6.00 |
| Creamer | 10.00 | 30.00 | Sherbet, Footed | 10.00 | 17.50 |
| Cup | 6.00 | 20.00 | Sugar | 10.00 | 30.00 |
| Goblet, 5", 7 oz. | 17.50 | | | | |

---

# VITROCK, "FLOWER RIM"   HOCKING GLASS COMPANY, 1934-1937

Colors:   White and white w/fired-on colors, usually red or green.

Vitrock, "Flower Rim", pattern was Hocking's answer to the Platonite made by Hazel Atlas. Many kitchenware pieces were also made in this line. You can see more Vitrock in my *Kitchen Glassware of the Depression Years*.

The major claim to fame of Vitrock is its confusion with Indiana Custard. Note that the creamer and sugar are shaped like Princess except the Vitrock does not have a sugar lid. Fired-on colored plates (like those shown) make great accessory items for special occasions (Christmas and Valentine's Day).

| | White | | White |
|---|---|---|---|
| Bowl, 4" Berry | 3.00 | Plate, 7¼" Salad | 1.50 |
| Bowl, 5½" Cream Soup | 8.00 | Plate, 8¾" Luncheon | 2.00 |
| Bowl, 6" Fruit | 4.00 | Plate, 9" Soup | 7.00 |
| Bowl, 7½" Cereal | 3.00 | Plate, 10" Dinner | 4.00 |
| Bowl, 9½" Vegetable | 7.00 | Platter, 11½" | 17.50 |
| Creamer, Oval | 3.00 | Saucer | 1.00 |
| Cup | 2.00 | Sugar, Oval | 3.00 |

**Please refer to Foreword for pricing information**

# WATERFORD, "WAFFLE"  HOCKING GLASS COMPANY, 1938-1944

Colors:    Crystal, pink; some yellow, white; 1950's, Forest Green.

Add a cup to the list of items that were made in the Miss America style. The other known items in this style were shown in the seventh edition. Why no more of these are found is still a mystery.

Crystal Waterford is one of our best selling patterns in the shop. The only problem has been in finding enough to keep all those collectors happy. There do not seem to be enough water goblets, cereal bowls and cup and saucers to go around—no matter how many I find. There is a demand for the crystal trimmed in red, but I have seen very little of that. There are two styles of crystal sherbets found. The scalloped base is the one most often seen.

A few white ash trays with fired-on green and pink (colors shown in Oyster and Pearl) have been found over the years. The pink is known as "Dusty Rose" and the green as "Springtime Green". These sell in the price range of the crystal ones.

Pink Waterford butter dishes, pitchers and cereal bowls still top the list of most wanted items. Some collectors have been willing to overlook minor inner rim imperfections on the cereal bowls just in order to own some.

| | Crystal | Pink | | Crystal | Pink |
|---|---|---|---|---|---|
| * Ash Tray, 4″ | 6.00 | | Plate, 6″ Sherbet | 1.50 | 3.50 |
| Bowl, 4¾″ Berry | 4.00 | 7.00 | Plate, 7⅛″ Salad | 2.00 | 4.50 |
| Bowl, 5½″ Cereal | 9.00 | 14.00 | Plate, 9⅝″ Dinner | 5.00 | 11.00 |
| Bowl, 8¼″ Large Berry | 6.00 | 12.00 | Plate, 10¼″ Handled Cake | 5.00 | 9.50 |
| Butter Dish and Cover | 22.00 | 175.00 | Plate, 13¾″ Sandwich | 5.00 | 20.00 |
| Butter Dish Bottom | 5.00 | 25.00 | Relish, 13¾″, 5-Part | 13.00 | |
| Butter Dish Top | 17.00 | 150.00 | Salt and Pepper, 2 Types | 7.50 | |
| Coaster, 4″ | 1.50 | 4.00 | Saucer | 1.00 | 3.50 |
| Creamer, Oval | 2.50 | 7.50 | Sherbet, Footed | 2.50 | 6.50 |
| Creamer (Miss America Style) | 20.00 | | Sugar | 2.50 | 6.50 |
| Cup | 4.00 | 10.00 | Sugar Cover, Oval | 2.50 | 17.50 |
| Goblets, 5¼″, 5⅝″ | 12.00 | | Sugar (Miss America Style) | 20.00 | |
| Goblets, 5½″ (Miss America Style) | 25.00 | 60.00 | Tumbler, 3½″, 5 oz. Juice | | |
| Lamp, 4″ Spherical Base | 22.50 | | (Miss America Style) | | 40.00 |
| Pitcher, 42 oz. Tilted Juice | 17.50 | | Tumbler, 4⅞″, 10 oz. Footed | 8.50 | 12.00 |
| Pitcher, 80 oz. Tilted Ice Lip | 22.50 | 100.00 | | | |

*With Ads $10.00

**Please refer to Foreword for pricing information**

# WINDSOR, "WINDSOR DIAMOND"   JEANNETTE GLASS COMPANY, 1936-1946

Colors:   Pink, green, crystal; some Delphite, amberina red, ice blue.

No other pieces of blue Windsor have been found. I would not mind finding a set in blue myself! I will be content with these two pieces for now. Cups, saucers and dinner plates have been found in Amberina to go with the pitcher and tumbler shown here.

There are two styles of sugar and butter lids in crystal. Both styles are shown on the crystal butter tops. The pointed top may have been redesigned into the more rounded style and then that style was continued into the making of Holiday a few years later. That is only an educated guess; but it does seem logical.

The crystal punch bowl is still a conversation piece. The pointed edge 10½" bowl fits upon an inverted comport and has been found with a dozen cups to make the set. Saucers in crystal are in shorter supply than the cups because of this. In recent years that comport was made in crystal and a multitude of sprayed-on colors. These are easily distinguished because a beaded edge was added to the newer comport.

Do green candlesticks exist? The pink ones (shown) are still difficult to find; so is the smaller pitcher. The 16 oz. pitcher is similar in style to the one found in Holiday. The trays found without handles (shown in crystal) are not often found in pink.

| | Crystal | Pink | Green | | Crystal | Pink | Green |
|---|---|---|---|---|---|---|---|
| * Ash Tray, 5¾" | 11.50 | 30.00 | 40.00 | Pitcher, 5", 20 oz. | 5.00 | | |
| Bowl, 4¾" Berry | 2.50 | 5.00 | 7.00 | Pitcher, 6¾", 52 oz. (Red | | | |
| Bowl, 5" Pointed Edge | 3.00 | 8.00 | | $350.00) | 11.00 | 18.50 | 35.00 |
| Bowl, 5" Cream Soup | 4.50 | 12.50 | 15.00 | Plate, 6" Sherbet | 1.50 | 2.50 | 3.50 |
| Bowl, 5⅛", 5⅜" Cereals | 5.00 | 11.00 | 12.00 | Plate, 7" Salad | 3.00 | 9.50 | 10.00 |
| Bowl, 7⅛", Three Legs | 6.00 | 15.00 | | ** Plate, 9" Dinner | 3.50 | 9.50 | 9.50 |
| Bowl, 8" Pointed Edge | 8.00 | 20.00 | | Plate, 10¼" Handled Sandwich | 4.00 | 9.00 | 10.00 |
| Bowl, 8", 2-Handled | 4.50 | 11.00 | 14.00 | Plate, 13⅝" Chop | 7.50 | 20.00 | 20.00 |
| Bowl, 8½" Large Berry | 4.50 | 10.00 | 11.00 | Plate, 15½" Serving | 7.00 | | |
| Bowl, 9½" Oval Vegetable | 5.00 | 12.00 | 15.00 | Platter, 11½" Oval | 4.50 | 9.50 | 11.00 |
| Bowl, 10½" Salad | 6.00 | | | Relish Platter, 11½" Divided | 7.50 | | |
| Bowl, 10½" Pointed Edge | 20.00 | 85.00 | | Salt and Pepper, Pr. | 12.50 | 27.50 | 37.50 |
| Bowl, 12½" Fruit Console | 20.00 | 65.00 | | Saucer | 1.50 | 2.50 | 3.00 |
| Bowl, 7" x 11¾" Boat Shape | 12.00 | 19.00 | 22.00 | Sherbet, Footed | 2.50 | 6.00 | 7.00 |
| Butter Dish | 22.50 | 37.50 | 70.00 | Sugar and Cover | 4.50 | 15.00 | 17.50 |
| Cake Plate, 10¾" Footed | 6.00 | 11.50 | 13.00 | Sugar and Cover (Like "Holiday") | 4.00 | | |
| Cake Plate, 13½" Thick | 5.00 | 11.50 | 12.50 | Tray, 4" Square | 2.50 | 4.50 | 6.50 |
| Candlesticks, 3" Pr. | 15.00 | 55.00 | | Tray, 4⅛" x 9" | 3.00 | 6.50 | 7.50 |
| Candy Jar and Cover | 10.00 | 25.00 | | Tray, 8½" x 9¾", w/Handles | 5.00 | 18.50 | 19.50 |
| Coaster, 3¼" | 2.50 | 7.00 | 10.00 | Tray, 8½" x 9¾", No Handles | | 55.00 | |
| Comport | 3.00 | 12.00 | | Tumbler, 3¼", 5 oz. | 6.00 | 11.00 | 20.00 |
| ** Creamer | 3.00 | 7.50 | 8.00 | *** Tumbler, 4", 9 oz. | 5.00 | 10.00 | 17.50 |
| Creamer (Shaped as "Holiday") | 4.00 | | | Tumbler, 5", 12 oz. | 7.50 | 20.00 | 27.50 |
| Cup | 2.50 | 6.00 | 7.00 | Tumbler, 4" Footed | 5.00 | | |
| Pitcher, 4½", 16 oz. | 17.50 | 95.00 | | Tumbler, 7¼" Footed | 9.00 | | |

*Delphite—$40.00      **Blue—$45.00      ***Red—$50.00

**Please refer to Foreword for pricing information**

# Reproductions

## NEW "ADAM"  PRIVATELY PRODUCED OUT OF KOREA THROUGH ST. LOUIS

### IMPORTING COMPANY

The new Adam butter is being offered at $6.50 wholesale. Identification of the new is easy.
**Top:** Notice the veins in the leaves.
**New:** Large leaf veins do not join or touch in center of leaf.
**Old:** Large leaf veins all touch or join center vein on the old.
A further note in the original Adam butter dish the veins of all the leaves at the center of the design are very clear cut and precisely moulded, whereas in the new these center leaf veins are very indistinct - and almost invisible in one leaf of the center design.
**Bottom:** Place butter dish bottom upside down for observation.
**New:** Four (4) "Arrowhead-like" points line up in northwest, northeast, southeast, and southwest directions of compass.
**Old:** Four (4) "Arrowhead-like" points line up in north, east, south and west directions of compass.
There are very bad mold lines and very glossy light pink color on those butter dishes I have examined but these could be improved.

## NEW "AVOCADO"  INDIANA GLASS COMPANY Tiara Exclusives Line, 1974 . . .

Colors: Pink, frosted pink, yellow, blue, red amethyst, green?

In 1979 a green Avocado pitcher was supposedly run. It was supposed to be darker than the original green and was to be limited to a hostess gift item. I was supposed to get one for photographing purposes. However, I've never seen said pitcher. Did they make it?

The pink they made was described under the pattern. It tends to be more orange than the original color. The other colors shown pose little threat as these colors were not made originally.

I understand that Tiara sales counselors tell potential clientelle that their newly made glass is collectible because it is made from old molds. I don't share this view. I feel it's like saying that since you were married in your grandmother's wedding dress, you will have the same happy marriage for the fifty-seven years she did. All you can truly say is that you were married in her dress. I think all you can say about the new Avocado is that it was made from the old molds. TIME, SCARCITY and PEOPLE'S WHIM determine collectibility in so far as I'm able to determine it. It's taken nearly fifty years or more for people to turn to collecting Depression Glass--and that's done, in part, because EVERYONE "remembers" it; they had some in their home at one time or another; it has universal appeal. Who is to say what will be collectible in the next hundred years. If we all knew, we could all get rich!

If you like the new Tiara products, then by all means buy them; but don't do so DEPENDING upon their being collectible just because they are made in the image of the old! You have an equal chance, I feel, of going to Las Vegas and DEPENDING upon getting rich at the Black Jack table.

# Reproductions (Cont.)

## NEW "CAMEO"

Colors: Green (shakers); yellow, green, pink (child's dishes).

Although the photographer I left this shaker with opted to shoot the side without the dancing girl, I trust you can still see how very weak the pattern is on this reproduction of Cameo shaker. Also, you can see how very much glass remains in the bottom of the shaker; and, of course, the new tops all make this very easy to spot at the market. These were to be bought wholesale at around $6.00; but did not sell well.

The children's dishes pose no problem to collectors since they were never made originally. The sugar and creamer are a shade over 1½ inches tall and the butter dish is just 3¾ inches from handle to handle. There are now thirty or more children's pieces made in miniature from original pieces. These are "scale models" of the larger size. This type of production I have no quarrel with as they aren't planned to "dupe" anyone.

## NEW "CHERRY BLOSSOM"

Colors: Pink, green, blue, delphite, cobalt, red, iridized colors.

**Please use information provided only for the piece described. Do no apply information on tumbler for pitcher, etc.**

Several different people have gotten into the act of making reproduction Cherry Blossom. We've even enjoyed some reproductions of reproductions! All the items pictured on the next pages are extremely easy to spot as reproductions once you know what to look for with the possible exception of the 13" divided platter pictured at the back. It's too heavy, weighing 2¾ pounds and has a thick, ⅜" of glass in the bottom; but the design isn't too bad! The edges of the leaves aren't smooth; but neither are they serrated like old leaves.

I could write a book on the differences between old and new scalloped bottom, AOP Cherry pitchers. The easiest way to tell the difference is to turn the pitcher over. My old Cherry pitcher has nine cherries on the bottom. The new one only has seven. Further, the branch crossing the bottom of my old Cherry pitchers LOOKS like a branch. It's knobby and gnarled and has several leaves and cherry stems directly attached to it. The new pitcher just has a bald strip of glass halving the bottom of the pitcher. Further, the old cherry pitchers have a plain glass background for the cherries and leaves in the bottom of the pitcher. In the new pitchers, there's a rough, filled in, straw-like background. You see no plain glass. (My new Cherry pitcher just cracked sitting in a box by my typing stand -- another tendency which I understand is common to the new)!

As for the new tumblers, the easiest way to tell old from new is to look at the ring dividing the patterned portion of the glass from the plain glass lip. The old tumblers have three indented rings dividing the pattern from the plain glass rim. The new has only one. (Turn back and look at the red cherry tumbler pictured with Cherry Blossom pattern). Further, as in the pitcher, the arching encircling the cherry blossoms on the new tumblers is very sharply ridged. On the old tumblers, that arching is so smooth you can barely feel it. Again, the pattern at the bottom of the new tumblers is brief and practically nonexistent in the center curve of the glass bottom. This was sharply defined on most of the old tumblers. You can see how far toward the edge the pattern came on the red cherry tumbler pictured with the pattern. The pattern, what there is, on the new tumblers mostly hugs the center of the foot.

Now for a quick run down of the various items.
**2 handled tray - old:**1⅞ lbs; ³⁄₁₆" glass in bottom; leaves and cherries east/west from north/south handles; leaves have real spine and serrated edges; cherry stems end in triangle of glass. **new:** 2⅛ lbs; ¼" glass in bottom; leaves and cherries north/south with the handles; canal type leaves (but uneven edges); cherry stem ends before cup shaped line.
**cake plate - new:** color too light pink, leaves have too many parallel veins which give them a "feathery" look; arches at plate edge don't line up with lines on inside of the rim to which the feet are attached.
**8½" bowl - new:** crude leaves with smooth edges; veins in parallel lines.
**cereal bowl - new:** wrong shape, looks like 8½" bowl, small 2" center. **old:** large center, 2½" inside ring, nearly 3½" if you count the outer rim before the sides turn up.
**plate - new:** center shown close up; smooth edged leaves, fish spine type center leaf portion; weighs 1 pound plus; feels thicker at edge with mold offset lines clearly visible. (See next page). **old:** center leaves look like real leaves with spines, veins, and serrated edges; weights ¾ pound; clean edges; no mold offset.
**cup new:** area in bottom left free of design; canal leaves; smooth, thick top to cup handle (old has triangle grasp point).
**saucer - new:** off set mold line edge; canal leaf center.

## NEW CHERRY BLOSSOM (Cont.)

First of all, notice the cup bottom and the close up of the center design on the reproduction plate. Once you learn to recognize these "fake" leaves, you'll be able to spot 95 percent of the reproduction Cherry Blossom. These new leaves look like orderly docking stations at the local marina with a straight canal going down the center. Old Cherry Blossom dishes have real looking leaves, complete with main stem, delicate veins branching from that stem, and serrated edges. Notice the smooth edges of the reproduction leaves.

The Cherry child's dishes were first made in 1973.

First to appear was a child's cherry cup with a slightly lop-sided handle and having the cherries hanging upside down when the cup was held in the right hand. (This defiance of gravity was due to the inversion of the design when the mold, taken from an original cup, was inverted to create the outside of the "new" cup). After I reported this error, it was quickly corrected by re-inverting the inverted mold. These later cups were thus improved in design but slightly off color. The saucers tended to have slightly off center designs, too. Next came the "child's butter dish" which was never made by Jeannette. It was essentially the child's cup without a handle turned upside down over the saucer and having a little glob of glass added as a knob for lifting purposes. You could get this item in pink, green light blue, cobalt, gray-green, and iridescent carnival colors. A blue one in pictured on the preceding page.

Pictured are many of the colors made so far in the butter dishes and shakers begun in 1977. Some shakers were dated '77 on the bottom and were marketed at the ridiculous price of $27.95, a whopping profit margin! Shortly afterward, the non dated variety appeared. How can you tell new shakers from old--should you get the one in a million chance to do so?

First, look at the tops. New tops COULD indicate new shakers. Next, notice the protruding ledges beneath the tops. They are squared off juts rather than the nicely rounded scallops on the old (which are pictured under Cherry Blossom pattern). The design on the newer shakers is often weak in spots. Finally, notice how far up inside the shakers the solid glass (next to the foot) remains. The newer shakers have almost half again as much glass in that area. They appear to be ¼ full of glass before you ever add the salt!

Butter dishes are naturally more deceptive in pink and green since those were the only original colors. The major flaw in the new butter is that there is ONE band encircling the bottom edge of the butter top; there are TWO bands very close together along the skirt of the old top. Using your tactile sense, the new top has a sharply defined design up inside; the old was glazed and is smooth to touch. The knob on the new is more sharply defined than the smoothly formed knob on the old butter top. Today, with thousands of newly-made butters on the market, tactile sense is not as good an indication as it once was.

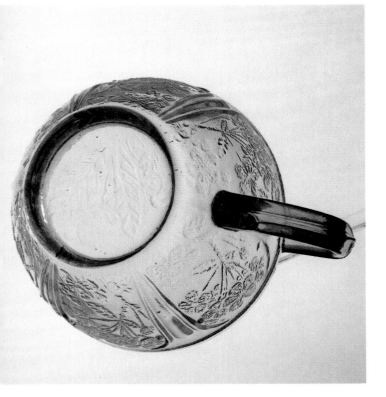

# Reproductions (Cont.)

## NEW "MADRID" CALLED "RECOLLECTION"     Currently being made.

I hope you have already read about Recollection Madrid on page 112. The current rage of Indiana Glass is to make Madrid in blue, pink and crystal. These colors are being sold through all kinds of outlets ranging from better department stores to discount catalogs. In the past few months we have received several ads stating that this is genuine Depression glass made from old moulds. None of this is made from old glass moulds unless you consider 1976 old. Most of the pieces are from moulds that were never made originally.

The blue is becoming a big seller for Indiana according to reports I am receiving around the country. It is a brighter, more florescent blue than the originally found color.

Look at the top picture! None of these items were ever made in the old pattern Madrid. The new grill plate has one division splitting the plate in half, but the old had three sections. A goblet or vase was never made. The vase is sold with a candle making it a "hurricane lamp". The heavy tumbler was placed on top of a candlestick to make this vase/hurricane lamp. That candlestick gets a workout. It was attached to a plate to make a pedestaled cake stand and to a butter dish to make a preserve stand. That's a clever idea, actually.

The shakers are short and heavy and you can see both original styles pictured on page 113. The latest item I have seen is a heavy 11 oz. flat tumbler being sold in a set of four or six called "On the Rocks" for $7.99. The biggest giveaway to this newer glass is the pale, washed out color. (It really looks washed out in the bottom photograph here. This is a little over done, but all the new is almost that bad.)

The bottom picture shows items that were originally made. The only concern in these pieces are the cups, saucers and oval vegetable bowl. These three pieces were made in pink in the 1930's. None of the others shown were ever made in the 1930's in pink, so realize that when you see the butter dish, dinner plate, soup bowl, or sugar and creamer. These are new items! Once you have learned what this washed out pink looks like by seeing these items out for sale, the color will let know when you see other pieces. My suggestion is to avoid pink Madrid except for the pitcher and tumblers.

The most difficult piece for new collectors to tell new from old is the candlestick. The new ones all have raised ridges inside to hold the candle more firmly. All old ones do not have these ridges. You may even find new candlesticks in black.

A special thanks to John and Trannie Davis for providing the "Recollection" glass shown in these photographs! Atlanta stores had it before Lexington's did!

# Reproductions (Cont.)

## NEW "MAYFAIR"

Colors: Pink, green, blue, cobalt (shot glasses), 1977 onward. Pink, green, amethyst (cookie jars), 1982 to date.

Only the pink shot glass need cause any concern to collectors because the glass wasn't made in those other colors originally. At first glance, the color of the newer shots is often too light pink or too orange. Dead give away are the stems of the flower design, however. In the old that stem branched to form an "A" shape; in the new, you have a single stem. Further, in the new design, the leaf is hollow with the veins molded in. In the old, the leaf is molded in and the veining is left hollow. In the center of the flower on the old, dots (another) cluster entirely to one side and are rather distinct. Nothing like that occurs in the new design.

As for the cookie jars, at cursory glance, the base of the cookie has a very indistinct design. It will feel smooth to the touch its so faint. In the old cookie jars, there's a distinct pattern which feels like raised embossing to the touch. Next, turn the bottom upside down. **The new bottom is perfectly smooth.** The old bottom contains a 1¾" mold circle rim that is raised enough to catch your fingernail in it. There are other distinctions as well; but that is the quickest way to tell old from new.

In the Mayfair cookie lid, the new design (parallel to the straight side of the lid) at the edge curves gracefully toward the center"V" shape (rather like bird wings in flight); in the old, that edge is flat, straight line going into the "V" (like airplane wings sticking straight out from the side of the plane as you face it head on).

The green color of the cookie, as you can see from the picture, is not the pretty, yellow/green color of true green Mayfair. It also doesn't "glow" under black light as the old green does.

So, you see, none of these reproductions give us any trouble; they're all easily spotted by those of us now "in the know"!

## NEW "MISS AMERICA"

Colors: Crystal, green, pink, ice blue, red amberina, cobalt blue.

The new butter dish in "Miss America" design is probably the best of the newer products; yet there are three distinct differences to be found between the original butter top and the newly made one. Since the value of the butter dish lies in the top, it seems more profitable to examine it.

In the new butter dishes pictured, notice that the panels reaching the edge of the butter bottom tend to have a pronounced curving, skirt-like edge. In the original dish, there is much less curving at the edge of these panels.

Second, pick up the top of the new dish and feel up inside it. If the butter top knob is filled with glass so that it is convex (curved outward), the dish is new; the old inside knob area is concave (curved inward).

Finally, from the underside, look through the top toward the knob. In the original butter dish you would see a perfectly formed multi-sided star; in the newer version, you see distorted rays with no visible points.

Shakers have been made in green, pink and crystal. The latest batch of shakers are becoming more difficult to distinguish from the old! The shakers will have new tops; but since some old shakers have been given new tops, that isn't conclusive at all. Unscrew the lid. Old shakers have a very neatly formed ridge of glass on which to screw the lid. It overlaps a little and has neatly rounded off ends. Old shakers stand 3⅜" tall without the lid. New ones stand 3¼" tall. Old shakers have almost a forefinger's depth inside (female finger) or a fraction shy of 2½ inches. Most new shakers have an inside depth of 2", about the second digit bend of a female's finger. (I'm doing finger depths since most of you will have those with you at the flea market, rather than a tape measure). In men, the old shaker's depth covers my knuckle; the new shaker leaves my knuckle exposed. Most new shakers simply have more glass on the inside the of shaker--something you can spot from twelve feet away! The hobs are more rounded on the newer shaker, particularly near the stem and seams; in the old shaker these areas remained pointedly sharp!

New Miss America tumblers have ½" of glass in the bottom, have a smooth edge on the bottom of the glass with no mold rim and show only two distinct mold marks on the sides of the glass. Old tumblers have only ¼" of glass in the bottom, have a distinct mold line rimming the bottom of the tumbler and have four distinct mold marks up the sides of the tumbler. The new green tumbler doesn't "glow" under black light as did the old.

New Miss America pitchers are all perfectly smooth rimmed at the top edge above the handle. All old pitchers that I have seen have a "hump" in the top rim of the glass above the handle area, rather like a camel's hump. The very bottom diamonds next to the foot in the new pitchers "squash" into elongated diamonds. In the old pitchers, these get noticeably smaller, but they retain their diamond shape.

# Reproductions (Cont.)

## NEW SANDWICH (Indiana) INDIANA GLASS COMPANY

### Tiara Exclusive Line, 1969 . . .

Colors: Amber, blue, red, crystal, green.

The smoky blue and amber shown here are representative of Tiara's line of Sandwich which is presently available. (See Sandwich pattern for older amber color).

The bad news is that the crystal has been made now and there are only minute differences in this new and the old. I will list the pieces made in crystal and you can make yourself aware of these re-issues if you collect the crystal Sandwich.

Ash Tray Set
Basket, Handles, 10½"
Bowl, 4" Berry
Bowl, 8"
Butter Dish & Cover
Candlesticks, 8½"
Cup, 9 oz.
Cup (Fits Indent in 6 oz. Oval Sandwich Plate)
Decanter & Stopper, 10"
Goblet, 5¼", 8 oz.
Pitcher, 8" Tall, 68 oz. Fluted Rim
Plate, 10" Dinner

Plate, 8" Salad
Plate, 8½" x 6¾" Oval Sandwich
Sandwich Tray, Handled
Saucer, 6"
Sherbets
Tray, 10" (Underliner for Wine Decanter & Goblets)
Tumbler, 6½" High, 12 oz.

## NEW "SHARON" Privately Produced 1976 . . .

Colors: Blue, dark green, light green, pink, burnt umber

A blue Sharon butter turned up in 1976 and turned my phone line to a liquid fire! The color is Mayfair blue--a fluke and dead giveaway as far as real Sharon is concerned.

When found in similar colors to the old, pink and green, you can immediately tell that the new version has more glass in the top where it changes from pattern to clear glass, a thick, defined ring of glass as opposed to a thin, barely defined ring of glass in the old. The knob of the new dish tends to stick up more. In the old butter dish there's barely room to fit your finger to grasp the knob. The new butter dish has a sharply defined ridge of glass in the bottom around which the top sits. The old butter has such a slight rim that the top easily scoots off the bottom.

In 1977 a "cheese dish" appeared having the same top as the butter and having all the flaws inherent in that top which were discussed in detail above. However, the bottom of this dish was all wrong. It's about half way between a flat plate and a butter dish bottom, bowl shaped; and it is over thick, giving it an awkward appearance. The real cheese bottom was a salad plate with a rim for holding the top. These "round bottom cheese dishes" are but a parody of the old and are easily spotted. We removed the top from one in the picture so you could see its heaviness and its bowl shape.

The butter/cheese dishes wholesale to dealers for around $6.00.

## NEW "SHARON" (Con't.)

Some of the latest reproductions in Sharon are too light pink creamer and sugar with lid. They are pictured with the "Made in Taiwan" label. These sell for around $15.00 for the pair and are also easy to spot as reproductions. I'll just mention the most obvious differences. Turn the creamer so you are looking directly at the spout. In the old creamer the mold line runs dead center of that spout; in the new, the mold line runs decidedly to the left of center spout.

On the sugar, the leaves and roses are "off" but not enough to DESCRIBE it to new collectors. Therefore, look at the center design, both sides, at the stars located at the very bottom of the motif. A thin leaf stem should run directly from that center star upward on BOTH sides. In this new sugar, the stem only runs from one; it stops way short of the star on one side. OR look inside the sugar bowl at where the handle attaches to the bottom of the bowl. In the new bowl, this attachment looks like a perfect circle; in the old, its an upside down "v" shaped tear drop.

As for the sugar lid, the knob of the new lid is perfectly smooth as you grasp its edges. The old knob has a mold seam running mid circimference. You could tell these two lids apart blind folded!

While there is a hair's difference between the height, mouth opening diameter, and inside depth of the old Sharon shakers and those newly produced, I won't attempt to upset you with those sixteenth and thirty seconds of a degree of difference. Suffice it to say that in physical shape, they are very close. However, as concerns design, they're miles apart. The old shakers have true appearing roses. The flowers really LOOK like roses. On the new shakers, they look like poorly drawn circles with wobbly concentric rings. The leaves are not as clearly defined on the new shakers as the old. However, forgetting all that, in the old shakers, the first design you see below the lid is a ROSE BUD. It's angled like a rocket shooting off into outer space with three leaves at the base of the bud (where the rocket fuel would burn out). In the new shakers, this "bud" has become four paddles of a windmill. It's the difference between this 🌱 and this 🦋 .

The shakers wholesale for around $6.50 a pair.

Candy dishes have been made in pink and green. These candy jars are among the easiest items to discern old from new. Pick up the lid and look from the bottom side. On the old there is a 2″ circle knob ring; on the new the ring is only ½″. This shows from the top also but it is difficult to measure with the knob in the center. There are other major differences but this one will not be mould corrected easily. The bottoms are also simple to distinguish. The base diameter of the old is 3¼″ and the new only 3″. Quality of the new is rough, poorly shaped and molded on the example I have, but I do not know if that is true of all reproductions of the candy. I sure hope so!

221

**Publications I recommend**

## DEPRESSION GLASS DAZE

### THE ORIGINAL NATIONAL DEPRESSION GLASS NEWSPAPER

Depression Glass Daze, the Original, National monthly newspaper dedicated to the buying, selling and collecting of colored glassware of the 20's and 30's. We average 60 pages each month, filled with feature articles by top notch columnists, readers "finds", club happenings, show news, a china corner, a current listing of new glass issues to beware of and a multitude of ads! You can find it in the DAZE! Keep up with what's happening in the dee gee world with a subscription to the DAZE. Buy sell or trade from the convenience of your easy chair.

Name_____ Street_____

City_____ State_____ Zip_____

☐ 1 Year - $15.00    ☐ Check enclosed    ☐ Please bill me

☐ MasterCard    ☐ VISA    (Foreign subscribers - please add $1.00 per year)

Exp. date_____Card No._____

Signature_____

Order to D.G.D., Box 57GF, Otisville, MI 48463-0008 - Please allow 30 days

A colorful magazine devoted to keeping glass collectors informed about all kinds of glass - antique to contemporary collectibles. Filled with articles, pictures, price reports, ads, research information and more! 12 "BIG" issues yearly.

Name_____ Street_____

City_____ State_____ Zip_____

☐ New    ☐ 1 year - $15.95    ☐ Single Copy $2.00

☐ Renewal    ☐ 1 year Canada or Foreign $17.50 (U.S. Funds please)

Orders to P.O. Box 7188GF, Redlands, CA 92373

**Heisey Club Membership To:**

**Heisey Collectors of America**
Box 27GF
Newark, OH 43055
Dues: $15.00 Yearly

# Books by Gene Florence

# Schroeder's Antiques Price Guide

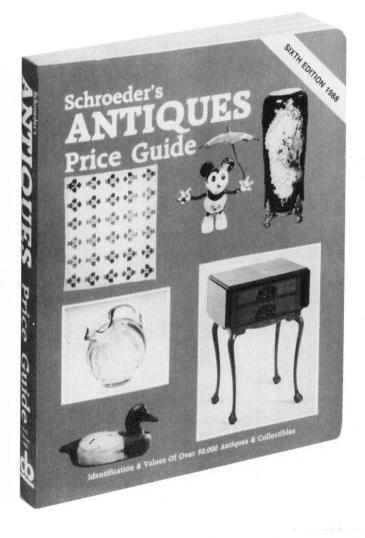

*Schroeder's Antiques Price Guide* has climbed its way to the top in a field already supplied with several well-established publications! The word is out, *Schroeder's Price Guide* is the best buy at any price. Over 500 categories are covered, with more than 50,000 listings. But it's not volume alone that makes Schroeder's the unique guide it is recognized to be. From ABC Plates to Zsolnay, if it merits the interest of today's collector, you'll find it in Schroeder's. Each subject is represented with histories and background information. In addition, hundreds of sharp original photos are used each year to illustrate not only the rare and the unusual, but the everyday "fun-type" collectibles as well -- not postage stamp pictures, but large close-up shots that show important details clearly.

Each edition is completely re-typeset from all new sources. We have not and will not simply change prices in each new edition. All new copy and all new illustrations make Schroeder's THE price guide on antiques and collectibles.

The writing and researching team behind this giant is proportionately large. It is backed by a staff of more than seventy of Collector Books' finest authors, as well as a board of advisors made up of well-known antique authorities and the country's top dealers, all specialists in their fields. Accurancy is their primary aim. Prices are gathered over the entire year previous to publication, from ads and personal contacts. Then each category is thoroughly checked to spot inconsistencies, listings that may not be entirely reflective of actual market dealings, and lines too vague to be of merit. Only the best of the lot remains for publication. You'll find *Schroeder's Antiques Price Guide* the one to buy for factual information and quality.

No dealer, collector or investor can afford not to own this book. It is available from your favorite bookseller or antiques dealer at the low price of $11.95. If you are unable to find this price guide in your area, it's available from Collector Books, P. O. Box 3009, Paducah, KY 42001 at $11.95 plus $1.00 for postage and handling.

8½ x 11, 608 Pages                                                                                     $11.95

**COLLECTOR BOOKS**

*A Division of Schroeder Publishing Co., Inc.*